Spellcasters

SPELLCASTERS

Witches and Witchcraft in
History, Folklore, and
Popular Culture

PAULINE BARTEL

TAYLOR TRADE PUBLISHING

Dallas, Texas

Copyright © 2000 by Pauline Bartel

Designed by Barbara Werden

Published by Taylor Publishing Company
1550 West Mockingbird Lane
Dallas, Texas 75235
www.taylorpub.com

Library of Congress Cataloging-in-Publication Data

Bartel, Pauline C.
    Spellcasters : witches and witchcraft in history, folklore, and
popular culture / Pauline Bartel.
        p.   cm.
    Includes index.
    ISBN 0-87833-183-2 (cloth)
    I. Witchcraft—History.   I. Title

BF1566. B27 2000
133.4'3'09—dc21   00-042588

10   9   8   7   6   5   4   3   2   1

Printed in the United States of America

To Mary Bartel, Anna Szelowski, and Bertha Raskowski—
mother, aunt, and friend—three wise women
who are much loved.

Contents

ℐℓℴ

Preface

~

VERITABLE mountain of material exists on the subject of witches and witchcraft. Why then add to the profusion with this volume? Because some of the more important books tend to be terribly dry, while some of the more popular books tend to be terribly unreliable. My aim in writing *Spellcasters: Witches and Witchcraft in History, Folklore, and Popular Culture* was to present a coherent overview of the subject in an engaging yet scholarly style and to explore aspects of witches and witchcraft that I find most fascinating.

Within these pages, you will find a wide scope of information. Chapters 1 and 2 focus on the origins and folklore of witches and witchcraft. Chapter 3 discusses the Great European Witch Hunt, including its events, why it began, and why it ended. Chapters 4, 5, and 6 discuss the Salem Witch Trials and present a number of theories to explain what happened in Salem. Chapters 7 and 8 detail the Craft today and the basics of Witchcraft. Chapter 9 provides a witches who's who, a compendium of interesting individuals who have affected witchcraft. And Chapter 10 explores the influence of witches and witchcraft in popular culture, including books, music, film, and television.

While each chapter could be a book unto itself, I have chosen not to serve a full-course literary banquet but to offer readers a tantalizing taste of information in each chapter. For those who wish further nibbles, the bibliography is designed to satisfy the heartiest of appetites.

To facilitate ease of reading, I have adapted modern-day spelling and punctuation to the historical excerpts and quotations. Because I believe in allowing historical persons to speak for themselves, I have also presented their words unembellished with authorial paraphrasing wherever possible.

I have capitalized the religious terms Witchcraft, Witch, Wicca, Wiccan, Craft, Neo-Pagan, and Neo-Paganism. I have used lower case letters when referring to witchcraft and witches in general. I use the words "magick" and "magickal" to refer to energy manipulation and to differentiate them from "magic" and "magical," which refer to illusionary manipulation. Pulling a rabbit out of a hat or sawing a person in two are examples of illusionary manipulation. Magick, on the other hand, is a real and powerful religious practice.

I have used the abbreviations B.C.E. ("Before Common Era") and C.E. ("Common Era") instead of B.C. and A.D., respectively.

Numerous Wiccan practitioners graciously assisted me in preparing this book by providing secondary research sources including books, journal articles, and audio and videocassettes and by allowing me to interview them for primary research. I am most grateful for their support, and I respect their wishes to remain anonymous in this volume. To each person who helped in any way, large or small, my most sincere thank you for your assistance. I hope *Spellcasters* will not disappoint.

Introduction

❧

N *The Wizard of Oz,* beautiful, dazzling Glinda materializes from a bubble of light before young Dorothy, newly arrived in Munchkinland, and asks: "Are you a good witch or a bad witch?"

The image of witches throughout history, folklore, and popular culture has reflected this black-and-white dichotomy. Bad witches are portrayed mostly as ugly, old hags dressed in black, wearing cone-shaped hats. Bad witches fly through the air on broomsticks. Bad witches cast evil spells to harm their foes and kill babies for demonic rituals.

The Wicked Witch of the West in *The Wizard of Oz*

threatened to kill Dorothy for possession of the ruby slippers. The witch in the fairy tale "Hansel and Gretel" lured the children to her magickal cake-and-bread cottage with the intention of fattening them up and eating them. In *The Blair Witch Project* three college kids disappeared in an atmosphere of malevolent mystery near Burkittsville, Maryland, while investigating a local witch legend.

By contrast, good witches are portrayed mostly as lovely, young women who grant wishes with the whirl of a wand, the wiggle of a nose, or the wave of a hand. Glinda, The Good Witch of the North, helped Dorothy return to Kansas with the chant "There's no place like home" and with three clicks of the heels of the ruby slippers. Samantha Stephens of "Bewitched" used her powers to rescue husband Darrin and their friends from various business as well as domestic catastrophes. As a young witch-in-training, Sabrina, the Teenage Witch, experienced the often fickle results of witchcraft while attempting to help boyfriend Harvey.

This black-and-white dichotomy is rooted in ancient times when people believed that special individuals could manipulate—for good or for evil—the supernatural power that controlled the world. When spells, rituals, and incantations cured illnesses, increased the harvest, or brought rains to parched land, magick materialized in the world. However, people also knew that magick could turn malevolent if the sorcerer or witch chose to bring plague to the house of an enemy, to ruin crops, or to raise destructive storms.

Far from black and white is the etymology of the word "witch." Many authorities believe that the word derived from the Old English words "wicce" and "wicca," referring to female and male practitioners, respectively, who are "wise ones," working in concert with the Divine Force.

Some experts believe that "wicce" and "wicca" stemmed from the root "wikk," which relates to magic and sorcery, or from the verb "wiccian," which means "to cast a spell." Others suggest that the root is "wit" meaning "wisdom." Many witches were considered the wise ones of a village, and witchcraft is considered the Craft of the Wise. Still other authorities think that the words are derived from the Indo-European roots "wic" and "weik," meaning "to bend or to turn." Seemingly, witches "bend" the forces of nature in order to effect change.

The word "witch" is a gender-neutral designation, applying today to both women and men. The term "warlock," popularly used to refer to a male witch, derives from the Old English "waer" meaning "truth" and "leogan" meaning "to lie." "Warlock" originally meant "one who breaks the faith" or "liar." By tradition, a warlock is a sorcerer or wizard who gained his power through a pact with the Devil. Contemporary Witchcraft does not share Christianity's belief in the Devil; thus, "warlock" is considered a pejorative term by modern-day followers of Witchcraft.

Although a witch can be either male or female, over the centuries the magickal arts became associated primarily with women. Their customary roles in society as cooks, healers, and midwives gave women ample opportunity to practice magick.

As cooks, women gathered plants to transform into magickal potions. People believed that witches brewed magickal potions in cooking pots or cauldrons. In fact, women as witches are often portrayed stirring bubbling cauldrons, brimming with nefarious ingredients.

As healers, women harnessed the medicinal secrets of herbs and ointments to create folk remedies that cured illnesses. When villagers died unexpectedly, healers could be accused of having used magick against their patients. People believed that witches could either cure or kill, depending upon their intent. Thus, people both tolerated and feared witches.

As midwives, women aided mothers in bringing new life into the world. During times of high infant mortality, midwives were convenient targets for accusations of killing children through sorcery. People believed that witches sacrificed unbaptized infants to the Devil, ate the roasted flesh of children at sabbats, and used their remains in potions and ointments.

Women were also suspected of practicing sorcery because of the belief that women were inferior to men intellectually and morally. This belief existed from the earliest days of Christianity and reached its height in the late fifteenth century with the publication of the *Malleus Maleficarum* or "Hammer of Witches." According to the book's authors, women are "intellectually like children" and "more carnal" than men. The *Malleus Maleficarum* indicted women as witches by concluding that "all witchcraft comes from carnal lust, which is in women insatiable."

The concept that carnal lust drove women to witchcraft became pertinent when witchcraft was prosecuted as a crime. Prevailing beliefs held that women surrendered to the sexual temptations of the Devil, secured their powers through pacts with the Devil, and engaged in sexual intercourse with the Devil and his demons. These beliefs strengthened the image of the woman as witch.

More women than men were persecuted and executed as witches during the Great European Witch Hunt from the fifteenth to eighteenth centuries and during the Salem Witch Trials of 1692 and 1693. Typical methods of punishment included torture, hanging, and burning at the stake.

Over time, witch hunts declined when the social, economic, and religious conditions that fueled the frenzy no longer existed. Laws making witchcraft a crime were repealed, and sorcery reverted to the realm of folk magick. However, the archetype of the witch as a malevolent force who conjures spirits, changes shape, and casts evil spells remains a potent universal image.

In the 1950s, Witchcraft was revived as a Neo-Pagan religion with adherents honoring the feminine aspect of the Divine—the Goddess—through seasonal cycles and the practice of benevolent magick. Interest in Neo-Pagan Witchcraft surged throughout the 1960s and 1970s due to renewed fascination with the occult and the rise of feminism. Through the 1980s and 1990s, Neo-Pagan Witchcraft attracted individuals who felt disconnected from Christianity and other mainstream religions.

Today those who practice Neo-Pagan Witchcraft—called Wicca, the Craft, the Old Religion, or Witchcraft—face fear, hate, and prejudice from a public that confuses Wiccans with Satanists. As a result, many keep secret their participation in the Craft, while others seek publicity in order to educate society and to secure civil rights as Wicca flourishes in the twenty-first century.

Spellcasters shines a light on the shadowy realm of witches and witchcraft, revealing their impact on history, folklore, and popular culture in Europe, the United States, and around the world. Welcome to an illuminating adventure.

Spellcasters

꙳ꙮ꙳

ONE

The Origins of Witches and Witchcraft Around the World

ᔆᔆᑭ

T the dawn of time, human beings trembled in the face of awesome, bewildering powers. Flashes of lightning. Thunder. Hard rains and swift floods. Burning sun. Luminous moon. Ice and fire. Birth and death. Sickness. The cycle of the seasons. They attributed these mysterious powers to spirits unseen: the goddesses and the gods who ruled their world. People etched the walls of their caves with crude drawings, perhaps to remind them of the goddess who bestowed life to all things or the god who ensured a good hunt.

Human beings worshiped nature-based deities such as the Mother Goddess, who represented the earth's fertility, and the male Horned God, whose death and resurrection represented the earth's regenerative power. The Mother Goddess was known as Astarte in Syria, Ceres in Rome, Cybele in Phrygia, Demeter in Greece, Ishtar in Babylon, and Isis in Egypt. The Horned God was associated with Cernunnos, the Celtic god of fertility, animals, and the underworld; Pan, the Greek god of the woodlands; Janus, the Roman god of beginnings whose two bearded heads look to the future and to the past; Osiris, the Egyptian god of the underworld; and Dionysus, the Greek god of fertility and wine.

Early people held festivals and celebrations to honor their goddesses and gods. Anglo-Saxons honored their spring goddess, Eostre. Romans celebrated the spring festival of Floralia, honoring Flora, the goddess of the flowering of plants.

The Mayans paid tribute to the maize god, Ah Mun, with a gruel of maize and water, offered in intricately painted vessels. The gruel mixture symbolized life and rebirth. For the Inuit, or Eskimo, the sea provided a bounty of food, and masked rituals honoring the moon spirit guaranteed continued beneficence.

In India, the Hindu god of fire, Agni, was honored with fire feasts. In Japan, the Shinto sun goddess, Amaterasu, was venerated at her main shrine at Ise.

Ancient Egyptians commemorated the rebirth of the sun at the end of the year, while Persians celebrated the return of the god of light, Mithra. According to the myth, Mithra was a child of the earth, born on December 25 bearing a torch and wielding a knife. He later rode the life-giving cosmic bull and slayed the beast, spilling its blood which then fertilized the earth's vegetation. These Egyptian and Persian traditions merged in ancient Rome and became Saturnalia, a festival to Saturn, the god of harvests, held from December 17 to 24. Work and war ceased; gifts were exchanged; homes were decorated with greenery, candles, and lamps.

MAGICK MATERIALIZES

But the goddesses and the gods could be unpredictable. Plentiful herds of animals might disappear when frigid winds swept the land. Abundant crops sometimes shriveled under the glare of an unrelenting sun. Human beings probably despaired when they saw that their world was not within their control.

However, special individuals emerged from the chaos to intervene with the goddesses and the gods. Shamans, medicine people, sorcerers, and witches used spells, rituals, and incantations to manipulate—for good or evil purposes—the grand power that controlled the world. Thus, magick materialized in the world. And in caves, human beings drew images of the magick: pictures of people enacting rituals that guaranteed successful hunting.

This was homeopathic or sympathetic magick, a common type of sorcery involving representations of the person to whom the magick is directed. Those who practice sympathetic magick believe that by imitating the desired effect, they can produce it. For example, someone who wishes to cause the death of an enemy may fashion a wax doll to resemble the foe then toss the doll into a fire, destroying the image of the adversary.

Those who practice contagious magick believe that items belonging to a person can influence that person even at a distance. For example, a lock of hair or a fingernail can be used in a spell against the person to whom they belong.

Witches also engaged in folk magick, so called because the sorcery affected the lives of ordinary folk. In cultures throughout the world, witches blended herbs, flowers, and plants into concoctions that cured illnesses. They cast spells to draw rain clouds to the land. They performed rituals to increase the flow of a cow's milk. They spoke mysterious incantations to destroy an enemy's home.

WITCHES AS WOMEN

These witches, usually women, were both revered as healers and feared as spellcasters in the villages in which they lived. Within them resided great power to nurture or to destroy love, health, or prosperity through their communications with spirits. This ability set them apart from others in the village, and often they lived isolated from the inhabitants, by choice or by design.

Over time, isolation bred speculation, and fear of witches predominated. Communities felt imperiled by the presence of witches who could cause plague and famine, ruin crops, kill livestock, and raise storms. Fear fed superstitious beliefs. Those beliefs included the folklore that witches had the power to fly, that they kept demons in the form of animals to do their bidding, and that they were old hags.

The face of the witch was definitely female. According to Selma R. Williams, coauthor of *Riding the Nightmare: Women and Witchcraft,* "As society moved from open field to clustered community, man and woman ceased working together, side by side. Organization, authority, and power gradually slithered into the domain of man alone." Women were considered inferior both physically and mentally. However, with their great powers, witches clearly threatened male dominance. Fortunately, for men, witches were easy to identify and deal with.

Many women died before reaching the age of 40, so any woman in her 50s or beyond was suspect. Beyond childbearing age, such women were considered worthless to society, especially if they were infirm or crippled. In times of scarcity, precious food and fuel were not wasted on crones who would repay the kindness with curses.

Midwives were also considered to be witches. According to Williams, "If a midwife could bring both mother and child safely through the throes of childbirth, she doubtlessly was calling on the supernatural. On the other hand, if either mother or child died, the midwife-witch was demonstrating her unearthly power for evil."

WITCHES AS ENEMIES OF THE STATE AND THE CHURCH

Evil acts of witches, called maleficia, were condemned and punished throughout the known world. Before the Middle Ages, witchcraft was usually a civil crime, punishable by fines, imprisonment, and banishment. However, Roman law distinguished between malefic witchcraft and beneficial magick. Beneficial magick, which included healing and divination, was not only tolerated but officially sanctioned, whereas malefic witchcraft was a crime. According to Ronald Hutton, author of *The Pagan Religions of the Ancient British Isles,* "The pagan Romans, like most ancient peoples and modern tribal societies, prescribed the death penalty for those who killed or who harmed property by witchcraft: in a system which believes in magic and has capital punishment for normal murder and arson, there is no other logical situation."

When Christianity took root and flourished throughout much of Europe, the Church proclaimed that all pre-Christian goddesses and gods were false. The Church introduced veneration of the saints to replace worship of the goddesses and the gods. The Holy Mother, the Virgin Mary, was substituted for the Mother Goddess, and Jesus was her Divine Child who was sacrificed and resurrected. The Horned God became the Devil. The Church also assimilated many pre-Christian feasts and festivals into the Roman Catholic religious calendar. Thus, Saturnalia became Christmas; spring festivals became Easter. Churches were built on sites sacred to those who worshipped the nature-based deities. However, the Church's stance on witches vacillated throughout the centuries.

At times, the Church viewed witchcraft and sorcery as relics of superstition; at other times, the Church viewed witchcraft and sorcery as heresy wrought by the Devil and warranting suppression. Christian theologians reflected these divergent opinions, as well.

Two early theologians, Origen (185–254 C.E.) and St. Augustine (354–430 C.E.) proclaimed that the practices of magick, sorcery, and divination were possible only through pacts with the Devil. Two other influential figures, St. Boniface (675–754 C.E.) and St. Agobard (circa 770–840 C.E.), held that witchcraft and sorcery were dubious remnants of paganism.

Despite this divergence of opinion within the Church, canon law reflected moderation and leniency for witches and witchcraft. The Church believed in attacking gods and goddesses rather than attacking human beings.

Nevertheless, many people continued to honor the nature-based deities and to practice the spells and rituals of magick. According to Margot Adler in *Drawing Down the Moon,* they were ridiculed with the sobriquet "pagan," a word from the Latin "paganus," meaning "country dweller." "Paganus" is derived from "pagus," the Latin word for a village or rural area. Adler states that by the third century, the word "pagan had become a derogatory term in Rome," meaning that the individual was considered a "hick."

In a footnote, Adler indicates that Edward Gibbon, author of *The Decline and Fall of the Roman Empire,* attributed a different interpretation to the word: "With the rise of the Roman military, 'pagan' became a contemptuous epithet meaning 'nonsoldier.' The Christians considered themselves soldiers of Christ and those who refused the sacrament of baptism were reproached with the term 'pagan' as early as the reign of Emperor Valentinian (365 C.E.) and the word was introduced into Imperial law in the Theodosian Code."

Robin Lane Fox in *Pagans and Christians* concurs: "Christians first gave them their name, pagani. . . . In everyday use, it meant either a civilian or a rustic. Since the sixteenth century the origin of the early Christians' usage has been disputed, but of the two meanings, the former is the likelier. Pagani were civilians who had not enlisted through baptism as soldiers of Christ against the powers of Satan. By its word for nonbelievers, Christian slang bore witness to the heavenly battle which coloured Christians' view of life."

According to Adler, "Centuries later the word 'pagan' still suffers the consequences of political and religious struggles, and dictionaries still define it to mean a godless person or an unbeliever, instead of, simply, a member of a different kind of religion."

During the decline and fall of the Roman Empire, Germanic peoples spread throughout Europe, carrying with them their fear of witches. Powers of malevolent witchcraft were attributed to women, and the archetype of the old woman as witch appeared frequently in literature. The literature of the ancient Slavic peoples reflects a similar archetype.

In ancient Spain and Gaul, religious and civil laws against witchcraft practices and beliefs were common. Charlemagne and other rulers declared that witchcraft was an evil superstition and advocated severe penalties, including death, for those convicted of witchcraft.

In 906, the Church promulgated its official stance that witchcraft was mere fantasy. The *Canon Episcopi* defined witchcraft as Devil worship but declared it to be "in every way false" because "such phantasms are imposed on the minds of infidels" by the Devil. The document declared that:

> . . . some wicked women, perverted by the Devil, seduced by illusions and phantasms of demons, believe and profess themselves, in the hours of the night, to ride upon certain beasts with Diana, the goddess of pagans, and an innumerable multitude of women, and in the silence of the dead of the night to traverse great spaces of earth, and to obey her commands as of their mistress, and to be summoned to her service on certain nights.

The *Canon Episcopi* stated that witches did not have the ability to fly or to change themselves into animals. Anyone who was "so stupid and foolish" to believe that they could was "beyond doubt an infidel." However, the document granted that while these fantastic feats were physically impossible, individuals could perform them in spirit.

Despite the Church's position, attitudes toward witchcraft were changing. The lines of distinction between beneficial witchcraft and malefic witchcraft blurred until both were considered heresy, a crime punishable by death.

Those who clung to the old ways and continued to heal with herbs, cast spells for good harvests, or foretell the future were considered not only enemies of the Church and threats to the state but disciples of the Devil. Determined to obliterate the last, tenacious vestiges of paganism, religious and civil authorities initiated persecutions. Witchcraft was clearly a threat to the Church, which feared the overthrow of Christendom by Satan. Thus, the Church used an arsenal of weapons against witchcraft, particularly the Bible.

The Bible contains numerous references to "witch." However, some scholars believe the term distorts the meaning of the original Hebrew word, which translates to "a woman who uses spoken spells to harm others." The most well-known of these Biblical references is Exodus 22:18: "Thou shalt not suffer a witch to live."

Leviticus 20:27 states, "A man also or woman that hath a familiar spirit, or that is a wizard, shall surely be put to death: they shall stone them with stones: their blood shall be upon them."

Deuteronomy 18:10–11 warns, "There shall not be found among you any one that maketh his son or daughter to pass through the fire, or that useth divination, or an observer of times, or an enchanter, or a witch, or a charmer, or a consulter with familiar spirits, or a wizard, or a necromancer."

Galatians 5:19–20 holds that "Now the works of the flesh are manifest, which are these: Adultery, fornication, uncleanness, lasciviousness, idolatry, witchcraft, hatred, variance, emulations, wrath, strife, seditions, heresies."

Chapter 28 of I Samuel tells the story of the so-called Witch of Endor, who conjured the spirit of Samuel for King Saul of Israel. The Old Testament castigates sorcerers and magickians as being anti-God, and their offenses deserve to be punished by death. The New Testament denounces them as immoral individuals.

WITCHES AS HERETICS

From the eleventh century on, the Church wielded the wrath of God, ferreting out and condemning heretics to death by burning. Various religious sects were specific targets, including the Albigenses in eastern Europe and southern France, the Cathars who populated most of Europe, and the Waldenses of southern France. In addition to heresy, these groups also faced accusations of witchcraft and Devil worship.

In 1184, Pope Lucius III directed bishops to investigate any departure from Church teachings. In 1233, Pope Gregory IX established the papal Inquisition, appointing Dominicans as Inquisitors and decreeing that they would report only to the Pope. This led to the Church's reversal of the *Canon Episcopi*. One of the most influential voices against the position of the *Canon*

Episcopi was renowned theologian St. Thomas Aquinas (circa 1227–1274 c.e.). He held that witches engaged in "miracles" such as having intercourse with demons, flying through the night skies, changing into other shapes, and raising storms. He wrote in *Sententiae* that "Magicians perform miracles through personal contracts made with demons."

The connection between witches and demons was further strengthened throughout the thirteenth and fourteenth centuries by a shift in philosophical thought away from that of Plato and toward that of Aristotle. Platonic philosophy argued for the existence of natural magick which was morally neutral. Aristotelian philosophy argued that natural magick did not exist; hence, magick must spring from either the Divine or the demonic.

Beginning in 1320, the Church put on trial those accused of heretical witchcraft, and fifteen years later, the definition of heretical witchcraft expanded to include flying, attending sabbats, and worshipping the Devil.

One of the most famous individuals executed as a heretic in the fifteenth century was Joan of Arc, the French peasant who led troops against the English and won for the dauphin his crown as King Charles VII of France. As a girl of 13, Joan began hearing the voices of St. Michael, St. Catherine, and St. Margaret and began seeing visions that directed her to aid the dauphin. In 1429, she secured an audience with him and convinced him of her divine mission to defeat the English and to restore him to the throne of France. Furnished with troops, Joan raised the siege of Orleans in May 1429, and two months later Charles VII was crowned king.

In September 1429 Joan unsuccessfully besieged Paris, an English stronghold, and the following spring she was captured during an attempt to seize Compiegne. The Duke of Burgundy, an English ally, imprisoned Joan in his castle. He relinquished her to another ally of the English, the Bishop of Beauvais, in exchange for 10,000 francs.

Joan spent one year and one week imprisoned in a bleak dungeon, often chained to a wooden block that secured her neck, arms, and feet. At times her jailers locked her in irons and threatened her with torture unless she confessed. She responded, "Even if you tear me limb from limb, and even if you kill me, I should not respond otherwise; and if I did speak otherwise, I should always thereafter say that you had made me answer so by force."

At a formal ecclesiastical trial in front of thirty-seven clerical judges, Joan faced seventy charges, including being a sorceress, witch, diviner, false prophetess, invoker of evil spirits, and conjurer. She was accused of being "given to the arts of magic" and of being a heretic. Most of the charges could not be substantiated and were subsequently dropped. However, the Inquisitors moved forward with twelve charges, among which were accusations of her wearing men's clothing, her ability to see visions, and her heresy in refusing to acquiesce to the authority of the Church.

During the trial, evidence favorable to Joan was expunged from the official record. The scribe Guillaume Manchon admitted later that when the proceedings recorded in French were translated into Latin, the judges forced him "to change the meaning of words." Manchon also revealed that two men secreted behind a curtain in the courtroom "wrote and reported what was charged against Joan and suppressed her excuses."

The court condemned her as a heretic. As she was about to be given over to the English for execution, Joan signed a confession stating that her visions and voices had been false and that she would submit to the authority of the Church. The court sentenced her to life imprisonment.

While in prison, Joan recanted her confession. She was condemned as a relapsed heretic and sentenced to burn at the stake. The Maid of Orleans faced the pyre on May 30, 1431. Her executioner later reported that the flames had refused to consume her heart. He found Joan's heart intact and untouched amid the ashes. Joan was canonized a saint in 1920 by Pope Benedict XV.

To the early Church, the fate of Joan of Arc symbolized the world engulfed in the flames of turmoil. Europe was wracked by wars, the Crusades, plagues, and peasant revolts. According to Starhawk, an American Witch, feminist, peace activist, and author, "The stability of the medieval Church was shaken, and the feudal system began to break down. The Christian world was swept by messianic movements and religious revolts, and the Church could no longer calmly tolerate rivals."

Through the middle of the fifteenth century, the Church issued numerous papal bulls against witchcraft. Pope Sixtus IV linked witchcraft to heresy in bulls issued in 1473, 1478, and 1483. His successor, Pope Innocent VIII, issued a bull in 1483; its force ignited the Inquisition against witches as no other document had done before.

WITCHCRAFT AROUND THE WORLD

Anthropologists report that belief in witchcraft permeates human society around the globe. However, the term "witchcraft" assumes varied meanings throughout different cultures and during different historical time frames. The word possesses both negative and positive connotations.

Although popular usage of the terms "witchcraft" and "sorcery" are synonymous, many anthropologists distinguish between the two words. Witchcraft is defined as an innate psychic ability to harm others without the use of spells or rituals. Sorcery is defined as the efforts of ordinary individuals to harm others using deliberate techniques and external means. The witch seems to effect harm unintentionally, while the sorcerer seems to effect harm deliberately.

Anthropologists first observed this distinction of the Azande people of central Africa. The distinction in terms has been found also in other tribal peoples in nonliterate cultures as well as in several European societies in early modern times. Nevertheless, in some societies in medieval Europe, sorcery was performed for beneficial rather than for harmful purposes.

Compounding the anthropological complexity of the origins of witchcraft is the fact that the Kalahari San and Andaman Islanders do not maintain a belief in witchcraft. The Javanese believe in sorcery but not in witchcraft. People in Arab and Muslim cultures also do not believe in witchcraft, although they do believe in the evil eye, a lingering look or envious glance believed to cause illness, misfortune, or death.

Anthropologists hold that belief in witchcraft often occurs in small communities where lifelong personal relationships are the bedrock of social interaction. Thus, belief in witchcraft affords individuals a logical way to explain misfortunes and provides the society a method of social control. For example, the person who fears being accused of or attacked by witchcraft tends to be more prudent in his or her behavior toward others. Those who are accused of causing misfortune through witchcraft are considered pariahs and serve as unwitting scapegoats for events such as sudden death or unexplained accidents. However, anthropologists point out that members of these small communities do not necessarily dwell on their fears related to witchcraft. Instead, they acknowledge the threat of witchcraft and accept the danger as they live their daily lives.

MODERN-DAY AFRICAN BELIEFS

A fascinating study of African witchcraft was conducted in the late 1920s by Sir Edward E. Evans-Pritchard, and his findings were published in the classic *Witchcraft, Oracles and Magic Among the Azande*. The Azande of central

Africa believe that witchcraft—called mangu—is responsible for all misfortunes, great and small. They believe that mangu exists as a hereditary element in a witch's stomach. Male witches pass mangu to their sons, and female witches pass mangu to their daughters.

According to the Azande's beliefs, many people do not realize that they possess mangu. While the person sleeps at night, the witchcraft spirit rises from the abdomen and attacks the spirit of the victim. Thus, the witch is unaware that his or her spirit has been about creating mayhem. However, the victim knows that he or she has been attacked, since nightmares herald witch attacks. Another witch or a witch doctor observing the victim can also determine when an attack is taking place because the witchcraft spirit generates a tiny, bright light.

The victim or the victim's relatives can identify the witch using divination techniques. One method—the ant hill oracle—involves sticking two branches in an ant hill and asking the ants a question such as "Are my in-laws bewitching me?" The Azande believe that if the ants eat the left branch, the answer is yes. If the ants eat the right branch, the answer is no.

The iwa oracle involves the use of a rubbing board, consisting of a tiny table with a board that fits over it like a cover. The rubbing board is similar to a Ouija board. An Azande native sprinkles fruit or plant juice on the table then slides the board across it. While asking a "yes" or "no" question, the native commands the board to stick for a positive response and to glide for a negative response. The native may recite a list of those suspected of witchcraft, and the name uttered when the board sticks is the guilty person.

If these divination methods fail to yield a conclusion, the Azande native can consult the benge oracle. Similar to strychnine, benge is a native poison that affects fowl, particularly chickens, in a strange manner. When exposed to benge, some chickens die within minutes from an allergic reaction, while others survive with no apparent ill effects.

Consulting the benge oracle involves the witchcraft victim, the oracle operator who administers the benge, and the oracle questioner who frames the question to elicit a clear answer. The questioner determines from the victim the nature of his or her inquiry and carefully poses the query to the benge, ordering the potion to kill the chicken to indicate "yes" and to spare the chicken to indicate "no." The oracle operator then administers the benge and jerks the chicken about to circulate the poison. Next, the three participants wait for the answer to manifest. According to Arthur S. Gregor, author of *Witchcraft & Magic: The Supernatural World of Primitive Man,* "The Zandes have a tremendous respect for the benge oracle and, if they had the means and the hens, would consult it not only for detecting witches but about almost anything troubling them. But costs run high. A man with problems can run through an entire flock of chickens in short order."

If the chicken dies and the answer points to a particular person, he or she is considered guilty of witchcraft. A wing from the chicken is detached and mounted on a stick, and the stick is delivered by an impartial courier to the guilty person. The usual reaction of the witch is to claim innocence and to beg the mangu to cease afflicting the victim. Usually thereafter the victim recovers from the affliction. If the victim doesn't recover, the failure of the oracle is explained by circumstances such as the oracle poison being too old or the oracle being affected by another person's use of witchcraft.

Unlike the Azande people, the Tswana people of Botswana believe that all witchcraft is done deliberately and with malice. They distinguish between "day sorcerers"—baloi ba motshegare—who on occasion use herbs and other preparations to harm a specific enemy, and "night witches"—baloi ba bosigo—who regularly gather at night in small groups and terrorize the countryside.

"Night witches" are mostly thought to be elderly women who gain admittance to the groups by causing the death of a family member, often a firstborn child. New members are said to receive either a special ointment that wakes them when the coven is to convene or an injection of magickal medicine in the thumb. When the thumb itches, the sensation awakens the witch so that she can join the coven. The women eschew clothing for their activities, preferring to smear their bodies with white ashes or the blood of their victims. They glide through the night, riding on hyenas and keeping their owl familiars close by as they perpetrate their offenses.

One of their nightly activities is robbing graves for cadaver parts. The women use a special ritual that allows the corpse to rise from the grave. They claim the parts they need for their spells then return the body to its resting place.

Living humans also become their victims. The "night witches" slip through walls and locked doors and silently assault sleeping persons by cutting their flesh. The fiends then place pebbles or pieces of rotted flesh into the cuts that soon fester and sicken the victims.

Beliefs in both "day sorcerers" and "night witches" are strong among many Africans, although fanciful stories of the latter are taken lightly. However, Africans take stories of "day sorcerers" and their practice of poisoning food or drink seriously. Some reports allege that the poison transforms itself into a miniature crocodile that eats away the insides of the victim, leading to an excruciating death. Other reports point to the true workings of poison, moving slowly through the body until it becomes too late to either save the victim or to identify the poisoner.

Contemporary people in eastern, southern, and western Africa cling still to the belief in witches, despite their beliefs in God and in the spirits of their ancestors as intermediaries with the Divine. Africans believe that at the heart of witchcraft is unresolved anger.

In modern African cities dotted with skyscrapers, office workers complain via electronic mail that jealous colleagues use witchcraft to thwart promotions. Successful business-people seek diviners to bestow protection upon new products to prevent witchcraft complications from competitors. Politicians who lose elections secretly blame opponents for using witchcraft against them.

Belief in witchcraft is considered primitive, and religious and civil authorities work vigorously to discourage its practice. However, numerous recent incidents demonstrate the present-day impact of witchcraft:

- Stunned silence gripped a courtroom in Busia, western Kenya, when the tools of a suspected witch were displayed. The items included animal claws, rags, human hair, shirt buttons, horns, ashes, coins, and herbs.
- An elderly man was stoned and burned to death in South Africa's Northern Transvaal Province after he was accused of directing a lightning bolt to strike and kill a school-age boy.
- A woman in Kitwe, Zambia, was caught in a tug of war between residents who attempted to kill her and police who struggled successfully to protect her. The woman had been accused of murdering a boy so that she could transfer his intelligence to her son.
- In Zambia, AIDS-related deaths in the region have been blamed on witchcraft. The village of Chiawa hired a witch finder to "cleanse" witchcraft from the area. Within a four-month period, the witch finder's method of administering a "tea" to uncover suspected witches had killed sixteen people.
- The Kenyan soccer team was thoroughly searched by authorities in Zaire after the home team complained that the visiting team had brought amulets to assure victory in the match.

While the traditional image of the witch is that of an unearthly creature who flies, dances naked on graves, copulates with animals, walks backwards, eats salt when thirsty, and hangs upside down from a tree when relaxing, the actual image is as familiar as the person next door or in the next cubicle. The African witch is someone the person knows well, such as a neighbor, colleague, or family member; and the witch wishes to harm that individual.

Suspected witches are often those who are poor and on the fringes of society, but the accusation of witchcraft also touches well-to-do, successful individuals. Research conducted by the Lands Institute of Dares-Salaam indicates that belief in witchcraft is an impediment to economic development in the northern district of Handeni La Tanzania. The fear is pervasive that if people are prosperous, they will become either targets of witchcraft accusations or recipients of bewitchment because of jealousy.

When individuals believe they have been bewitched, they consult specialists for "cleansing" rituals. Priests of traditional religions, mediums, or diviners conduct these complex ceremonies. For witchcraft affecting an entire community, witch hunters are called in to reveal the perpetrators of the witchcraft.

Witch-detection ordeals range from benign to deadly. In a benign test, the witch hunter asks suspected witches to swallow pieces of magickal bread. The person who has difficulty swallowing is considered to be the witch. In a deadly test, the witch hunter asks suspected witches to drink a poisonous mixture of herbs. Such a test left fifteen dead in Zambia. Sometimes just the fear generated by witch-detection ordeals is enough to make guilty witches confess.

The traditional punishment for witchcraft in many African communities was banishment or death. Today, witch hunts and the hangings of suspected witches are on the rise in some African countries. For example, in Kenya, where witchcraft is not a crime, the accused are prosecuted only for the intent to cause fear and harm. When the courts fail to deliver the kind of justice that communities demand, mob violence often results. In 1992, more than 300 people accused of witchcraft were lynched as witches in Kenya.

In response to the widespread violence in South Africa, the Ministry of Safety and Security of South Africa's Northern Transvaal Province established a Commission of Inquiry into Witchcraft, Violence, and Ritual Killings. The commission's May 1996 report indicated that thousands of people have faced accusations of witchcraft, have been driven from their homes, and have lost their property. Hundreds have been killed by vigilante mobs. Suspected witches were accused of transforming themselves into bats and birds, changing people into zombies, and killing victims by drawing down lightning bolts or poisoning them with toxic herbs.

Alarming statistics of witchcraft deaths brought together nearly two hundred police and government officials for a September 1998 conference in Thohoyandou, South Africa, to develop strategies to reduce the violence. From April 1994 to February 1995, ninety-seven women and forty-six men were accused of witchcraft in South Africa and subsequently killed by mobs. From January to June 1998, the Northern Province alone reported 386 crimes against suspected witches, including murder, assault, and property damage. Murder occurs most often during the rainy season, when people believe that witches use lightning to destroy their enemies.

Halting crimes against suspected witches will be an enormous challenge for authorities. In a culture that not only believes in malevolent witches but also considers violent reactions to witchcraft morally justifiable as self-defense, attitudes may be entrenched.

ABORIGINES OF AUSTRALIA

In 1894, English biologist and anthropologist Sir Walter Baldwin Spencer joined the Horn Scientific Expedition on an exploration of central Australia. There he met Francis James Gillen, an Australian anthropologist conducting independent studies of the Aborigines. Spencer and Gillen formed a fast friendship which blossomed into a professional collaboration.

The two amassed extensive information about Aboriginal customs, rituals, and beliefs, including those related to witchcraft. Spencer and Gillen discovered that the Aborigines had a strong belief in the power of sorcerers. For example, the various tribes believed that:

- Magick causes death. Since every death within a tribe is blamed on magick, the friends and relatives of the deceased consult the medicine man for the identity of the sorcerer. Then, one or more individuals stalk and kill the sorcerer to avenge the death.
- Medicine men can cure and kill. While their main function is to cure illnesses caused by malevolent magick, medicine men are also able to bring sickness and death to enemies of their tribes by repeating special incantations. Some medicine men can transform themselves into eagle-hawks, enabling them to fly to the camps of rival tribes to attack their victims.
- Pointing a charmed bone or stick at enemies can kill them, even at a distance. Along with pointing the implement repeatedly at the victim, the

sorcerer mutters a curse, which translates to: "May your heart be rent asunder. May your backbone be split open and your ribs torn asunder. May your head and throat be split open." The practice of "pointing" is conducted in strict secrecy. Were the perpetrator to be caught, he or she would mostly likely be put to death.

᠙ Spears can be charmed by singing an incantation over the weapon to endow it with magickal, poisonous properties called *Arungquiltha.* Anyone struck by an acknowledged "sung" spear, even if the wound is superficial, believes in the certainty of his or her death, unless counter-magick is conducted by a medicine man.

᠙ Hair-girdles are magickal possessions. When a man dies, his hair is cut off by the male members of his family and woven into a hair-girdle presented to the deceased's eldest son. This girdle is a valued, magickal possession that grants to the wearer all the warlike qualities of the deceased, ensures that his weapons have accurate aim, and enhances the wearer's skills as a sorcerer.

᠙ Wives are obtained through sorcery. When a man desires a wife, he takes a wooden Churinga—a sacred, engraved object, oval in shape and about six to eight inches long—and two or three friends into the bush. Throughout the night the men sing courtship songs and chant love phrases, addressed to the desired woman. At daylight, the native strikes the ground once with the Churinga then whirls it round and round until it hums. The humming sound travels to the ear of the woman, causing affection to grow within her and compelling her to respond to the summons.

Spencer and Gillen published their findings in *The Native Tribes of Central Australia* (1899) and in *The Northern Tribes of Central Australia* (1904).

A later scholar, sociologist, and anthropologist W. Lloyd Warner studied the Murngin people of northern Australia in the 1930s. Warner discovered this tribe's belief that sorcerers could perform mystical operations on their enemies. The victims would die later, not knowing the cause of the fate that had befallen them.

DOBU ISLANDERS

From November 1927 to May 1928, New Zealand-born anthropologist Reo Franklin Fortune studied the natives of the D'Entrecasteaux Islands, a cluster of islands in Papua New Guinea in the southwest Pacific, north of Australia. He published his findings in the book *Sorcerers of Dobu: The Social Anthropology of the Dobu Islanders of the Western Pacific* (1932).

The dense forests of Dobu Island revealed to Fortune a volcanic land and a volatile people whose lives were permeated by sorcery. Dobuans had a reputation among the islanders as being the grand masters of the black arts.

Cannibals and head hunters, the inhabitants of Dobu were treacherous, distrustful people who viewed anyone—relative, friend, or neighbor—as a potential sorcerer. Strangers were especially suspect, and Dobuans constructed special trails around their hamlets to divert travelers away from them.

Within the communities, fear was rampant. Rather than jointly raising yams, the principal food crop, husbands and wives kept separate gardens, guarding their respective patches with spells and rituals.

Farmers believed that once the root vegetable sent its vines into the air, the yams grew restless underground. This restlessness caused them to wander out of the garden at night and into a neighbor's garden. The Dobuans feared that the yams would find the neighbor's garden more appealing, especially since the neighbor had no doubt cast a spell to keep them from returning home. Thus, a farmer secured the shoots of the vines to their main stem and recited a spell to tie the yams to the home garden.

Since neighbors were plotting against them, farmers felt justified in using a stealing ritual to attract the yams of their neighbors. However, physically invading a neighbor's garden to steal yams was despised throughout the community. That act proved that the farmer's magick was weak and ineffective.

The farmer with the strongest magick had the largest crop of yams. Among many native peoples, a bountiful harvest usually calls for festivals and celebrations. However, just the opposite occurred among the Dobuans. Farmers harvested their crops secretly and concealed them in hidden storehouses. The common assumption was that the farmer with the largest crop had stolen from the neighbors.

Another type of theft that Dobuans feared was loss of affection through love sorcery. Adultery was prevalent. When a man seduced a neighbor's wife, he was envied throughout the community because his love sorcery was stronger than that of the woman's husband. The community scorned the husband. He usually retaliated by raging against the sorcery, aiming malevolent spells at the rival, and breaking his wife's cooking pots. If those actions failed to restore his status, the husband resorted to suicide.

Dobuans also feared that their good health would be stolen through sorcery. In a nefarious twist on the Golden Rule, Dobuans believed in doing unto others what others would do unto them, but doing it first. Thus, almost every native was a repository of various disease spells. Some Dobuans were renowned for having a monopoly on particular diseases. Therefore, if an individual came down with a specific illness, the person knew exactly who was responsible for the disease. The sick were reviled as weaklings; and when death occurred, Dobuans blamed the loss of life on sorcery, too.

Plotting the deaths of their neighbors was a tradition among the Dobuans. According to Reo Fortune, after one particular sorcerer decided to murder his "good friend," the sorcerer undertook serious training for the deed. He ingested large quantities of ginger and other potent spices to "hot up" his spells. Since he feared that the spells might poison him as well, the sorcerer diluted the spells by drinking copious amounts of water.

On the appointed day, the sorcerer crept up on his unsuspecting victim in his garden. The sorcerer leaped out of the bushes, uttered a bloodcurdling scream, and pounced on the man. Collapsed on the ground, the man writhed violently and mumbled incoherently. Within a few days, he was dead.

Dobuans believed in the efficacy of their death spells but were not averse to augmenting spells with poison. Housewives were vigilant when preparing meals so that no one tampered with the cooking pots. Accepting food from strangers was verboten. Even taking food from a friend was dangerous unless the friend ate his or her portion first.

Friendships were viewed with suspicion since they could be preludes to death spells. By tradition, a friend was not allowed to enter another person's home. Instead, the friend remained at the entrance to the home. If the friend was offered food, the friend had to eat with his or her back to the family. This guarded against the friend casting a spell against the household. Before a man left the village for a trading expedition, he performed a ritual to close the mouths of the family, friends, and neighbors he left behind. This prevented them from casting spells against him.

Anthropologists suggest that in a society without police or courts of law, sorcery affords individuals the opportunity to express their jealousy and hatred toward others in magickal rituals rather than in violent acts. Thus, sorcery maintains order and keeps the peace.

Reo Fortune reported that a farmer who wished to protect his fruit trees from robbery placed a disease spell on the orchard. Except in cases of extreme famine, no one dared to snatch the fruit. Another farmer found that one of his pigs had been killed and discovered footprints near the carcass. The farmer gathered the soil with the footprints and confronted his neighbor whom he suspected of committing the deed. The farmer threatened that he would perform sorcery on the footprints unless the neighbor made restitution for the lost animal. The neighbor paid the debt.

Fortune experienced personally the impact of the threat of sorcery. The anthropologist planned to leave a Dobuan village temporarily for business elsewhere but intended to return to continue his work. Before his departure, he pretended to place a dangerous spell of protection on his equipment. Almost immediately, the residents in the neighborhood fled into the surrounding forest.

THE NAVAHOS

American anthropologist Clyde Kluckhohn developed a lifelong interest in Navahos in 1922 when he moved to New Mexico for health reasons. While there, he became acquainted with a nearby tribe, learned their language and customs, and studied their beliefs and rituals. He published his findings in *Navaho Witchcraft* (1944).

Kluckhohn found that Navaho witchcraft provided relief from the tensions created by living together in small groups. Belief in witches affords social control by reining in those who stray from established economic and social norms.

Individuals and families conducted simple rituals to assure luck in travel and trade and for protection of crops and herds. For protection against witchcraft, a Navaho kept in his house pieces of turquoise and miniature carvings of sheep and horses. When he traveled, he wore a small sack containing magickal elements called "medicine." Typical medicines were animal teeth and claws, beeswax, seeds, roots, feathers, and stones.

More complex rituals for healing were conducted by a medicine man, who received payment based on his skill and the length of the ritual. For example, if a Navaho awoke feeling ill and discovered footprints outside his hut, he or she would realize that a witch had visited during the night and had cast a spell. To remove the spell, the Navaho consulted the local medicine man to perform the proper ritual.

Navahos believed that diseases were caused by witches shooting porcupine quills, wildcat whiskers, or pieces of bones from dead bodies at the intended victim with a type of bean shooter. When a Navaho discovered such a foreign body imbedded in the skin, the individual called upon the medicine man to extract the offending object. The medicine man performed a successful extraction and then offered to return the disease to the witch for an added fee.

Kluckhohn observed that Navahos also used witches as scapegoats, blaming witches for their misfortunes. For example, when a Navaho lost his beloved to another, he would conclude that the other man had used a witch's love potion to win her affection. If a Navaho acquired a horse during a trade and then realized later that the horse was lame, he would blame the original owner for using witchcraft to blind his eyes to the animal's defects.

Witchcraft was also used among the Navahos to "stifle dissent and independent thinking," according to Arthur S. Gregor, author of *Witchcraft & Magic: The Supernatural World of Primitive Man.* Gregor states:

> In 1884 there was a faction among the Navaho Indians who refused to yield to the whites and wanted to continue armed resistance. Manuelito, the Navaho chieftain, however, was convinced that the only hope for his tribe lay in surrender to the federal troops. How was he to silence the militants? If he betrayed them to the United States Army his own people would turn against him. He therefore denounced them as witches and then had them executed. Not one man dared protest against the slaying of those who were labeled witches.

NATIVES OF CHIAPAS, MEXICO

Indian villagers in Chiapas, Mexico, who become ill rely first on folk remedies to make them well. If they don't improve, they visit the local healer called a "curandero." If the local curandero is unable to effect a cure, villagers blame witchcraft for their maladies and seek the person tormenting them.

The natives of Chiapas believe that witches own familiars called "nawales." Owners of nawales can transform themselves into their familiars and roam through the village streets at night. In their animal shapes, they enter a neighbor's house unseen and nibble on the neighbor's soul each night until the neighbor becomes ill.

Uncovering the identity of the witch is tricky. The afflicted person must decide who in the village is angry or holding a grudge against him or her. After the identity of the suspected witch is known—usually a defenseless or powerless person—the afflicted person asks the curandero to visit the witch to ask that the witchcraft cease. Often, as the illness runs its natural course, the afflicted person recovers. However, if the illness progresses, the afflicted person goes witch hunting.

Witch hunting involves waiting for a time when the witch is not fully aware, perhaps when the witch is sleeping off a night in the cantina. Then the person thrusts a shotgun into the witch's hut and pulls the trigger.

After news of the killing spreads through the village, the elders convene for a trial to determine if the murdered person was indeed a witch. The afflicted person gives testimony, and reliable witnesses describe events related to the incident. After considering the evidence, the elders usually conclude that the murdered person was a witch. Thus, the afflicted person is deemed to have rid the community of a supernatural threat, and the person is hailed as a hero.

MORE MAGICKAL BELIEFS FROM AROUND THE WORLD

- In southern Italy, sorcerers who wished to harm an enemy named a lemon after the foe and pushed needles or splinters of wood into the fruit.
- In Wales, women were cautioned never to spin or knit in or near a field because witches would tangle the yarn.
- In Japan, following a house burglary, residents sought footprints of the thieves and burned mugwort (*Artemisia vulgaris*) in them. The homeowner believed that this made the robbers' feet sore, preventing them from running far and allowing the police to capture them easily.
- In China, sorcerers produced rain by placing five frogs on the altar of the god of the soil. Since frogs live in water, the Chinese believed that the creature controlled this element. The croakings of the frogs called for rain, encouraging the god to deliver the desired downpour.
- In Uganda, sorcerers stopped heavy rains by building fires and fanning the smoke toward the sky, preventing the clouds from falling.
- In Madagascar, a child's first haircut was a solemn occasion. The hair from the right side of the head was sacrificed to the family's ancestors to obtain a favorable life for the child. The hair from the left was secretly buried or thrown into running water to prevent a sorcerer from using it in a malevolent spell against the child.

- In Austria, on May Day at twilight, entire villages conducted a ceremony called "Burning Out the Witches." At the sound of the evening church bell, bundles of twigs attached to poles were ignited. Men and boys rang bells and banged pots and pans. Women waved censers of burning incense, and girls unchained dogs to run through the streets, yelping and barking. Everyone yelled repeatedly, "Witch flee, flee from here / Or it will go ill with thee." Residents ran seven times around the village, screaming and continuing the racket to drive the witches from their hiding places.
- In Germany, a sudden stiffness in the small of the back was blamed on witchcraft and called a "witch-shot."
- In the Highland region of Scotland, farmers believed that a witch could destroy an entire herd of livestock by hiding a small bag filled with magickal charms in a cleft of the stable.
- In England, farmers who believed that their flocks were bewitched burned alive one of the animals in order to destroy the witch embodied in the animal and to release the rest of the flock from the spell.
- In Lithuania, farmers kindled bonfires on Midsummer's Eve to prevent witches from using charms and spells to steal milk from cows.
- In France, on Midsummer's Eve, peasants gathered bunches of St. John's wort (*Hypericum perforatum*) and hung them on the walls of their houses to serve as witch detectors. If a witch crossed the threshold, the blossoms immediately dropped their yellow heads.
- In Ecuador, bewitching shamans among the Jivaro Indians dispatched "wakani" or spirit birds to fly around their victims, frightening them into insanity and then death.

When inexplicable events occur in the world, magick and witchcraft offer easy explanations. When witch-related folklore is part of the fabric of a culture, people are more prone to believe in the power of witches. The rich tapestry of this folklore provides insight into the attitudes, fears, and desires of people all over the world.

✺ *La Vecchia Religione* or The Old Religion ✺

According to Raven Grimassi, author of *Italian Witchcraft: The Old Religion of Southern Europe* and *Hereditary Witchcraft: Secrets of the Old Religion*, some valid evidence of pre-Christian Italian Witchcraft exists in documented sources:

✺ The ancient Roman poet Horace related the story of an Italian witch called Canidia in *Epodes of Horace* (30 B.C.E.). He wrote of Proserpine and Diana bestowing power to the Witches who worshipped them, of Witches gathering in secret to perform their mysterious rituals, and of a book of incantations (i.e., *Libros Carminum*) containing a spell for calling the moon down from the sky. Grimassi cites other ancient Roman writers such as Lucan and Ovid whose works address the same themes.

✺ Charles Leland, in his 1889 book *Aradia, or the Gospel of the Witches*, discussed Witches who gathered skyclad, or naked, at the time of the full moon, worshipping a goddess and a god by singing, dancing, and feasting on cakes and wine. Grimassi asserts that "these concepts clearly pre-date the Gardnerian movement of the 1950s from which modern Wicca evolved."

✺ Italian folklorist Lady Vere de Vere noted in an article included in *La Rivista of Rome* in 1894 that "the Community of Italian Witches is regulated by laws, traditions, and customs of the most secret kind, possessing special recipes for sorcery."

✺ J. B. Andrews, in volume 3 of *Folk-Lore: Transactions of the Folk-Lore Society*, 1897, indicated that "The Neapolitans have an occult religion" and that the Witches of Naples practice knot magick, prepare herbal potions, create protective amulets, and engage in the healing arts. According to Andrews, the knowledge possessed by the Witches was by tradition "given by the mother to the daughter."

✺ Sally Scully of the Department of History at the University of San Francisco contributed an article to the *Journal of Social History* that discussed the seventeenth century witchcraft trial of Laura Malipero, known as "la strega famosissima" or "the most famous witch" in Venice. In 1654, Malipero's home was searched by officials of the Inquisition, who uncovered numerous handwritten spells; suspicious herbals; and several copies of a magickal book, apparently being hand copied, in various states of completion. According to Raven Grimassi, "This serves as partial evidence that Italian Witches were passing magical traditions through personal hand written books (what Wiccans would call a Book of Shadows)."

Grimassi relates that many Italian Witches acknowledge the historical existence of "The Holy Strega" or "The Beautiful Pilgrim," a woman named Aradia di Toscano, thought to have been born in Tuscany circa 1313. The tale reflects that Aradia was taught the Old Ways by her aunt. As a young woman, Aradia experienced spiritual enlightenment, prompting her to assemble a group of followers and travel throughout the country, teaching the secrets of the Old Religion. According to T. C. Lethbridge in his book *Witches*, "Aradia was sent to earth to teach this art to Mankind. That is, she was, in the opinion of her devotees, a personage, known in Hindu Religion as an Avatar, who taught them how to harness magic power. Aradia, at some far-off time, may have been as much an historical person as Christ, Krishna or Buddha."

The historical Aradia created a revival of Italian Witchcraft also known as Stregheria. Stregheria traces its roots back to ancient Etruscan religion. The modern Arician system of Stregheria, also known as the Arician Tradition or the Arician Ways, differs from modern-day Wicca in a number of ways:

- For most Streghe in Italy, the chief name for the God is Tagni, while the chief name for the Goddess is Uni.
- The feminine expression of the Deity assumes four individual aspects that are associated with the four phases of the moon. Italian Hereditary Witches relate the dark phase of the moon to Umbrea, the goddess of shadows and secrets. They relate the new, waxing crescent moon to Diana, the goddess of the hunt. They relate the full moon to Losna, the goddess who is the Great Mother. They relate the old, waning crescent moon to Manea, the goddess of night spirits and departed souls.
- Rituals are structured, and Streghe believe in adding to but never removing elements from their rites.

According to Grimassi, "We believe our tradition follows what we would call elder Wicca, the Old Religion, from which many of the elements of modern-day Wicca have been derived."

TWO

The Folklore of Witches and Witchcraft

✦

HE old hag soaring through the night air on a broom-stick. The witch and her constant companion, a black cat. A coven of witches gathered together to worship the Devil and to eat children. These are only a few of the images of witches and witchcraft that originated in folklore and that persist to this day. How and why did these beliefs begin?

THE POWER OF FLIGHT

In the Middle Ages and during the Renaissance, people believed that witches had the power to fly. According to folklore, a witch mounted a shovel, pitchfork, or broom; soared into the sky; and zoomed through the air at lightning speed toward her destination.

Scholars have speculated about the origins of the modes of transportation for witches. Some believe that the broom is associated with the folk image of the flying witch because it was the main implement used in the home by women and because most witches were female. By custom, a woman used her broom to signal to her neighbors that she was away from home. She either propped the broom outside the door or pushed the broom up the chimney. Thus, the folklore evolved that witches launched themselves into the air on their brooms from outside their homes or through the chimney.

Other scholars believe that the association of witches with shovels and pitchforks is a remnant from the days of ancient pagan fertility rituals. Pagans who worshipped nature-based deities mounted shovels and pitchforks and rode them through the fields, leaping and dancing among the rows to ensure a bountiful crop.

According to popular belief, witches brewed flying ointments in their cauldrons by combining fat from dead, unbaptized babies, bat's blood, and special herbs. The witch smeared the concoction on herself or on her broom and then was whisked away to a sabbat by the magickal ointment. In 1560 in Italy, a witch anointed herself with a flying ointment then fell into a trance. Later, when she emerged from her stupor, she described an airy journey over mountains and rivers.

In 1662, Isobel Gowdie, who was tried for Witchcraft in Scotland after voluntarily confessing to participating in covens and cavorting with the Devil and his demons, testified about the night flights she took with her sister witches: "We take our windle-straws or beanstalks and put them between our feet and say thrice, 'Horse and hattock, Horse and pellatis, ho!' and immediately we fly to wherever we would. We fly like straws when we please."

Johannes Wierus, a sixteenth century demonographer, recorded two recipes for flying ointments. One recipe called for hemlock, water of aconite, poplar leaves, and soot. The other recipe called for infant's fat, juice of cowbane, aconite, cinquefoil, deadly nightshade, and soot. Today, scientists speculate that the hallucinogenic herbs used in the recipes were absorbed by the skin and that the physiological reactions—dizziness, irregular heartbeat, confusion, delirium, and hallucinations—merely simulated the sensation of flying.

Dr. Will-Erich Peuckert, a twentieth century researcher at the University of Göttingen in Germany, concocted a flying ointment from a medieval recipe.

The recipe called for a base of hog's lard plus ingredients such as deadly night-shade, thornapple, henbane, wild celery, and parsley. Dr. Peuckert and a colleague tested the ointment on themselves, and the two succumbed to a trancelike sleep. They remained in that state for twenty hours, each dreaming of airborne flights to distant mountain tops where they engaged in demon rituals. When they awakened, both men suffered from headaches and depression yet both were astounded at the seeming reality of their dreams.

This experiment may explain why medieval witches who used such magickal ointments believed that their experiences had been real and may also explain why many of the witches' confessions of flight contain similar details.

As early as 906, the Church's *Canon Episcopi* declared that witches did not have the ability to fly physically but that witches could fly in spirit. However, the Church altered this position during the time leading up to the Inquisition. While doubting that witches could fly, Inquisitors and demonologists accepted confessions of flight as incriminating evidence against suspected witches.

Folklore states that one way to keep witches grounded is by ringing church bells. People believed that the sound created by bells generated great spiritual power to chase away evil spirits. During the Middle Ages, on nights such as Samhain (All Hallow's Eve) or Beltaine when villagers feared that witches would be traveling to sabbats, church bells pealed continuously to prevent witches from flying over the village. To augment the church bells, villagers banged on pots and pans or rang bells of their own. Accused witches testified at their trials that as they glided through the air on the way to sabbats, the sound of bells ringing in the night threw them off their brooms and onto the ground.

KEEPING FAMILIARS

A demon in animal form, a familiar serves a witch in her diabolical enterprises. Scholars speculate that the association between witches and familiars may have its roots in the ancient belief in fairies: supernatural beings and nature spirits such as brownies, elves, dwarfs, trolls, gnomes, and leprechauns who could be helpful, mischievous, or malevolent.

During the Great European Witch Hunt, accused witches often testified that they had been taught their magickal arts by fairies, perhaps hoping to be judged less harshly than if they admitted to being students of the Devil. Nevertheless, the Church considered these spirit entities to be minor demons, providing further evidence that the witch and her familiar were in league with the Devil.

Familiars often take the shape of a cat, toad, or owl. However, any animal or insect that lingered around an accused witch was suspected of being her familiar. People believed that the Devil gave familiars to witches or that witches purchased or inherited familiars from other witches.

The cat has been linked to witches since ancient times, especially black cats, which represented darkness and death. In medieval Europe, black cats were customarily hunted, captured, and burned alive.

Cats have also been used in witches' spells, the most notorious being the spell attributed to Scotland's John Fian and his North Berwick Witches in their plot to drown James VI and Queen Anne. During the trial of the witches in 1590 and 1591, testimony was given that Fian and his coven had christened a cat, tied each of its paws to the limb of a corpse, then tossed the cat into the ocean with the incantation "Hola!" This caused fierce storms to buffet the royal ship, but James and his young bride survived the journey from Scandinavia to Scotland.

The toad was another animal shape taken by familiars. Toads have been associated with evil since the days of the ancient teacher and prophet of Persia, Zoroaster (circa 600 B.C.E.), who declared that all toads should be killed because of their malevolent nature. This judgment may have been prompted because of the toad's natural defense mechanism: When attacked or injured, a toad secretes a thick, white poison through its skin. This hallucinogenic substance, which can be lethal, is known scientifically as bufotenine. In folklore, the poison is called "toad's milk." People believed that witches dispatched their toad familiars to poison enemies.

Witches also used toads as ingredients in various spells and rituals. If she wanted to kill an enemy by torture, a witch baptized a toad with the enemy's name. Then she tortured the toad to death, believing that the same fate would befall the enemy. Combining a toad's spittle with sow thistle sap made a lotion that the witch applied to make herself invisible. As a cure for drunkenness, a witch mixed the ashes of a burned toad with brandy.

Familiars also took the shape of owls. Since ancient times, the owl has been associated with sorcery and the dark side of life. The Egyptians saw the owl as the symbol of night, cold, and death. While the Greeks honored the owl as a sacred symbol of wisdom, the Romans viewed it as a sign of impending death. Screeching owls announced the murder of Caesar, and, according to folklore, the hooting of an owl presages illness or death.

The Aztecs believed that owls were evil spirits, and North American Indians saw the owl as an omen of death or as a messenger from the realm of the dead. Medicine men among the Chippewa cause starvation among their enemies by feeding an owl magickal ingredients and commanding the bird to fly to the house of the enemy. Africans fear owls because they—as well as bats, hyenas, and baboons—are known to be the familiars of sorcerers.

Witches often kept more than one familiar. A sixteenth century woman from Essex confessed that she had three familiars, Littleman, Prettyman, and Daynty, who took the shape of mice. Elizabeth Clark, the first person to fall victim to seventeenth century English witch hunter Matthew Hopkins, testified under torture that she owned five familiars: a kitten, a legless spaniel, a black rabbit, a polecat, and a magickal creature named Vinegar Tom. Vinegar Tom resembled a greyhound but had the head of an ox, and Clark testified that the creature could transform itself into a headless 4-year-old child.

The witch and her familiar enjoyed a symbiotic relationship. The familiar offered protection to the witch and did her bidding; the witch nourished the familiar with her blood. Familiars sucked the blood from her finger or from any outgrowth on the witch's skin such as a wart, birthmark, extra nipples, red spots, freckles, or unusual bumps. These so-called "witch's marks" were evidence that a witch had a familiar and were used as proof to convict an individual of witchcraft.

During the witch hunts of the Middle Ages and the Renaissance, Inquisitors in England and Scotland were especially obsessed with exposing accused witches through their familiars. These Inquisitors embraced the Biblical directive that anyone "that hath a familiar spirit . . . shall surely be put to death" (Leviticus 20:27) and the warning from the *Malleus Maleficarum* (1486) that a familiar "always works with her [the witch] in everything." They also used the legal clout of the Witchcraft Act of 1604, which forbade anyone to "consult, covenant with, entertain, employ, feed, or reward any evil and wicked spirit to or for any intent or purpose."

When a witch was arrested, she was stripped and examined for signs of "witch's marks." If marks were found, the witch was bound and left alone in a jail cell. Secretly, the jailers watched for the witch's familiar to materialize to offer aid and comfort to the witch. Any creature that moved toward her, even a rat or a cockroach, was deemed to be her familiar.

In the 1556 trial of the Chelmsford Witches of Essex, England, Elizabeth

Francis testified that her grandmother, Mother Eve, had taught her the art of witchcraft and had presented to Francis a white-spotted cat named Sathan that was the Devil in disguise. According to the trial records, Mother Eve taught Francis to feed the cat with bread and milk. Francis also testified that "every time he did anything for her, she said that he required a drop of blood, which she gave him by pricking herself, sometime in one place and then in another, and where she pricked herself there remained a red spot which was still to be seen."

The witch, the keeping of familiars, and the bearing of any "witch's mark" entered the permanent record of folklore through lines of verse such as those from Thomas Gay in 1726:

> *Teaz'd with their cries her choler grew*
> *And thus she sputter'd. Hence ye crew.*
> *Fool that I was to entertain*
> *Such imps, such fiends, a hellish train!*
> *Had ye been never hous'd and nurst*
> *I, for a witch had n'er been curst.*
> *To you I owe, that crouds of boys*
> *Worry me with eternal noise;*
> *Straws laid across my pace retard,*
> *The horse-shoe's nailed (each threshold's guard)*
> *The stunted broom the wenches hide,*
> *For fear that I should up and ride;*
> *They stick with pins my bleeding seat,*
> *And bid me show my secret teat.*

SABBATS AND DEVIL WORSHIP

People believed that witches congregated for Satanic worship, sexual orgies, and rapacious feasting at diabolical celebrations called sabbats. Historians disagree about the derivation of the word "sabbat." Some believe that the word comes from the French "s'esbattre," meaning "to frolic." Others think the word comes from the Greek "sabaoth," meaning "armies" or "hosts"; still others conclude that the word comes from the Hebrew "shabbath," meaning "to rest."

The word "sabbat" seems to have emerged as a term to describe a gathering of witches during the time of the Christian witch hunts in the fourteenth and fifteenth centuries. Some historians speculate that the connotation of the word blends images of seasonal pagan rituals still practiced during that time, such as the Druidic festivals of Beltaine and Samhain; the ancient Greek and Roman celebrations of Bacchanalia and Saturnalia; and the Church propaganda that heretical sects such as Cathars and Waldenses engaged in secret, lascivious rites.

Among those the Church considered heretics were witches and Jews. Thus, some historians theorize that "sabbat" was an anti-Semitic term used to equate the purportedly obscene gatherings of witches to the solemn day of rest and worship practiced by the Jews. Historians also note that the word "synagogue" was used as a synonym for "sabbat."

The term "synagogue" first appeared in 1182 when Walter Map described the alleged activities of a group of heretics assembled to worship the Devil:

> About the first watch of the night, when gates, doors, and windows have been closed, the groups sit waiting in silence in their respective synagogues, and a black cat of marvelous size climbs down a rope which hangs in their midst. On seeing it, they put out the lights. They do not sing hymns or repeat them distinctly, but hum through clenched teeth and pantingly feel their way toward the place where they see their lord. When they have found him they kiss him, each the more humbly as he is the more inflamed by frenzy—some the feet, more under the tail, most the private parts.

As witchcraft became associated with heresy, many details of heretical Devil worship were ascribed to witches, whom the Inquisitors presumed also gathered in groups. The word "sabbat" appears only twice in fifteenth-century literature. However, by the later years of that century, the term was most often applied to gatherings of witches.

Details about sabbats emerged from the trial records of the Inquisition, most often from torture-induced confessions of accused witches. These details formed the template for other accused individuals under duress to use to describe a typical gathering of witches. Inquisition records reveal that sabbats were held at night in isolated locales such as in caves, on mountaintops, and within the cover of thick forests. Witches and their familiars arrived at sabbats astride flying broomsticks or on the backs of demons that had transformed themselves into animals.

The guest of honor was the Devil, appearing as a goat, toad, crow, or other shape. According to Henri Bouguet, a judge presiding at the trial of accused witch Rolande de Vernois: "The Devil presented himself at the Sabbat in the form of a huge black cat."

The Devil began the sabbat by calling out the names of his followers and questioning them about evil deeds they had committed since the last gathering. Then the witches disrobed and honored the Devil with the "osculum infame" or "kiss of shame" on his buttocks. A fourteenth-century Latin tract describing the practices of the Waldenses, a heretical religious sect in the Vaudois area of the Alps, noted: ". . . the devil appears to them in the shape and form of a cat, and they kiss him individually under the tail."

After the "kiss of shame," the witches conducted blood sacrifices of unbaptized infants and welcomed new initiates to the Devil's demonic army. King James I wrote in *Daemonologie* (1597) that: "It is a certain rule Witches deny their Baptism when they make Covenant with the Devil." This was one of the common elements of initiation reported in many witch-hunt trials. Pierre de Lancre, a seventeenth-century witch hunter, claimed that witches disavowed their faith by reciting: "I renounce and deny God, the blessed Virgin, the Saints, baptism, father, mother, relations, heaven, earth and all that is the world."

Initiates also proclaimed an oath of allegiance to the Devil. For example, witches in Scandinavia reportedly placed into small bags the shavings from metal clocks and a number of weighty stones then tossed the bags into a nearby body of water. The witches vowed: "As these shavings of the clock do never return to the clock from which they are taken, so may my soul never return to heaven."

Witches in Scotland placed one hand on the top of their heads and the other hand on the bottom of one foot and announced that everything between the hands was consecrated to the Devil's service.

After the witches proclaimed their allegiance, the Devil baptized them; bestowed upon each a new, secret name; and offered his black book, into which each initiate added his or her signature in blood. Sometimes the Devil marked the new witches as his own by clawing or biting them. Other times the Devil had the initiates desecrate the cross by spitting on it or grinding it into the dirt.

Following the initiation, the witches engaged in frenzied intercourse with the Devil and his demons before joining in riotous feasting, preferring the roasted flesh of babies. French demonologist Jean Bodin wrote in *De Mago-*

rum Daemonomania (1580): "Witches eat human flesh, especially the flesh of children, and publicly drink their blood. But if they cannot procure children, they exhume human corpses from the grave or take from gibbets the bodies of hanged men."

At the conclusion of the feasting, the witches danced in the moonlight or set off for populated areas to raise storms, kill animals, sink ships, and perpetrate other malevolent deeds. Their revelry ended before dawn, and the witches returned home. Some accused witches testified that they attended sabbats weekly; others confessed that they attended sabbats just one or two times a year.

Historians and writers argued throughout the years about the veracity of claims that witches participated in sabbats. According to demonologist Henri Bouguet in *Discours des Sorciers* (1590): "Unfortunately, the Sabbat did—and does —take place; formerly in deserted wasteland, on the hill-side, in secluded spots, now, as often as not, in the privacy of vaults and cellars, and in those lone empty houses innocently placarded 'To Be Sold.'"

However, in 1761, French cleric Dom Augustin Calmet wrote: "To attempt to give a description of the Sabbat is to attempt a description of what does not exist and what has never existed save in the fantastic and disordered imagination of warlocks and witches. The pictures which have been drawn of these assemblies are merely the fantasy of those who dreamed they had actually been borne, body and soul, through the air to the Sabbat."

Contemporary writer Rosemary Ellen Guiley states in *The Encyclopedia of Witches and Witchcraft*: "Most likely, the witches' sabbat was a fabrication of the witch-hunters, who seized upon admission of attendance at a gathering, meeting or feast and twisted it into a diabolical affair. Victims who made such confessions were pressed to name others who had attended the sabbats. In this manner, sometimes entire villages became implicated in Devil-worship."

MEMBERSHIP IN COVENS

In *A History of Witchcraft, Sorcerers, Heretics, and Pagans*, Jeffrey Burton Russell states: "Another contribution of heresy to witchcraft is the idea that witches met in groups. Sorcerers almost always practised [sic] magic singly, but heretics worked in communities. The Alpine Italian heretics of the fourteenth century met in assemblies of seven to forty-seven, with an average meeting of about twenty." Thus, by extension, people believed that witches were also members of secret organizations, and these were called covens.

The derivation of the word "coven" is murky. Some historians believe that the word is derived from the Latin word "coventus," which means "assembly" or "coming together." In the *Canterbury Tales*, Chaucer described the meeting of thirteen people as a "covent." In 1662, confessed Scottish witch Isobel Gowdie described a squad of witches as a "covine."

References to covens of witches appear in literature beginning in the twelfth century, but many of the citations contain the admonition that covens were illusionary deceptions wrought by the Devil. Only during the Renaissance was the existence of covens embraced with fervor.

The 1324 trial of Alice Kyteler in Ireland yielded the earliest mention of the word in connection with a witch trial. Kyteler stood accused of being one of a thirteen-member coven. During the sixteenth and seventeenth centuries, accused witches were often tortured until they admitted their membership in covens, after which they were compelled to reveal the names of other members. By the early eighteenth century, the image of a coven as a working circle of witches was an entrenched popular belief.

This belief was promulgated in the early twentieth century by British anthropologist Margaret A. Murray, who believed that ancient covens were highly organized and widespread. In her book *The Witch-Cult in Western Europe*, Murray theorized that witchcraft in the Middle Ages and during the Renaissance was not a heretical phenomenon of Christianity. She believed that witchcraft practices were the vestiges of a pagan, earth-based, fertility religion that had originated in Paleolithic times. Many scholars dispute Murray's theories. While acknowledging that some practitioners of pagan religion who still met in secret groups may have been swept up in the net of the Inquisition, most scholars believe that the majority of accused witches were women with herbal knowledge and healing power, living alone and apart from their communities.

Another popular belief was that covens numbered thirteen individuals, consisting of twelve followers and a leader who was either the Devil or a person who dressed in animal skins and horns to represent the Devil. Murray lent credence to this belief by citing trial records from 1567 to 1673 that documented eighteen covens each having thirteen members. She pointed to five thirteen-member covens in England, nine in Scotland, and one each in France, Germany, Ireland, and the United States. However, many scholars deem Murray's data to be erroneous.

Still, the thirteen-member coven retained its resonance in folklore. The number 13 has been associated with bad luck and evil power since ancient times. Those who suffer from triskaidekaphobia, fear of the number 13, point to the fact that Christ and his twelve apostles, including Judas the betrayer, numbered thirteen at the Last Supper.

In *Power of the Witch,* author Laurie Cabot states: "The association with Jesus was probably just another attempt by the Inquisition . . . to draw unfavorable analogies between Christianity and paganism by creating the myth that Witches pervert Christian customs." According to Cabot, the power of the number 13 stems from its association with the old lunar calendar and its thirteen full moons.

THE FEAR OF WATER

Associated since ancient times with purity and holiness, water entered folklore as an earthly element that witches feared. People believed that they could stop a witch from pursuing them by crossing a body of running water, and the Catholic Church taught that holy water would deter witches.

During the Middle Ages and Renaissance, villagers sprinkled holy water on houses to chase away witches and to stop them from drawing lightning bolts to the dwellings. Villagers also doused crops and animals with holy water to prevent bewitchment. If an animal fell under a witch's curse, a dose of holy water poured down the animal's throat broke the spell. Holy water became a household staple, obtained from the holy-water carrier who passed through villages on a regular route. During the witch hunts, Inquisitors kept vials of holy water nearby to ward off spells from the witches on trial.

According to King James I of England in *Daemonologie,* upon making a pact with the Devil, witches denied their baptism. "Water being the sole element thereof, and when they are heaved into the water it refuseth to receive them but suffers them to float." The belief that water would reject a witch became a tool that the Inquisition used against accused individuals in an ancient test of guilt or innocence called "swimming."

When an accused witch was "swum," he or she was cross-bound, meaning that the right thumb was bound to the left toe and the left thumb was bound to the right toe. The person was then plunged into a body of water, usually three times in succession. Those who floated were deemed guilty, while those who sank were deemed innocent. However, many of those deemed innocent subsequently drowned because friends and relatives on shore could not pull them out in time. Those deemed guilty by the water test were also doomed but by death in another form. For example, two accused witches were "swum" in Hartford, Connecticut, in 1633. They floated, were declared guilty, and then were hanged.

The process of swimming was conducted differently in Russia. There, accused witches had a rope tied around the waist and were lowered into a deep section of a river. Upon sinking, the accused were yanked back to shore and safety. Upon floating, the witches were pulled out, and a burning brand in the shape of a cross was applied to their bodies. The cross served a dual purpose, warning the populace that the individuals were witches and neutralizing their power.

A variation on swimming comes from Babylonia. The code of laws developed by Hammurabi (1792–1750 B.C.E.) stated that a person accused but not proved guilty of practicing black magick was to be thrown into a river. If the accused witch drowned, his or her property would be forfeited to the accuser. If the accused witch did not drown, the accuser would be executed, and the accuser's property would be forfeited to the one who had been accused of witchcraft.

One leading proponent of swimming was Englishman Matthew Hopkins, a notorious professional witch hunter responsible for the deaths of at least 230 alleged witches. However, most judges held that swimming was not irrefutable proof because many witch hunters could manipulate their victims to float or the accused could manipulate themselves to sink. One prominent religious leader who agreed was Increase Mather. In his 1684 *An Essay for the Recording of Illustrious Providences,* Mather disputed vigorously the arguments about swimming offered by King James I in *Daemonologie* and opposed its use in witch trials.

In 1219, King Henry III declared swimming illegal in England, but the method later became a favorite of witch hunters in Europe, the British Isles, and North America from the sixteenth to the eighteenth centuries. Swimming was again outlawed in England in 1712, and those who continued to use the technique were charged with murder when their victims drowned. Swimming continued as a spontaneous reaction of lynch mobs throughout the years, but the practice finally ceased in the nineteenth century.

SHAPE-SHIFTING

People believed that witches could change themselves and other humans into animals, birds, and insects. Common forms included a cat, dog, hare, crow, owl, or bat. The origins of this belief may be found in ancient literature and folklore.

In Homer's *Odyssey*, the fair-haired enchantress Circe transformed Odysseus's men into swine. In fairy tales and folktales, wicked witches routinely punished people by turning them into toads, frogs, or other creatures. In the Scottish Highlands, large, wild "Elfin Cats" that roam the land are considered to be witches who have changed shape. The creatures have arched backs, black coats with erect fur, and a white spot on the breast, the very image of the Halloween cat.

Accusations of metamorphosis were a staple in witch-hunt trials. In 1663 in Newcastle, England, Jane Milburne claimed that when she failed to invite Dorothy Strangers to a wedding supper, Strangers changed herself into a feline, and along with other cats appeared at the Milburne home, scratching, howling, and raising an infernal din.

John Louder of Salem, Massachusetts, who had exchanged angry words with his neighbor Bridget Bishop, testified in a sworn statement in June 1692:

> I did see a black pig in the room coming towards me, so I went towards it to kick it, and it vanished away. Immediately after, I sat down in a narrow bar and did see a black thing jump into the window and came and stood just before my face, upon the bar. The body of it looked like a monkey, only the feet were like a cock's feet, with claws, and the face somewhat more like a man's than a monkey. . . . So the thing spoke to me and said, 'I am a messenger sent to you, for I understand you are troubled in mind, and if you will be ruled by me you shall want for nothing in this world.' Upon which, I endeavored to clap my hands upon it, and said, 'you devil, I will kill you.' But [I] could feel no substance, and it jumped out of the window again, and immediately came in by the porch, although the doors were shut, and said 'you had better take my counsel.' Whereupon, I struck at it with a stick, but struck the groundsill and broke the stick, but felt no substance. . . . Then it vanished away, and I opened the back door and went out. And going towards the house end, I espied said Bridget Bishop in her orchard, going towards her house.

Accused witches sometimes confessed to changing shape. In 1649, Englishman John Palmer of St. Albans admitted that he had changed himself into a toad and had waited for a man with whom he had had a disagreement. When the man passed by, he kicked the creature. Palmer confessed that after he metamorphosed back to his original shape, he had an achy shin.

In 1662 Scotland's Isobel Gowdie declared that she and the members of her coven used incantations to turn themselves into hares, crows, cats, and other animals. Gowdie revealed the incantation they repeated three times in order to change into cats:

> *I shall goe intill ane catt,*
> *With sorrow, and sych, and a blak shott;*
> *And I sall goe in the Divellis nam,*
> *Ay will I com hom againe.*

She also revealed the incantation they repeated three times in order to change back into human form:

> *Catt, catt, God send thee a blak shott.*
> *I am in a cattis liknes just now,*
> *Bot I sal be in a womanis liknes ewin now.*
> *Catt, catt, God send thee a blak shott.*

According to folklore, witches changed themselves into other shapes in order to roam unsuspected through the countryside, to gain entry into an enemy's household, or to escape capture. For example, in Navarre in 1547 a witch waiting to face the Inquisitors slathered a magickal ointment on her body, transformed into a screech owl, and flew away.

Many witches believed that their magick ointments effected their metamorphosis. However, some alchemists and demonologists believed that the hallucinogenic ingredients used in the ointments fostered the illusion of having changed shape in the same way that flying ointments simulated flight. Alchemist Giovanni Batista Porta wrote in *Natural Magick* in 1562 about the experiences of two men who had applied a hallucinogenic ointment and believed that they had become a fish and a goose. Porta recorded:

> . . . the man would seem sometimes to be changed into a fish; and flinging out
> his arms, would swim on the ground; sometimes he would seem to skip up,

and then dive down again. Another would believe himself turned into a goose, and would eat grass, and beat the ground with his teeth, like a goose: now and then sing, and endeavor to clap his wings.

Although folklore attributed to witches the ability to change form, expert opinion varied. French demonologist Jean Bodin believed that witches could effect shape-shifting, while Puritan minister Increase Mather denounced the process as "fabulous," writing:

> But it is beyond the power of all the Devils in Hell to cause such a transformation; they can no more do it than they can be Authors of a true Miracle . . . Though I deny not but that the Devil may so impose upon the imagination of Witches so as to make them believe that they are transmuted into Beasts.

To prove his point, Mather shared the story of a woman jailed as a suspected witch who told her jailer that she could change herself into a wolf. After anointing herself with a magickal lotion, the woman descended into a deathlike sleep. Her frightened jailer could not rouse her either by making noise or by delivering blows to her. Three hours later, she awoke and described how she had traveled to a nearby location and while in the shape of a wolf had attacked and killed a sheep and cow. An investigation of her claim was conducted, and both a sheep and cow were found dead in the area described by the woman. Mather attributed the "mischief" to the Devil and believed that Satan had deluded the woman into thinking she had perpetrated the slaughter.

The ability of a witch to change into a wolf was a terrifying concept for most people. When villages were attacked by wolves, the residents often believed that the animals were in fact witches. In 1573 in Lyon, France, Gilles Garnier was accused of being a wizard who transformed himself into a wolf. Accused of attacking, killing, and devouring children, Garnier was condemned and burned alive for his crimes.

A seventeenth-century French folktale perpetuates such fears. A hunter attacked by a giant wolf slices off one of the wolf's paws. The wolf escapes, and the hunter pockets the paw as a souvenir and returns home to show his friends. When he later withdraws the paw, it has become a woman's hand with a familiar ring on one of the fingers. The hunter calls for his wife, who shows him the bloody stump where her hand once was and admits that she is a witch. She confesses that she had changed into a wolf so that she could travel to a sabbat. The tale ends with the wife being burned at the stake.

The notion that witches can change themselves into wolves and coyotes is also part of the Navaho belief system. Called "Big Trotter," the wolf is the most common animal shape chosen by witches. Called "Little Trotter," the coyote is regarded by Navahos as the champion of disorder, trickery, and witchcraft. Both animals travel swiftly, cover ground furtively, and disappear seemingly into thin air, which proves their supernatural power.

According to James Burbank, author of *Vanishing Lobo: The Mexican Wolf and the Southwest*, "greater fluidity" exists between the human and animal worlds for Navahos. Thus, they believe that transforming into an animal is well within the power of witches, most of whom are men in the Navaho tradition.

A Navaho can always tell whether an encounter with a wolf is caused by a Yenaldlooshi, which means "he who trots along here and there on all fours with it [an animal skin]." A genuine wolf runs with its tail held out behind it, while a Yenaldlooshi or "skinwalker" runs with its tail hanging straight down. Navahos believe that shooting a wolf at night and following the tracks of the wounded animal will lead to a man with a suspicious injury.

THE ARCHETYPE OF THE EVIL WITCH

What accounts for the almost universal commonality of witch imagery and witchcraft beliefs in cultures around the world? According to historian Jeffrey Burton Russell:

> The worldwide similarity of sorcery beliefs constitutes the most curious and important dilemma in the study of witchcraft. When we find, centuries and continents apart, the idea of a night-hag seducing men and murdering children or a sorceress riding a broomstick, we are not entitled to dismiss the question of how these similarities arose.

One theory that explains such similarities is that of the "collective unconscious," a term coined by Swiss psychologist and psychiatrist Carl Jung. Jung theorized that all human beings share a common collection of universal primordial ideas and images. This "collective unconscious" may be genetically coded in the human brain and may be inherited by succeeding generations.

Jung believed that these ideas and images manifested themselves as archetypes such as the fair maiden or the brave knight. The archetype of the evil witch occurs consistently in folklore, legends, and fairy tales in most cultures around the world. The following fairy tales provide a taste of the evil-witch archetype.

From Germany: "Hansel and Gretel"

Once upon a time, a little boy named Hansel and a little girl named Gretel lived at the edge of a forest with their father and stepmother. Their father, a poor woodcutter, spent long days in the forest, chopping trees.

Hansel and Gretel knew that their stepmother did not love them. When they played in the yard, she scolded them for being noisy. When they sat quietly in the corner, she slapped them for being lazy. When it was time to eat, she threw stale crusts of bread on their plates.

Then into the land came a terrible famine, and no one had food to trade for wood. Soon the cupboards were nearly bare in the woodcutter's home. "How shall we feed the children?" the woodcutter moaned to his wife.

"How shall we feed ourselves?" his wife wanted to know. She proposed a plan: taking Hansel and Gretel deep into the forest, giving them a bit of bread, then leaving them there. "They will never find the way home," the stepmother said, "and we will be rid of them forever."

Hansel and Gretel heard what their stepmother planned to do. Gretel wept softly, and Hansel comforted her. "Don't worry, dear Gretel. I will save us."

The next morning, Hansel and Gretel were awakened by their stepmother. "Get up, you lazy children," she said. "You are going with us into the forest to gather sticks." Hansel and Gretel jumped out of bed, dressed, then went to the kitchen. Their stepmother gave them each a portion of bread. "Save this for your dinner," she told them. "If you eat it now, you'll receive no more later."

Hansel and Gretel, their father, and stepmother started on the path into the forest. Hansel crumbled up the bread that his stepmother had given him and dropped pieces along the path behind him to show him the way back home.

When they had reached the deepest part of the forest, their father and stepmother left Hansel and Gretel by a roaring fire. Their stepmother told them: "Your father and I will go on ahead to cut wood. Stay here, and we will return to fetch you later." Gretel shared her bread with Hansel, and soon the two fell asleep beside the fire.

They awoke when the silver orb sprinkled moonlight on the forest path.

But when Hansel looked for the bread crumbs he had left on the path, he realized that the birds of the forest had eaten them all.

Hansel and Gretel walked and walked through the forest, gathering only a few nuts and berries to eat. They spied a beautiful white bird, singing in the trees, and decided to follow the bird when it spread its wings and flew away. The bird lead them to a clearing where they saw a wondrous sight: a cottage with a roof made of cake, walls made of bread, and windows made of barley sugar. Hansel and Gretel were so hungry, they ran to the house and began nibbling on a shutter.

From inside the house, a voice called out: "Nibble, nibble, little mouse. Who is nibbling on my house?" Then the owner of the voice appeared, a very old woman leaning on a stick and smiling. At first Hansel and Gretel were frightened, but the old woman looked kind and did not scold them. "We are lost and hungry," Hansel told her. "Then come into the house, you poor dears. I will take care of you," the old woman said.

The old woman spread a bountiful meal in front of Hansel and Gretel, and they ate until they were full. Then the old woman led them to two snowy-white beds. "Rest your weary heads, my dears, and forget all of your troubles," she told them.

Hansel and Gretel had more trouble than they knew. For the kindly old woman was a wicked witch in disguise. She had built her cake-and-barley-sugar cottage to lure unsuspecting children to her door. Once she had them under her spell, she fattened them up then roasted and ate them.

The wicked witch seized Hansel from his bed and carried him to a small cage in the yard, locking him in. "Scream all you like," she told him. "No one can hear you but me." Then the wicked witch woke Gretel and ordered her to carry water into the kitchen for cooking. "I must cook something special for your brother. When he is fat enough, I will eat him," the wicked witch said.

Gretel sobbed as she did the wicked witch's bidding. Gretel fetched the water, stoked the flames of the fire, and helped cook rich food for Hansel. The wicked witch gave Gretel only scraps to eat.

Every morning, the witch hobbled to Hansel's cage. "Stick out your finger, Hansel, so I can see how fat you are," she commanded. Hansel held out a bone instead because he knew that witches could not see very well. After a month, the wicked witch lost patience. She told Hansel: "Fat or thin, into the oven you will go today."

She ordered Gretel to light the fire and to prepare the kettle. Gretel sobbed piteously, knowing the fate that awaited her poor brother. "Be quiet!" the witch screamed and, having lost patience with Gretel, decided to eat her, too.

"First, we must bake bread," the witch announced. "I've kneaded the dough. Crawl in the oven to see if it is hot enough."

Gretel saw a way to save Hansel. "The oven is too small. I can't fit in," she said.

"You stupid girl. The oven is big enough for *me* to get in. Just watch." The witch put her head in the oven. At that moment, Gretel pushed the wicked witch into the oven, slammed the iron door, and slid the bolt into place. The wicked witch howled for a time, but the flames of the oven soon burned her to death.

Gretel ran to Hansel's cage, unlocked the door, and proclaimed: "The witch is dead! We are free!" The children hugged one another and jumped for joy. They returned to the witch's house because they were no longer afraid, and in every corner they found chests, brimming with precious jewels. They filled all of their pockets with diamonds, emeralds, rubies, and pearls, then set off to find the way back to their home.

Soon they recognized their father's house in the distance. They ran into the yard and pounded on the front door. When the woodcutter saw that Hansel and Gretel had returned, tears of joy streamed down his face. He welcomed the children and told them that their stepmother had died.

Hansel and Gretel emptied their pockets of their treasures from the witch's house. "We are rich," they shouted. "We will never go hungry again." The woodcutter, Hansel, and Gretel rejoiced that they were all together again, and they lived happily ever after.

From Japan: "Witch Cat"

Kowashi and his sweet, gentle mother lived happily in a small house in a tiny village at the foot of a large mountain in Japan. One day Kowashi noticed that his mother's teeth had grown sharp and pointed. He also noticed that his mother enjoyed chewing on fish bones.

That night Kowashi's neighbor, a fish peddler, came home late to the village, carrying a large fish in his basket. All of a sudden, a pack of wild cats attacked the fish peddler, biting and scratching him in hopes of taking his fish. The fish peddler struck the cats over and over again with a club, but the blows did not seem to affect them.

"Call Old Woman Kowashi," one of the cats shouted.

Almost immediately from the mountain pass bounded a big, tough gray cat, the largest cat the fish peddler had ever seen. He wasted no time. He whacked the gray cat on its head. At that moment, the sun came up, and all the cats disappeared. Shaken, the fish peddler ran to his house and locked the door.

When Kowashi woke up that day, his mother was in the kitchen preparing breakfast and gnawing on a fish bone. Kowashi also noticed that his mother had a mysterious cut on her head. As he ate his breakfast, he wondered how the wound had occurred.

As he worked at his job in the village, Kowashi thought about his mother, the cut on her head, and her fondness for fish bones. At the end of the day when Kowashi returned to his small house, his fish-peddler neighbor was waiting for him.

"Kowashi," the neighbor began. "I have a strange tale to tell you." Then the fish peddler told Kowashi about being attacked by the cats and about the tough gray cat called Old Woman Kowashi. Kowashi was shocked, but now he knew where the cut on his mother's head had come from.

"Mother, I am home," Kowashi said when he entered his small house. His mother was in the kitchen, busily licking a fish bone. When she saw him, she hissed and arched her back. Then Kowashi was sure. His mother wasn't his mother at all. A witch cat had killed Kowashi's mother and had taken her shape. Kowashi knew what he had to do.

He picked up his sword, and with one stroke he killed the imposter. When he looked down at the body, there lay a big, gray cat.

From the Hebrew Talmud: "The Rabbi and the 29 Witches"

In a deep, dark cave near a small village lived 29 wicked witches. They brewed deadly potions, raised bats and buzzards, and turned beautiful flowers into poisonous mushrooms.

Once a month, when the full moon rose high in the sky, the 29 witches mounted their broomsticks, flew out of their cave, and headed toward the village. They circled over the houses, shrieking, laughing, and howling. The villagers trembled in their beds. Their animals cowered in their barns. But if rain fell on the night of the full moon, the 29 witches stayed in their cave.

At each full moon, if the night was clear, the villagers hurried to their homes, locking their doors and bolting their windows behind them. Some hid in closets, and others pulled the bedcovers over their heads to block out the screeches and screams of the 29 witches. Then one old grandmother decided that enough was enough.

"I have never seen a full moon," she complained. "Before I die, I would like to see a full moon."

Her friends were shocked. No one in the village had ever seen a full moon. The witches had kept generations of villagers from gazing upon the smiling face of the full moon. What could she do to change that?

"I will go to see the Rabbi," the old grandmother said. "The Rabbi will know what to do."

But, at first, the Rabbi did not know what to do, so he considered the problem. The witches come only when the moon is full. But when the moon is full and it is raining, the witches do not come. He watched as the rain cascaded down the windows of his house, and he thought of a wonderful plan. He told the old grandmother: "If it is still raining tomorrow night have 29 of the bravest men of the village come to me. Tell each to bring a long, white robe tucked inside a clay pot with a tight cover."

The rain continued to fall the next night, and the 29 bravest men of the village gathered at the Rabbi's house with their robes and clay pots. "We are going to the witches' cave," the Rabbi said, "and with your help our village will soon be rid of the witches for good." The Rabbi and the 29 bravest men of the village set off. They marched out of the village, up and over the hills, and through dark forests toward the witches' cave, carrying on their heads their clay pots that held their long, white robes.

When they arrived at the witches' cave, many of the men were afraid. Even the Rabbi felt frightened, but he summoned his courage and told the men: "I will enter first. You stay here in the entrance to the cave and listen for my whistle. When you hear it the first time, put on your robes but keep them dry. When you hear it the second time, rush in, choose a witch, and dance with her. I will let you know what to do after that." The Rabbi put on his long, white robe; distorted his face into a fierce expression; and went into the cave.

"Witches, witches! Here I am," he called.

The witches stopped stirring their cauldron, startled to see a stranger arrive unexpectedly.

"Who are you?" they demanded.

"I am a witch," the Rabbi said.

The witches were puzzled. The stranger looked fearsome, but his clothes were dry. How could a witch fly through a cold, rainy night and still keep dry? They didn't know, so they asked him.

"Simple," the Rabbi answered. "As I fly on my broom, I dodge the raindrops."

The witches were impressed with the stranger's trick but wondered why he had come. They didn't know, so they asked him.

"Simple," the Rabbi answered. "If you show me some magick, I will show you some magick. We can learn some magick from each other."

The witches thought that was a good idea, so they invited the stranger in.

The Rabbi entered the main part of the cave and said: "I think I would like to see a great feast spread out before me."

The witches waved their hands and a bountiful banquet appeared on a great table in the center of the cave. The table groaned under the weight of meats, stews, breads, wines, fruits, cakes, puddings, plates, and goblets.

"That's a fine trick," the Rabbi said. "Let's eat!"

"We will as soon as you show us one of your tricks," one of the witches said.

"Of course," the Rabbi said and whistled once. "For my first trick, I will make appear 29 handsome men to dance with you during this banquet."

All of the witches cackled with delight. None of them had been asked to dance for at least four hundred years.

The Rabbi whistled again. Each of the 29 bravest men of the village rushed in, took a witch by the hand, and twirled her around the cave.

"For my next trick," the Rabbi announced. "I will show you how to dodge the raindrops. Let's go outside!"

Each of the 29 bravest men of the village whirled his witch from the center of the cave to the cave's entrance and to the outside. The rain poured down on the witches, and they began to shriek and hiss and moan. Steam rose from their black robes.

"You are not a witch!" they shrieked. "You fooled us!"

They were right. The Rabbi had guessed that the witches feared the rain for a reason. Before the eyes of the Rabbi and the 29 bravest men of the village, the witches shrank smaller and smaller as the raindrops melted them. Soon all that was left of the witches were 29 black robes and 29 black, pointy hats adrift in large puddles of water.

In no time, someone had run back to the village to tell everyone to come see that the witches were no more. The villagers rejoiced that the witches were gone, and—not wanting to let a marvelous feast go to waste—everyone ate at the bountiful table and danced the night away. And they lived happily ever after, especially on the nights of a full moon.

Expressed through folklore, legends, and fairy tales, ideas about witches and witchcraft inculcated humankind with the predominant image of the witch as the epitome of evil. Religious authorities battling for the supremacy of their doctrines and civil authorities charged with maintaining law and order believed that evil must be stopped. Witches became their target. The collision of the image of the witch with the zeal to destroy evil led to centuries of death for thousands of people, many of them women.

THREE

The Dark Days of the Great European Witch Hunt

IMES of anxiety," according to Barbara W. Tuchman in *A Distant Mirror*, "nourish belief in conspiracies of evil." Beginning in the eleventh century, the Church felt buffeted by threatening, malevolent forces. In 1095, the First Crusade marched into the Holy Land to loosen the grip of the Moslems. Eight other Crusades stretched into the thirteenth century, bringing into the West knowledge of alchemy, astrology, necromancy, and other forbidden magickal arts. Heretical religious sects flourished—the Albigenses in eastern Europe and southern France, the Cathars throughout much of Europe, the Waldenses or Vaudois in southern France.

In 1231 Pope Gregory IX established the papal Inquisition, and in 1233 he decreed that the Dominican order would serve as Inquisitors. The Inquisition's objective was rooting out and destroying the enemies of the Church, specifically non-Christians and heretics.

"The Church, in recognition of Christian mercy, never executed anyone for heresy," according to Jeffrey Burton Russell, author of *A History of Medieval Christianity: Prophecy and Order.* "It conducted the investigations, arraigned and tried the dissenters, and, if they were found guilty, turned them over to the secular arm for 'proper attention' . . . which meant hanging or the stake."

By 1320, the Church added heretical sorcery to its list of heresies. By 1335, the definition of heretical sorcery included attending sabbats, worshipping the Devil, and flying. Papal bulls issued in 1473, 1478, and 1483 linked sorcery to heresy, but the bull of 1484 was the coup de grace, bringing the powerful hammer of the Inquisition down on heretical sorcerers: witches.

The guidebook for identifying, prosecuting, and punishing witches—the *Malleus Maleficarum*—spread throughout Europe in 1486. The manual linked witchcraft with women, and most of the victims of the Inquisition turned out to be poor, lower-class women, many on the fringes of society.

Those same factors characterize the victims of the Great European Witch Hunt which began in the fifteenth century and ended by the mid-eighteenth century, coinciding with the Inquisition. According to Brian P. Levack in *The Witch-Hunt in Early Modern Europe*, "The various ecclesiastical and secular authorities who prosecuted witches from Spain to the Baltic and from Scotland to Transylvania were in a sense participating in a common enterprise: the destruction of a particularly dangerous heresy and form of rebellion that had spread throughout Europe."

The Great European Witch Hunt most affected the western and west-central lands of Europe, including the Holy Roman Empire, France, and Switzerland. Germany emerged as the hotbed of the persecutions in the late sixteenth century. Other areas touched by the Great European Witch Hunt include the British Isles, Scandinavia, Poland, Spain, and Italy.

Witch persecutions declined gradually in the late seventeenth and early eighteenth centuries, then came to an end. Scholars attribute the decline to sweeping changes in the social, economic, and religious conditions that had spawned the earlier witch-hunting mood. When the persecutions ended, the task fell to historians to calculate the human toll.

Scholars continue to argue about the exact numbers of accused witches prosecuted and executed during the Great European Witch Hunt. Many court records have been lost or destroyed, and the exact number of witch prosecutions and executions may never be known.

Early estimates ranged from 100,000 to 300,000, while other experts speculated that the number could swell to several million, if those who died in prison are included in the total. However, research that emerged in the late 1970s revised these estimates, and most experts today agree on figures of less than 15,000 recorded executions in Europe and North America and an estimated death toll of approximately 35,000 to 64,000.

What accounts for the discrepancy in totals? Scholars believe that earlier estimates had been inflated. Witch hunters often exaggerated their claims about the number of witches they burned, and historians writing about the phenomenon sometimes increased the numbers of prosecutions and executions to account for missing records. According to Jenny Gibbons in *The Virtual Pomegranate: A New Journal of Developmental Neopagan Studies,* "Historians stopped relying on witch-hunting propaganda and began to base their theories on thorough, systematic studies of all the witch trials in a particular area."

Numerous theories have been advanced to explain the hysteria of the Great European Witch Hunt. According to Robin Briggs in *Witches & Neighbors: The Social and Cultural Context of European Witchcraft,* "The persecution is almost always interpreted as a cover for some other hidden purpose, whether it be state-building, the imposition of patriarchy or religious bigotry. Although these explanations usually possess some genuine value, they always break down if they are applied in too mechanical or sweeping a fashion. The notion of a single primary reason behind these events is an obvious misfit, since on close investigation the causes turn out to be dauntingly complex."

ARRAS WITCHES

One of the earliest witch hunts in northern France occurred in Arras from 1459 to 1460. According to Brian P. Levack, "These trials took place in areas where Waldensian heretics were also being prosecuted, and since both they and the witches were accused of meeting secretly and practising cannibalistic infanticide, inquisitors probably viewed the two groups as related threats."

The hysteria began with the 1459 arrest of a hermit who was tortured until he confessed that he, along with a prostitute and an elderly poet, had attended a sabbat. The hermit was burned at the stake. His companions were arrested, tortured into confessing, and compelled to name others.

The ripples from this incident soon spread throughout Arras. Snared in the net of the Inquisition were old, poor women; prominent officials; wealthy residents; and members of the clergy, including bishops and cardinals. Anyone who opposed the persecutions was branded a witch and forced to face the Inquisitors. The property of those convicted was confiscated.

The Inquisitors probed the accused with leading questions, tortured them on the rack if they failed to implicate others, and promised that their lives would be spared if they acknowledged their crimes and guilt. However, those who confessed were instead dragged to the stake, condemned in public, and set afire. Victims screamed their innocence and their betrayal from the inferno until the relentless flames silenced their voices forever.

News of the mounting death toll trickled out of Arras and frightened off foreign merchants. Commerce declined severely in the trading and manufacturing center until the end of 1460 when Philip the Good, the Duke of Burgundy, ordered an end to the arrests and executions. The Bishop of Arras, who returned to the area after a long absence, and the Parlement of Paris ordered the release of all prisoners accused of witchcraft. In 1491, the Parlement of Paris condemned the actions of the Inquisition in Arras.

THE *MALLEUS MALEFICARUM*

In 1484, two Dominican Inquisitors, Heinrich Kramer and Jakob Sprenger, approached Pope Innocent VIII about the roadblocks they were encountering in their efforts to prosecute witches in areas of northern Germany. Local religious and civil authorities had demurred to welcome the Inquisition into their areas, claiming that the apostolic letters allowing the tribunal had failed to name their provinces, cities, and dioceses, specifically. Therefore, the authorities believed that their areas were exempt from the Inquisition.

Innocent VIII responded by issuing the Bull of 1484, *Summis desiderantes affectibus* ("Desiring with supreme ardor") which, in part, directed that "to prevent the taint of heretical pravity and of other like evils from spreading their infection to the ruin of others who are innocent, . . . by virtue of our apostolic authority . . . it shall be permitted to the said inquisitors . . . to exercise their office of inquisition and to proceed to the correction, imprisonment, and punishment of the aforesaid persons for their said offences and crimes, in all respects and altogether precisely as if the provinces, cities, territories, places, persons, and offences aforesaid were expressly named in the said letter."

With the papal edict in hand, Kramer and Sprenger launched campaigns against witches in the archdioceses of Mainz, Cologne, Treves, Salzburg, and Bremen. They also incorporated the Bull of 1484 as a narrative frontispiece in their exhaustive witch hunter's guidebook, *Malleus Maleficarum* or "Hammer of Witches," first published in Germany in 1486.

The first sentence of the work was designed to still the voices of Christian scholars and theologians who doubted the existence of witches: "Whether the belief that there are such beings as witches is so essential a part of the Catholic faith that obstinately to maintain the opposite opinion manifestly savours of heresy." The *Malleus Maleficarum* established as fact the existence of witches, the threat to Christianity they posed, and a connection between witchcraft and heresy.

Kramer and Sprenger divided the book into three parts. Within each part, the authors posed a series of questions and answered them using arguments supported by the works of Aristotle, the Scriptures, St. Augustine, St. Thomas Aquinas, and others. Part I discusses how witches in concert with the Devil and with "the permission of Almighty God" inflict upon men and animals a litany of evils, including tempting them with succubi and incubi, swaying their minds to love or hatred, preventing or destroying fertility, and causing the metamorphosis of men into beasts.

According to Selma R. Williams in *Riding the Nightmare: Women and Witchcraft*: "But whereas the Pope had berated men as well as women for the sins of witchcraft, Sprenger and Kramer subtly shifted the emphasis to give women preeminence as witches. In fact, they made the point even for those who never got past the title page, by using the feminine form of the word for witches, *Maleficarum*. (In direct contrast, the more commonly used Latin form, though in the masculine gender, was long accepted as referring to either sex as witch.)"

Kramer and Sprenger state at the beginning of the book:

Witchcraft is high treason against God's Majesty. And so they are to be put to the torture in order to make them confess. Any person, whatever his rank or position, upon such an accusation may be put to the torture, and he who is found guilty, even if he confesses his crime, let him be racked, let him suffer all other tortures prescribed by law in order that he may be punished in proportion to his offenses.

Note: In days of old, such criminals suffered a double penalty and were often thrown to wild beasts to be devoured by them. Nowadays they are burnt at the stake, and probably this is because the majority of them are women.

They strengthened their thesis by discussing "Why it is that women are chiefly addicted to evil superstition." They first provide an overview of "the general conditions of women" and as evidence cite the opinion of St. John Chrysostom (circa 390 c.e.): "What else is woman but a foe to friendship, an unescapable punishment, a necessary evil, a natural temptation, a desirable calamity, a domestic danger, a delectable detriment, an evil of nature, painted with fair colors!"

Kramer and Sprenger listed specific reasons why women were more liable than men to embrace witchcraft, specifically:

- They are more credulous; and since the chief aim of the devil is to corrupt faith, therefore he rather attacks them.
- Women are intellectually like children.
- Women are naturally more impressionable, and more ready to receive the influence of a disembodied spirit.
- They have slippery tongues, and are unable to conceal from their fellow-women those things which by evil arts they know; and, since they are weak, they find an easy and secret manner of vindicating themselves by witchcraft.
- Since they are feebler both in mind and body, it is not surprising that they should come more under the spell of witchcraft.
- All witchcraft comes from carnal lust, which is in women insatiable. Wherefore for the sake of fulfilling their lusts they consort even with devils.

Other outrageous claims include the conjectures that women are quicker to waver and to renounce their faith; that women are jealous; that women follow their own impulses without a thought to repercussions; and that, by their very nature, women are liars.

In Part II, Kramer and Sprenger detail "the methods by which the works of witchcraft are wrought and directed and how they may be successfully annulled and dissolved." They focused on the pacts that witches made with the

Devil, the horrid crimes of witch midwives, and the spells that witches cast to "stir up hailstorms and tempests and cause lightning to blast both men and beasts." To illustrate the evils, the authors shared fantastic stories garnered from the Inquisitions they had conducted and from other contemporary writers.

In Part III, Kramer and Sprenger describe judicial procedures for trying witches in both ecclesiastical and civil courts. They included guidelines for examining witnesses, admitting evidence, recognizing a witch, initiating interrogation, administering torture, handling confessions, and pronouncing and passing sentence. They advocated allowing hostile witnesses to testify, using torture to compel confessions, and lying to the accused: "The judge may safely promise witches to spare their lives, if only he will later excuse himself from pronouncing the sentence and will let another do this in his place."

Kramer and Sprenger submitted their treatise to the University of Cologne in 1487 for official endorsement, and the work received unanimous approbation by the doctors of the theological faculty.

The *Malleus Maleficarum* was a runaway best seller in Europe, second only to the Bible in popularity. Fourteen editions appeared between 1487 and 1520. At least sixteen editions were published between 1574 and 1669. The first English edition appeared in 1584.

According to Robin Briggs in *Witches & Neighbors: The Social and Cultural Context of European Witchcraft*, "The *Malleus Maleficarum* and its successors assembled an untidy mass of stories and superstitions that were pulled together within a theological and legal framework to form a fairly coherent pattern. The printing press, the courts and officials, and the churches then combined to spread the information across the continent, in a form that could readily absorb any further variants."

CHELMSFORD WITCHES

In England, witchcraft was associated with sorcery rather than with heresy. Thus, the Inquisition did not root itself in English soil. However, authorities there believed that witches were assisted by the Devil in performing malefic witchcraft against people or livestock.

The first law against witchcraft was passed by Parliament in 1542, replaced by a second anti-witchcraft law in 1563 which classified as a felony the invocation of evil spirits for either benevolent or malefic purposes, whether or not any harm resulted. For most offenses, the penalties involved mandatory prison sentences. However, if witchcraft resulted in the death of a human being, the ultimate penalty was imposed: death.

The strength of this law was tested in four major witch trials held in Chelmsford in Essex during the sixteenth and seventeenth centuries. In the first of these trials, Elizabeth Francis, Agnes Waterhouse, and Agnes's daughter Joan Waterhouse were charged with witchcraft in the summer of 1566.

Elizabeth Francis stood accused of bewitching a baby and faced the court on July 26. She confessed her guilt to the crime then astounded the court with additional revelations of sex, murder, abortion, and infanticide.

Francis testified that as a girl of 12 she had learned the art of witchcraft from her grandmother, Mother Eve, who gave to Francis a white-spotted cat named Sathan. The feline was a familiar whom Francis fed with bread and milk and rewarded with a drop of blood "every time he did anything for her." According to the trial records, Sathan served Francis well:

> She desired to have one Andrew Byles to her husband, which was a man of some wealth, and the Cat did promise her that she should, but that she must first consent that this Andrew should abuse her, and she did so.

Following their illicit sex, Byles refused to marry Francis. She sought revenge by commanding Sathan "to waste his goods, which he forthwith did, and yet not being content with this, she willed him to touch his body which he forthwith did whereof he died." After her lover's death, Francis believed that she was pregnant and "willed Sathan to destroy it, and he bade her take a certain herb and drink it, which she did, and destroyed the child forthwith."

Sathan promised Francis another husband but instructed her that she must submit to "fornication which she did, and thereof conceived a daughter that was born within a quarter of a year after they were married." Their home life was not happy, and Francis blamed the presence of the child. She commanded Sathan "to kill the child, being about the age of half a year old, and he did so."

Francis testified that after fifteen years keeping the cat grew tiresome, so she offered to trade Sathan to Agnes Waterhouse for a cake. Francis promised Waterhouse that the cat would be "a thing that she should be the better for so long as she lived." Waterhouse accepted and learned from Francis how to feed the cat its diet of bread, milk, and blood.

Agnes Waterhouse was tried the following day, July 27, on the charge of bewitching and causing the subsequent death of William Fynee. Like Elizabeth Francis, Waterhouse confessed to the crime and also bared her soul regarding other deeds. Waterhouse testified that she had willed Sathan to destroy the livestock, geese, and property of various neighbors and that the cat had also caused the death of another man. Although she denied rewarding the cat with her blood, officials discovered areas on her face and nose that were identified as witch's marks.

Waterhouse's 18-year-old daughter, Joan, was charged with bewitching a 12-year-old neighbor girl, Agnes Brown, who had refused Joan's request for bread and cheese. Brown testified that after the angry encounter with Joan, the 12-year-old was at home churning butter when she saw "a thing like a black dog with a face like an ape, a short tail, a chain and a silver whistle about his neck, and a pair of horns on his head." The demon dog made several visits, finally threatening the girl with a knife. Brown testified: "I said in the name of Jesus lay down thy knife, and he said he would not depart from his sweet dame's knife as yet, and then I asked of him who was his dame, and then he nodded and wagged his head to your house Mother Waterhouse."

When the verdicts were rendered, Elizabeth Francis was sentenced to one year in prison. Joan Waterhouse was acquitted, but her mother Agnes was convicted and sentenced to death by hanging. The execution was carried out on July 29.

The second major trial in Chelmsford occurred in 1579, when four women were accused of bewitchment. Elizabeth Francis appeared again as a defendant. Since her trial in 1566, Francis had continued to run afoul of the law. She had been found guilty of bewitching a woman who suffered a ten-day illness. For that infraction, Francis had been sentenced to one year in prison and four detentions in the public pillory. To the charges of 1579—causing the lingering demise of Alice Poole the previous year—Francis pleaded innocent. However, the court found her guilty, and she was hanged.

The second defendant, Ellen Smith, was accused of bewitching and causing the subsequent death of a 4-year-old girl. The child's mother testified that her daughter had cried "Away with the witch" moments before she died. Then the mother reported seeing a large, black dog exiting the family's house. Smith appealed to the court for mercy. Unfortunately, the fact that Smith's mother had been hanged as a witch years before may have prejudiced the court against her. Smith was found guilty and hanged.

Alice Nokes and Margery Stanton were the third and fourth defendants. Nokes was hanged. Although Stanton was accused of bewitching a gelding and a cow to death, the case against her was weak, and Stanton was released.

The third major witch trial in Chelmsford happened in 1589 when nine women and one man were accused of bewitching persons and property. The court accepted testimony from children about the existence of familiars in the cases. Four of the defendants were hanged; three were acquitted; the fates of the remaining three were unaccounted for in the trial records.

The last and bloodiest of the Chelmsford witch trials occurred in 1645, orchestrated by Matthew Hopkins, England's most infamous witch finder. Hopkins began his personal reign of terror at Chelmsford.

According to the jail calendar and materials published after the trials, Hopkins exposed at least thirty-eight men and women as witches, using evidence gathered from ninety-two individuals. Among the thirty-eight accused, seventeen were hanged, six were found guilty but received reprieves, four died while in prison, two were found not guilty. The fates of the remaining nine are unknown.

His first Chelmsford victim was Elizabeth Clark, an old woman with only one leg. By the time Hopkins was finished with her, Clark had confessed to sharing a bed with the Devil and keeping a number of familiars. She also named five other alleged witches in the community.

Hopkins employed a fierce repertoire of techniques. He coerced statements from witnesses, using suggestion and speculation. For example, Hopkins questioned a child who complained of nightmares and of being bitten during the night. Although the child's bed was infested with fleas, the probable source of the bites, Hopkins suggested that the bites came from a witch's familiar. The child agreed. In another instance, Hopkins extracted a statement from a witness that she had been tormented in the night by an imp. Hopkins encouraged her to speculate: Who might have sent the imp? The witness named one of the defendants.

He forced confessions from the accused, using various methods of brutal torture. Although English law technically forbade the use of torture in witch trials, Hopkins routinely beat and starved accused witches. He deprived them of sleep. They were walked back and forth in their cells until their feet blistered and became infected.

Once his victims were exhausted, Hopkins assaulted them with leading questions. Nods and one-word answers were sufficient as confessions. Hopkins and his henchmen rounded out the confessions by liberally adding vivid details about casting spells on people and property, effecting sickness and injury, and cavorting with evil familiars.

Next he moved on to skin pricking. He inserted needles into moles, blemishes, and warts which, if they proved insensitive to pain, were declared witch's marks. Reportedly, Hopkins resorted to using retractable needles to insure that the spots would be nonsensitive.

Last, Hopkins used the "swimming" test. When an accused witch was "swum," he or she was bound, then plunged into a body of water, usually three times in succession. Those who sank were deemed innocent. Those who floated were deemed guilty, pulled out of the water, and subsequently hanged.

His vehemence toward witches and witchcraft apparently stemmed from an incident in 1645 when, he claimed, a group of witches had attempted to kill him. Thereafter, he left his law practice in Manningtree; joined forces with partner John Stearne; and established an itinerant witch-hunting business, moving from village to village to eradicate witches. The partners exploited the public's fear of witchcraft and the political unrest generated by the English Civil War.

After his success in Chelmsford, Hopkins hired four assistants and expanded his witch-hunting operation throughout Essex, Suffolk, Huntingdonshire, Norfolk, Cambridge, and other counties. He adopted the sobriquet "Witch-finder General" and advertised that he had been appointed a witch hunter by Parliament. The backbone of his business was the "Devil's List," a coded roster containing the names of all the witches residing in England.

Hopkins stimulated business by gathering gossip, adding innuendo, and massaging suppositions into formal accusations of witchcraft. Business boomed, even though Hopkins and Stearne commanded exorbitant fees, charging villages and towns from four to twenty-six pounds for their services, depending upon the number of persons convicted.

Hopkins outdid himself in Suffolk later in 1645 when at least 124 individuals were arrested on witchcraft charges. He succeeded in bringing sixty-eight to the hangman's noose, including a 70-year-old clergyman who had confessed to making a pact with the Devil, keeping familiars, and casting spells on cattle.

Abruptly, the witch-hunting enterprise ended for Hopkins and Stearne in 1646. Mounting public criticism of their torture tactics, complaints about their excessive fees, and resistance from local authorities compelled them to end their partnership and to go their separate ways.

Hopkins amassed a stunning record during his short-lived career as a professional witch hunter. He is credited with the deaths of at least 230 alleged witches. This number exceeds the combined totals of all other witch hunters operating during the 160-year peak period of England's witch hysteria.

BRUTALITY IN GERMANY

The tiny states of Bamberg and Würzburg in Germany bore witness to some of the worst brutality of the witch hunts from the early 1600s to about 1632. Two ruling prince-bishops—who were also cousins—share responsibility for the torture, condemnation, and execution of scores of people during a single nine-year period.

Prince Bishop Phillipp Adolf von Ehrenberg terrorized his Würzburg subjects from 1623 to 1631. Prince-Bishop Gottfried Johann Georg II Fuchs von Dornheim, known as the Hexenbischof or "Witch Bishop," terrorized his Bamberg subjects from 1623 to 1632.

The Prince-Bishop's Chancellor revealed the horror in Würzburg in a letter he wrote to a friend in August 1629:

Ah, the woe and the misery of it—there are still four hundred strongly accused that they may be arrested at any hour. It is true that, of the people of my Gracious Prince here, some out of all offices and faculties must be executed: clerics, electoral councilors and doctors, city officials, court assessors, several of whom Your Grace knows. There are law students to be arrested. The Prince-Bishop has over forty students who are soon to be pastors; among them thirteen or fourteen are said to be witches. A few days ago a Dean was arrested; two others who were summoned have fled. The notary of our Church consistory, a very learned man, was yesterday arrested and put to the torture. In a word, a third part of the city is surely involved. The richest, most attractive, most prominent, of the clergy are already executed. A week ago a maiden of nineteen was executed, of whom it is everywhere said that she was the fairest in the whole city, and was held by everybody a girl of singular modesty and purity. She will be followed by seven or eight others of the best and most attractive persons. . . . And thus many are put to death for renouncing God and being at the witch-dances, against whom nobody has ever else spoken a word.

During his reign in Bamberg, Prince-Bishop von Dornheim encouraged a network of informers to spy on friends and neighbors and to report suspicious behavior. He maintained a cadre of lawyers, torturers, and executioners to handle the waves of witch accusations. Accusations were withheld from public scrutiny, and accused witches were denied legal representation. The condemned had their property seized by the authorities. Von Dornheim constructed two specially designed prisons. The "Drudenhaus" accommodated up to forty accused witches; the "Hexenhaus" or "Witch House" was even larger and boasted a state-of-the-art torture chamber.

The most harrowing example of the barbaric Bamberg terror was that of 55-year-old Johannes Junius, one of the state's burgomasters or mayors. Although all of the burgomasters perished under the crush of the Inquisition, the case of Junius is historically significant because he was able to leave behind a first-person account of the horrendous torture he endured.

His ordeal began with accusations of witchcraft leveled by several individuals. Junius was taken in for interrogation on June 28, 1628, and pleaded innocent to charges of having renounced God, of having been baptized by the Devil, and of having attended witches' sabbats. When Junius demanded to see evidence of his wrongdoing, the Inquisitors brought in six witnesses who spoke against him. Dr. Georg Adam Haas, the vice-chancellor of Bamberg, testified that two years earlier he and Junius had attended a witches' sabbat together. Another witness, Hopffens Elsse, swore that Junius had been a guest at a witches' dance during which a consecrated host was desecrated.

Junius denounced the witnesses and their testimony. He was jailed for two days, permitting him time to examine his situation and reconsider his plea of innocence. On June 30, the Inquisitors asked for his confession, but Junius refused. His refusal signaled the beginning of the torture.

He was subjected to thumbscrews, then legscrews. When those techniques failed to elicit a confession, the Inquisitors next stripped him, shaved his body, and searched for witch's marks. A curious patch of skin—bluish in color and resembling the shape of a four-leaf clover—was pricked three times, but Junius seemed oblivious to the pain. Then, the Inquisitors administered the strappado torture. Junius had his bound hands attached to a rope strung over a pulley affixed to the ceiling. He was hoisted toward the ceiling then dropped suddenly, leaving Junius a dazed, crumpled heap of humanity on the floor.

On July 5, the Inquisitors asked again for a confession. Junius complied, concocting a tale that he hoped would placate his persecutors and terminate his torture. However, the tale only partially appeased the Inquisitors, and Junius was returned to his cell for a period of additional thought and reflection. Two days later, he elaborated the tale further, but this rendering of events still did not satisfy the Inquisitors. They marched him up and down the streets of Bamberg, commanding him to identify the names and addresses of his witchcraft confederates. His list of accomplices was too short for the Inquisitors, so they tortured him again. Finally, at the end of July, Junius was condemned to be burned at the stake.

Before his execution, Junius wrote a letter to his daughter, a staggering accomplishment considering the fact that the bones in his hands had been crushed by thumbscrews early in his torture. The letter was smuggled out of prison and remains a shocking, first-person account of the horrors of the witch hunts:

Many hundred thousand good-nights, dearly beloved daughter Veronica. Innocent have I come into prison, innocent have I been tortured, innocent I must die. For whoever comes into the witch prison must become a witch or be tortured until he invents something out of his head and—God pity him—bethinks him of something. I will tell you how it has gone with me. . . . And then came also—God in highest heaven have mercy—the executioner, and put the thumb-screws on me, both hands bound together, so that the blood ran out at the nails and everywhere, so that for four weeks I could not use my hands, as you can see from the writing.

When at last the executioner led me back into the prison he said to me: "Sir, I beg you, for God's sake confess something, whether it be true or not. Invent something, for you cannot endure the torture which you will be put to; and even if you bear it all, yet you will not escape, not even if you were an earl, but one torture will follow another until you say you are a witch . . ."

And so I begged, since I was in wretched plight, be given one day for thought and a priest. The priest was refused me, but the time for thought was given . . . at last there came to me a new idea. . . . I would think of something to say and say it. . . . And so I made my confession, as follows, but it was all a lie. Now follows dear child, what I confessed in order to escape the great anguish and bitter torture, which it was impossible for me longer to bear. . . .

Then I had to tell what people I had seen [at the sabbat]. I said that I had not recognized them. "You old rascal, I must set the executioner at you. Say—was not the Chancellor there?" so I said yes. "Who besides?" I had not recognized anybody. So he said: "Take one street after another, begin at the market, go out on one street and back on the next. . . . And thus continuously they asked me on all the streets, though I could not and would not say more. So they gave me to the executioner, told him to strip me, shave me all over, and put me to the torture. . . .

Then I had to tell what crimes I had committed. I said nothing. . . . "Draw the rascal up!" so I said that I was to kill my children, but I had killed a horse instead. It did not help . . .

Now, dear child, here you have all my confession, for which I must die. And they are sheer lies and made-up things, so help me God. For all this I was forced to say through fear of the torture which was threatened beyond what I had already endured. . . .

Dear child, keep this letter secret so that people do not find it, else I shall be tortured most piteously and the jailers will be beheaded. So strictly is it forbidden. . . . I have taken several days to write this: my hands are both lame. I am in a sad plight. . . .

Good night, for your father Johannes Junius will never see you more. July 24, 1628.

Other individuals escaped the fate of Johannes Junius. They fled Bamberg and appealed to Emperor Ferdinand for assistance. Ferdinand issued mandates in 1630 and 1631, condemning the persecutions, but the bloodshed ceased only with the deaths of the prince-bishops of Bamberg and Würzburg.

TORTURE

"Common justice demands that a witch should not be condemned to death unless she is convicted of her own confession." This directive from the *Malleus Maleficarum* reflects only the veneer of justice, because in truth the handbook of the Inquisition pronounced the use of torture a reasonable means of securing confessions.

The worst incidents of torture used against accused witches occurred in Germany, France, Italy, Switzerland, and Scotland. Torture was less extreme in England, Ireland, Scandinavia, and North America.

Accused witches were first urged to confess; then they were stripped, shaved, and examined for blemishes that could be considered witch's marks. If the accused still refused to confess, they were threatened with "engines of torture." The torturer explained to the accused the type of torture that would be inflicted and the effects on the body, and this was often horrific enough to elicit a confession.

According to the *Malleus Maleficarum,* those who refused to confess even after enduring torture were obviously under the protection of the Devil. Stronger methods were then applied hours or days later to break the hold of the Devil. Torture continued until the accused confessed.

Various methods of torture included:

- ⑤ *The Rack:* The victim was placed on a board with wrists tied at one end and ankles tied at the other. The torturer turned rollers at either end of the board which pulled the victim's body in opposite directions. In 1652 Suzanne Gaudry of Rieux, France, was stretched on the rack, screaming ceaselessly her denial that she was a witch. When she could stand no more torture, she confessed. She was hanged, then burned.

- ⑤ *The Turcas:* In 1590 and 1591, Scotland's John Fian experienced the turcas, and his ordeal was described in the pamphlet, *Newes from Scotland*: "His nails upon all his fingers were riven and pulled off with an instrument called in Scottish a turcas, which in England we call a pair of pincers, and under every nail there was thrust in two needles over, even up to the heads."

- ⑤ *The Boots.* John Fian also experienced the boots, called "cashielaws" in Scotland. This device encased both legs from the knees to the ankles, pressing them together. Using a heavy hammer, the torturer pounded wedges between the victim's knees, squeezing the legs and cracking the bones. *Newes from Scotland* described Fian's experience: "Then was he, with all convenient speed, by commandment, conveyed again to the torment of the boots, wherein he continued a long time, and did abide so many blows in them, that his legs were crushed and beaten together as small as might be, and the bones and flesh so bruised, that the blood and marrow spouted forth in great abundance, whereby they were made unserviceable forever."

- ⑤ *Thumbscrews:* The victim's thumbs or toes were inserted into a press-type apparatus. The screw was turned, which lowered the top of the device onto the thumbs or toes, crushing them at the roots of the nails and causing blood to gush forth. In Prossneck, Germany, in 1629, a woman was placed in thumbscrews. Oblivious to her screams, the torturer and other officials left for a long lunch, allowing her to remain alone and in agony for three hours.

- 🕲 *The Strappado:* In Bamberg, Germany, in 1628, Johannes Junius underwent this torture in which the victim's bound hands were attached to a rope strung over a pulley affixed to the ceiling. The torturer hoisted the victim toward the ceiling then dropped the person suddenly, dislocating shoulders, hands, and elbows. Junius described this torture in a letter to his daughter: "Thereafter they first stripped me, bound my hands behind me, and drew me up in the torture. Then I thought heaven and earth were at an end, eight times did they draw me up and let me fell again, so that I suffered terrible agony." Torturers in France enhanced the effect of the strappado by tying stones to the victim's feet. Stones ranged in weight from forty to more than two hundred pounds.

- 🕲 *The Spider:* The spider was a clawlike device heated to red-hot then used to gouge flesh from the body. In Bavaria in the late 1500s, Anna Pappenheimer had her breasts cut off during the spider torture. Afterwards, her severed breasts were stuffed into her mouth, removed, then stuffed into the mouths of two of her sons who were also being tortured.

- 🕲 *The Wheel:* The victim was stretched and bound across the spokes and hub of a wheel. With a heavy weapon, the executioner broke the victim's legs and arms in several places. Then in a manner similar to that of a crucifixion, the wheel was propped upright so that the crowd could gaze at the victim taking the last gasps of life. Anna Pappenheimer's husband, Paulus, was broken on the wheel. In the crowd of onlookers was his 10-year-old son, Hansel.

- 🕲 *Ordeal By Water:* In this torture, the victim's arm was plunged into boiling water. For lesser offences, the arm was submerged to the wrist; for more serious offences, the arm was submerged up to the elbow. Following the ordeal, the arm was wrapped and then examined three days later. Signs of a burn meant that the victim was guilty. In 1595 in the village of Mierlo in Peelland, Netherlands, Judt van Dorren faced witchcraft accusations. The ordeal by water provided evidence of her guilt, and she was burned at the stake.

Accused witches were also whipped, garroted with ropes, dipped in boiling oil, and impaled on stakes. Red-hot irons were inserted into vaginas and rectums, scalding water was poured down throats, burning feathers coated with sulphur were applied to armpits and groins.

After confessing, victims received additional torture as part of their sentences. Most confessed witches were executed either by burning at the stake or by hanging. On the way to their executions, the condemned were often spat upon, flogged, and branded. Fingers, hands, and tongues were hacked off and nailed to the gallows.

Ironically, victims of the witch hunts paid for their evil deeds financially as well as physically. The salaries of the torturer, executioner, and other court officials were subsidized by funds confiscated from victims or their families. Other costs included any expenses for the torture itself, the meals and travel expenses of the torturer, hay for his horse, salaries of assistant torturers, and banquets for the judges after every court session.

When victims were sent to the stake, their families received bills for the coal, wood, and loads of peat used for the fire. For example, the expenses for executing two Aberdeen witches, Janet Wishart and Isabel Crocker, in February 1596 included:

40 Shillings	For 20 loads of peat to burn them
24 Shillings	For six bushels of coal
26 Shillings, 8 Pence	For four tar barrels
16 Shillings, 8 Pence	For fir and iron barrels
16 Shillings	For a stake and dressing of it
4 Shillings	For 24 feet of hangman's rope
8 Shillings, 4 Pence	For carrying the peat, coals, and barrels to the hill
13 Shillings, 4 Pence	To one justice for their execution

In Germany in 1757, the Archbishopric of Cologne issued an official price list or "Tariff for Torture" for various elements of execution, with this preamble: ". . . so many unsubstantiated and exaggerated claims for extra expenses have been made that it has become very costly for the chief court of the Elector Archbishop. Therefore, the archbishopric is compelled, in order to contain these demands, to set up the following rules in which every single operation has been given its due charge, which is forthwith promulgated."

The price list set the fee "For tearing apart and quartering by four horses" at 5 Reichsthaler, 26 Albus; "For cutting out the tongue entirely, or part of it, and afterwards for burning the mouth with a red-hot iron" at 5 Reichsthaler; and "For putting the ladder to the gallows, regardless whether one or several are hanged on the same day" at 2 Reichsthaler.

A number of critics and skeptics risked imprisonment and death by voicing protests about the witch trials and the attendant torture, including Thomas Hobbes of England; Michel de Montaigne of France; and Alfonso Salazar de Frias, the Grand Inquisitor of Spain.

One vociferous critic was German physician Johann Weyer, who published his views in the book *De Praestigiis Daemonum* in 1563. Weyer believed that most witches were old, delusional women suffering from melancholia and incapable of causing harm to their neighbors. Belief in witchcraft, according to Weyer, was the Devil's doing; and the Church was aiding the Devil in his handiwork by encouraging people to believe that witches possessed evil powers. Weyer acknowledged the existence of witches and sorcerers who made pacts with the Devil, but in Weyer's mind, the Devil caused the harm, not the witches and sorcerers. He also believed that these individuals were not the hapless outcasts that the Church was targeting and persecuting.

🌀 The *Benandanti* 🌀

While examining Inquisition archival records of investigations in the Venetian province of Friuli, Italian scholar Carlo Ginzburg made a startling discovery. He uncovered evidence of the existence of the *benandanti,* an agrarian cult that battled witches in annual fertility rituals during the sixteenth and seventeenth centuries.

The *benandanti,* a term meaning "those who walk well," were a group of men and women "born of the caul," that is, with the inner fetal membrane covering their bodies, especially their heads. This sign marked them as persons with supernatural powers to see witches and to heal the bewitched and as individuals destined to serve their villages at the changing of the seasons, called Ember Days.

At the times of solstices and equinoxes, the spirits of the *benandanti* were summoned at midnight by drums or by angels; they rose from their bodies and shape-shifted into butterflies, mice, cats, and hares; then they traveled the land, searching for an army of spirit witches. When they encountered one another, a battle ensued with each side beating the other with stalks. Victory on the part of the *benandanti* meant that crops would be abundant. Victory on the part of the witches meant that crops would be destroyed by storms. After the battle, the spirits of the *benandanti* leapt and danced about the fields before returning to their bodies.

The Inquisition learned about the activities of the *benandanti* in 1575. The Inquisitors were alarmed that the spirits of the *benandanti* left their bodies and shape-shifted into animals, that they traveled to meet with witches, and that they cavorted in fields. To the Inquisitors, this sounded too much like the witches' sabbat.

The Inquisition conducted interrogations and trials of the *benandanti* who testified that they were "fighting for Christ" during their fertility rites. After more than fifty years, the Inquisition finally convinced members of the *benandanti* that they were practicing rather than combatting witchcraft. By the last major trial of the *benandanti* in 1644, members had confessed to attending sabbats, signing Devil's pacts, desecrating the cross, and renouncing the Christian faith.

As court physician to the Duke of Cleves in the Netherlands, Weyer was successful in decreasing witch hunts there for a time. Then he was ousted by the Duke of Alba, a Catholic. Weyer's book raised a furor among his critics who urged that it be burned. Those who opposed Weyer's views wrote their own books, and those rebuttals served to inflame further witch hunts.

Weyer's book influenced Reginald Scot, an Englishman, who joined the chorus of voices opposing the torture and execution of witches. In 1584, Scot self-published an encyclopedic work *The Discoverie of Witchcraft* that contained the beliefs of the day concerning ghosts, the Devil, demonic possession, charms, omens, divination, fairies, spells, magick, and witchcraft.

Scot believed that the "extreme and intolerable tyranny" of the Inquisition had taken the lives of innocents falsely accused of witchcraft and the mentally disturbed who believed that they had made pacts with the Devil. According to Scot, the malevolent witch caused harm by natural means such as poisonings but not through any power derived from the Devil. Scot characterized the Pope as one who "canonized the rich for saints and banneth the poor for witches."

The Discoverie of Witchcraft lent strength to the skepticism about witches that spread throughout England. The clergy received the book favorably, but King James I ordered that the book be burned. Vigorous opposition to Scot's beliefs compelled the King to pen his own book, *Daemonologie,* in 1597.

A third opponent to the torture and execution of witches was German Jesuit Friedrich von Spee. In the 1620s, when witch hunts were rampant in Germany, von Spee was appointed to serve as confessor to the condemned witches in Würzburg. He began his duties with a firm belief in the reality of witches in Würzburg who did the bidding of the Devil. However, von Spee witnessed first hand the endless parade of victims—tortured to confession, denied fair trials, condemned with weak evidence—and altered his views. What he had seen had also altered him. By age 30, his hair had turned almost completely white "through grief over the many witches whom I have prepared for death; not one was guilty."

Von Spee was shocked by the trials, during which the accused were forced to name other witches. He feared that "there is nobody in our day, of whatsoever sex, fortune, rank, or dignity, who is safe, if he have but an enemy and slanderer to bring him into suspicion of witchcraft."

He was revolted by the torture: "Often I have thought that the only reason why we are not all wizards is due to the fact that we have not all been tortured. And there is truth in what an inquisitor dared to boast lately, that if he could reach the Pope, he would make him confess that he was a wizard."

In 1631, von Spee reacted by writing and publishing anonymously *Cautio Criminalis* or "Precautions for Prosecutors." In this book, von Spee launched a no-holds-barred attack on the witch hunters. He exposed the incentives that drove the Inquisitors to condemn large numbers of witches: Inquisitors received a payment for every witch burned and confiscated the assets of their victims. He denounced the claim that confessions were secured without torture. He explained that "no torture" actually meant light torture and that after a victim was arrested more severe torture followed, despite proclamations of innocence. He wrote: "She can never clear herself. The investigating committee would feel disgraced if it acquitted a woman; once arrested and in chains, she has to be guilty, by fair means or foul."

That von Spee had authored *Cautio Criminalis* was well known throughout the Jesuit community. Many in the order denounced the book and attempted to suppress it. However, the work was translated into French, Dutch, and Polish and spread from hand to hand throughout Europe.

WHAT FUELED THE GREAT EUROPEAN WITCH HUNT?

No consensus of opinion occurs among contemporary historians grappling with theories to explain what fueled the Great European Witch Hunt. While general causes of the hunt can be discussed—the Reformation, the Inquisition, the religious wars, misogyny, an attempt to eradicate paganism—a one-size-fits-all explanation seems impossible.

However, some scholars offer such explanations. Rossell Hope Robbins theorizes that the main motive behind the Great European Witch Hunt was the desire to confiscate the property of the condemned. Marvin Harris, in *Cows, Pigs, Wars & Witches,* posits that the main motive was to shift "responsibility for the crisis of late medieval society from both Church and state to imaginary demons in human form." According to Harris, "the distraught, alienated, pauperized masses blamed the rampant Devil instead of the corrupt clergy and the rapacious nobility. Not only were the Church and state exonerated, but they were made indispensable. The clergy and nobility emerged as the great protectors of mankind against an enemy who was omnipresent but difficult to detect."

However, Brian P. Levack believes that "the hunt was an amalgam of hundreds, if not thousands, of separate hunts that occurred at different places and at different times. Each of these hunts, like the larger composite phenomenon, has its own history and each is capable of detailed analysis."

Rejecting "all-encompassing explanations of the hunt," Levack instead "adopts a multi-causal approach which sees the emergence of new ideas about witches and a series of fundamental changes in the criminal law as the necessary preconditions of the witch-hunt, and both religious change and social tension as its more immediate causes."

Levack believes that an essential precondition was a body of beliefs about the malevolent nature of witches shared by both the common people and the ruling elite. Popular beliefs held that witches made pacts with the Devil, attended sabbats, had the power to fly, and could effect metamorphoses on themselves and on others. Since they accepted the reality of witches and maleficia, common people were inclined to blame their misfortunes on witchcraft.

However, belief in witches and witchcraft was even more critical for the ruling and administrative elite. Those individuals needed to embrace witchcraft as reality and to harbor deep-seated fears about witches. They also needed to understand that witchcraft was a crime because of the pacts witches made with the Devil and that witchcraft was a conspiracy against people and society. These were vital preconditions because the ruling and administrative elite controlled the judicial process.

According to Levack: "As the ruling elite in Europe became more educated; as more literature, including witchcraft treatises, began to reach small communities; and as news of witchcraft spread by word of mouth among provincial elites, witch-hunts became much more likely to occur." However, by the end of the seventeenth century, when skepticism about witches and witchcraft permeated the ranks of the elite, such disbelief led to judicial inaction, even in the face of a populace still clinging to outmoded witchcraft beliefs.

Changes in criminal law and criminal procedure were other necessary preconditions, in Levack's view. Until the Church classified sorcery as heresy, papal Inquisitors were unable to prosecute witches. Similarly, until a specific jurisdiction passed a law against witchcraft, no trials could take place because witchcraft was not considered a crime. For example, the Imperial criminal code, the *Carolina* of 1532, included references to the crime of witchcraft. This paved the way for witch hunts to be conducted throughout the Holy Roman Empire.

Certain criminal procedures had to be in place, as well, to guarantee the successful prosecution of witches. Thus, most European courts adopted an inquisitorial system of criminal procedure that allowed courts the right to accuse and interrogate suspects on their own authority and to use coercive tactics such as torture to secure confessions.

The last precondition was an atmosphere of anxiety among the populace about witchcraft. Commonly, this mood arose from public discussion about witchcraft, including sermons; from news of witch hunts and executions in neighboring or distant areas; from pamphlets and treatises about sensational witchcraft trials; and from official warnings about the dangers of witchcraft.

Enhancing the social tensions were religious changes, political crises, and natural calamities. According to Levack: "In dealing with the psychological foundations of witch-hunting it is important to note that in most cases no single factor produced a mood that made people eager to pursue witches. Usually a combination of circumstances, such as war, plague and famine or bad harvests, coupled with the promulgation of an official edict against witchcraft, were responsible."

Even with the intellectual, legal, and psychological foundations in place, witch hunts did not erupt spontaneously. A number of triggers served as catalysts for initial accusations of malevolent witchcraft.

The most common trigger was personal misfortune such as the sudden death of a family member, destruction of a farm animal, mysterious illness, or theft. In the absence of a plausible explanation, the victim often attributed the misfortune to witchcraft and pointed a finger of accusation at an alleged witch, someone the accuser had long suspected of practicing the magickal arts.

Other triggers for witch hunts were communal catastrophes such as hail storms which often wiped out entire fields of crops in moments, fires which grew out of control and ravaged many dwellings, or storms at sea which delivered people and property to watery graves. For example, witch hunts were launched in Scotland and Denmark after a storm in the North Sea in 1590 destroyed one of the ships in the royal fleet of James VI and his young bride, Queen Anne.

Levack characterizes another trigger, demonic possession, as both a personal and communal misfortune. This form of maleficia affected the individual with unusual symptoms such as fits, sensations of being bitten and pinched, and skin lesions. However, the maleficia often spread to others in the community, affecting them similarly. Levack points to French witch hunts in Aix-en-Provence in 1611, Lille in 1613, Loudun in 1634, and Louviers in 1642 as being triggered by demonic possession.

Witch hunts could also be triggered by individuals bringing deliberate and malicious accusations of witchcraft against their enemies, by people who observed a neighbor performing a ritual or casting a spell against another neighbor or by persons who admitted freely to engaging in demonic activities. For example, Isobel Gowdie of Scotland readily confessed to wild escapades with the Devil.

"The process of scapegoating in response to misfortune was probably the most common trigger of European witch-hunts," according to Levack.

While Levack believes that witches were scapegoats for misfortune, Walter Stephens, the Charles S. Singleton Professor of Italian Studies at Johns Hopkins University, thinks that witches were scapegoats for God.

According to Stephens, author of *Demon Lovers: Witchcraft, Sex, and Belief*, theologians ridiculed the belief in witches as ignorant superstition until the 1400s. However, by the 1430s, theologians had begun producing treatises "proving" the existence of witches. Stephens believes that "a massive increase in unacknowledged skepticism about Providence" prompted theologians in this endeavor. "To repel this literally unspeakable doubt," theologians struggled to find a physical means to prove the existence of the spirit world. Thus, they constructed the malevolent witch.

"To the witch was entrusted the task of demonstrating that the demonic world was not imaginary but a numinous parody of the divine which, by reversal, perversion, and antithesis, made the divine literal, visible, palpable, and real," Stephens writes in the *Journal of Medieval and Early Modern Studies*.

Theologians demonstrated that witches caused genuine harm, received the power of witchcraft from the Devil, and consorted with demons by citing the confessions of accused witches. How can a mere woman cause so much damage, an Inquisitor asks? The Devil helps me, the witch replies. How can a witch have intercourse with a partner that is imaginary, an Inquisitor asks? The demon takes physical shape, the witch replies. Thus, witches became "expert witnesses" to the magickal and sexual powers of demons. The "reality" of witches explained not only why misfortunes occurred, but through witches' connections to demons, also provided inverse physical proof of the existence of God.

"In their pre-scientific, Biblically based world view, the only alternative to witches and demons as an explanation of misfortune is a God not powerful enough to stop bad things from happening or not good enough to try," Stephens states.

In the view of scholar Robin Briggs, social and cultural tensions at the village level fueled the Great European Witch Hunt. "Witchcraft was not an objective reality but a set of interpretations, something which went on in the mind. Even as a crime it was 'transparent,' with a hole at the centre, since witches did not actually do most of the things alleged against them. In consequence it drew to itself a great range of conflicts and can only be explained properly in the context of the whole society within which it existed."

The society of the typical agrarian village in early modern Europe was characterized by interdependence, with members of neighboring households interacting daily by exchanging goods and services, and by a belief in witches and magick. According to Briggs, tensions arose when a person asked a neighbor for an item or a service and was turned away, even if the neighbor had a legitimate reason to refuse. The neighbor who refused to give recognized the breach of communal obligation; suffered guilt over what was considered an aggressive act; and projected this aggression onto the person who had been refused, expecting that this person would react with anger and resentment. Thus, if the neighbor suffered a misfortune subsequently, the eye of suspicion would be cast in the direction of the one who had been refused, the one who bore the presumed grudge, the one who had turned to magick to exact revenge.

According to Briggs: "Witchcraft was about envy, ill-will and the power to harm others, exercised in small face-to-face communities which, although they could often contain such feelings, found it almost impossible to disperse them. Those involved relied heavily on the cunning folk and their counter-magic, alongside a range of social and familiar pressures, to deal with suspect neighbours. Only at a few brief and limited points in time and space did they think of eradicating them completely. Witches were people you lived with, however unhappily, until they goaded someone past endurance." In Briggs's view, the half-century period between 1580 and 1630 witnessed a precipitous drop in living standards as well as in individual security and coincided with the majority of the witchcraft trials.

Since Briggs believes that witchcraft persecutions were mostly initiated at the village level and stemmed from a fear of witchcraft, he rejects the popular theory that misogyny was the motivation behind the persecutions. Briggs estimates that men account for 25 percent of the total number of executions for witchcraft in Europe. Specifically, he notes that:

- Of nearly 1,300 witches whose cases were appealed to the Parlement of Paris, slightly more than half were men. In approximately 500 cases that did not reach the Parlement, 42 percent of the accused were men.
- Of the accused in Iceland, 90 percent were men; in Estonia, 60 percent were men; in Finland, almost 50 percent were men.
- In more than 1,000 witchcraft cases from the Jura and the Alps, men comprised 22.5 percent.
- In the 547 witchcraft cases in Luxembourg, 31 percent of those tried were men.

Although men were represented among witch trial victims, clearly the majority of the accused were women. Thus, Briggs believes that the central question is "not why witchcraft was used as an excuse to attack women," but "why women were particularly vulnerable to witchcraft accusation."

As an answer, Briggs points to the societal and economic roles that brought women together for group or communal activities such as working in the fields, baking bread in shared village ovens, washing garments, fetching water from the village well, going to market and to religious rituals, and participating in spinning bees. According to Briggs, these activities naturally bred tensions, instigated quarrels, and fostered blame when subsequent misfortune occurred.

Women were also in charge of caring for animals and managing dairy products. "Milking cows were at the centre of many disputes with overtones of witchcraft," according to Briggs. "They were always liable to die, or lose their milk or their calves inexplicably, while the everyday arrangements for supplying milk generated a lot of friction, with resentments easily aroused among both producers and consumers."

According to Briggs: "Once the researcher plunges into the trials themselves it is this universe of local feeling and feuding which dominates the scene. It is indeed gendered, as was the society it reflected, but not in ways which made it easy for men to take charge of the whole process and use witchcraft persecution (formal or informal) as a simple agency of male power."

WHY THE GREAT EUROPEAN WITCH HUNT ENDED

According to Brian P. Levack, small witch hunts involving one to three persons and medium-sized witch hunts involving fewer than ten persons were localized and usually ended quickly when the accused witch was acquitted, given a jail sentence, or executed. Large witch hunts involving from ten to hundreds of persons were more widespread and often lasted for two, three, or four years. Large witch hunts ended for a variety of reasons.

One reason was "a loss of confidence in the process of witch-hunting." According to Levack: "The great majority of witches were old, poor women, and the frequency of their prosecution led to the creation of a stereotype of the witch that was accepted both by villagers and members of the elite. . . . In the early stages of most large witch-hunts the victims conformed to the stereotype, but as the hunts progressed a higher percentage of wealthy and powerful individuals, children and males were named. . . . This breakdown had the effect of arousing suspicions that innocent persons were being accused and of making men aware that the procedures of torturing confessed witches to obtain the names of accomplices could not be trusted. When the accusations reached into very high places, breakdown of the stereotype had the added effect of prompting the implicated officials to put an end to the trials."

In 1629 in Würzburg, accusations spread to children, law students, clergy, the Bishop's chancellor, and even the Bishop. The witch hunt soon ended.

Other reasons for the end of large witch hunts include exposure of deliberate fraud in accusations, social chaos in the community, and financial distress.

Deliberate fraud was uncovered in Hoarstones, England, in 1633 when Edmund Robinson, a boy about 10 years old, testified that he had attended a witches' sabbat and provided a list of names of the witches who were there. Seventeen of the women that the boy named were convicted. An investigation of the convictions was conducted, and the boy admitted that he had lied at the urging of his father "for envy, revenge and hope of gain." All of the convicted victims were acquitted and released, and this large-scale witch hunt ended immediately.

Social chaos erupted when the panic of the witch hunt threw the equilibrium of life into disarray in the town or village. For example, in Rottenburg, Germany, in 1585, authorities feared that the witch hunt that swept the town would destroy every woman in town. Thus, the witch hunt was halted.

Financial distress often ended large witch hunts. Witch hunters charged towns and villages for identifying witches in their midst. If accused persons were unable to pay their own jail costs, towns and villages assumed those costs. Therefore, considering the large number of accused witches who might be imprisoned during a large witch hunt, the financial burden of maintaining the suspects became a legitimate reason for discontinuing the hunt.

Levack believes that: "Large hunts came to an end as European communities, having experienced the social dysfunction that mass panics produce and having come to the conclusion that innocent people had suffered in the process, became determined to prevent the recurrence of such undertakings and establish legal procedures that would prevent the chain-reaction type of hunt from developing. These hunts also declined when the social, economic and religious conditions that helped to create a mood conducive to witch-hunting no longer prevailed."

As the Great European Witch Hunt was on the decline in the late seventeenth century, the seeds of witch hysteria were being planted on the shores of the New World. They blossomed between 1692 and 1693 in the seemingly serene New England village of Salem, Massachusetts.

⑨ "Mea Culpa": The Pope Apologizes for Sins ⑨ Committed Through the Ages

On November 10, 1994, the Vatican issued "Tertio Millennio Adveniente," the Apostolic Letter of John Paul II. In the address, the Pope reflected on the approach of the year 2000: "It is fitting that the church should make this passage with a clear awareness of what has happened to her during the last ten centuries. She cannot cross the threshold of the new millennium without encouraging her children to purify themselves, through repentance, of past errors and instances of infidelity, inconsistency, and slowness to act."

The Pope encouraged the Church to "become more fully conscious of the sinfulness of her children, recalling all those times in history when they departed from the spirit of Christ and His Gospel." He also recollected that one "painful chapter of history to which the sons and daughters of the Church must return with a spirit of repentance is that of the acquiescence given, especially in certain centuries, to intolerance and even the use of violence in the service of truth."

This groundbreaking proposal led to an in-depth study of the theological and historical implications of such repentance that was conducted by the International Theological Commission. As the commission drafted its report, the Vatican released a statement in October 1998 indicating that the Pope was reviewing Church sins related to the Inquisition. Witches were prosecuted with such zeal during the Inquisition that the term "Witch Hunt" has become associated with the deliberate seeking out and harassing of both religious and political opponents.

Recognizing the historical significance of the Pope's planned address, the Pagan community mobilized. Various Pagan leaders and sympathetic Christians formed the Committee for the Pope's Millennium Apology and drafted a letter supporting the Pope's anticipated act. In part the document stated: "This is a brave and laudable effort, heralding the beginning of a great healing between the Catholic Church and the groups that have, historically, been persecuted in its name. We note however, that early news releases concerning this event have not indicated that those accused of being Witches, and those indigenous (i.e., "Pagan") peoples who were forcibly converted by the Church will be included in your apology. This letter is a formal request for that omission to be rectified. As leaders of the contemporary Pagan/Wiccan community, we sincerely hope that Your Holiness will lead the way to mutual respect for all religions and spiritual paths by including all those who suffered from the tragedy of the Inquisition."

The letter dated, Samhain (October 31) 1999, contained the signatures of 238 Pagan leaders, 88 Pagan organizations, 14 Christian clergy, 41 academic scholars, and 1,256 other members of the worldwide Pagan community.

In March 2000, the long-anticipated International Theological Commission report was issued, a fifty-page document titled "Memory and Reconciliation: The Church and the Faults of the Past" that outlined the conditions and limits to the Holy Year act of repentance. The sweeping apology would be made for the human sins of the sons and daughters of the Church, not the Church itself which is "holy and immaculate." While stressing that many acts of centuries past could not be judged solely by contemporary standards, the document suggested that the Pope would only allude to responsibility by Catholics in the Holocaust, the Crusades, and the Inquisition.

On March 12, 2000, the Pope offered the Day of Pardon Mass at St. Peter's Basilica in Rome. The day marked the first Sunday of Lent, the forty-day period of repentance and reconciliation that precedes Easter. During his homily, John Paul II said: "We are asking pardon for the divisions among Christians, for the use of violence that some have committed in the service of truth, and for attitudes of mistrust and hostility assumed toward followers of other religions."

While the Pope's homily mentioned few groups or historical moments specifically, the Mass included special prayers for general categories of oppression. The religious significance of the apology was underscored by the presence of five cardinals and two bishops who stood before the Pope to confess on behalf of the Church some of the most significant Catholic transgressions.

Joseph Cardinal Ratzinger, who heads the Vatican's Congregation of the Doctrine of the Faith—the modern successor to the Inquisition—confessed to "sins committed in the service of truth." The Pope responded: "In certain periods of history Christians have at times given in to intolerance and have not been faithful to the great commandment of love, sullying in this way the face of the Church."

Francis Cardinal Arinze confessed to sins against women: "Let us pray for women, who are all too often humiliated and marginalized, and let us acknowledge the forms of acquiescence in these sins of which Christians too have been guilty." The Pope responded: "Lord God . . . at times the equality of your sons and daughters has not been acknowledged, and Christians have been guilty of attitudes of rejection and exclusion."

Dressed in purple robes, the color of penitence, the Pope proclaimed: "We are deeply saddened by the behavior of those who in the course of history have caused these children of yours to suffer."

FOUR

"The Evil Hand Is on Them" in Salem Village

LANKETS of snow smothered the countryside, icy wind gusts rattled the doors and windows of homes, and frigid temperatures held the citizens of Salem Village in a death grip during the winter of 1691–1692. Freed for a while from their agricultural labors, men and boys occupied themselves by hunting wild turkeys and deer in the forests, ice fishing on nearby ponds, or tending to various household chores that were postponed during the busy spring, summer, and fall months. But the dreary days and nights of winter in New England held no such diversions for the women and girls of Salem Village.

Confined by year-round tasks such as spinning, sewing, cooking, laundering, cleaning, and child rearing, the matrons of Salem Village accepted their lot as helpmates to their husbands and had long since resigned themselves to a tedious domestic Puritan existence. Such resignation had not yet hardened the spirits of the adolescent and teenage girls of the Village, however.

While helping to bake bread, churn butter, or mold candles, they fondly recollected romping through the woodlands in spring, picking berries on sun-dappled summer days, and playing with hoops and sticks during crisp autumn afternoons. The winter that unfolded before them promised endless months of unrelenting drudgery, broken only by attending Sabbath meetings.

These were most likely the thoughts in the minds of 9-year-old Elizabeth Parris—called Betty—and her 11-year-old cousin Abigail Williams. The girls were the daughter and the niece, respectively, of the Reverend Samuel Parris, the minister of Salem Village, and his wife Elizabeth.

Historian Marion L. Starkey describes Betty as "a really sweet, biddable little girl, ready to obey anyone who spoke with conviction, including, to her misfortune, her playmate Abigail." Characterizing her as "not carefree," Starkey notes that "she had been exposed too long to the hell-fire in her father's composition." The Puritan realities of predestination and damnation had been burned into Betty's psyche, causing her to cower under the weight of the inevitable consequences of sin.

Although Abigail had had similar exposure, her uncle's sermons had affected her differently. "From the eyes of this child," Starkey writes, "an authentic hellion looked out on a world it would make over if it got a chance." According to Starkey, "She . . . took damnation, death, and most other unpleasant things as something scheduled to happen to someone else, particularly to people she didn't like."

On cold November nights in 1691 when Parris and his wife attended to the needs of parishioners or conducted errands of mercy outside the home, Betty and Abigail were left in the care of Tituba, a reputedly half-Caribbean-Indian and half-black slave that Parris had acquired in Barbados. While her spouse, John Indian, was occupied with laboring in the field, tending the livestock, and maintaining the woodlot, Tituba was assigned the backbreaking domestic chores of boiling and pounding linens on seasonal wash days, carrying well water to the house, emptying the slops, and scrubbing and sanding the floors. "She found subtle ways of easing her lot," according to Starkey, "and one of these was idling with the little girls."

These idling moments probably began innocently with Tituba sharing stories about her life in Barbados. The strange, colorful tales must have captivated the imaginations of girls whose austere lives in Puritan New England most likely seemed dull and drab by comparison. On long, cold winter nights, Betty and Abigail probably shivered with excitement as Tituba spun her stories while the flames from the fireplace cast eerie shadows on the walls of the kitchen. Encouraged by the bold Abigail, Tituba expanded her evening offerings by sharing bits and pieces of tricks, spells, and voodoo chants that she recollected from her Caribbean days.

Betty may have suffered pangs of conscience from these secret sessions. She knew that flirting with dark, evil doings was wrong. Certainly she recognized the guilt she bore in keeping their activities from her parents. However, her affection for Tituba and pressure from Abigail most likely prevented Betty from exposing the slave woman to the wrath of the Reverend Parris. If Betty's father were to learn of their clandestine activities, he would deliver a swift and sound thrashing to Tituba. So Betty kept their secret while wrestling with the knowledge that they risked unleashing God's fury by their forbidden forays into the Devil's underworld.

Abigail, too, recognized the dangerous ground on which they treaded, but this only increased the excitement for her. Soon news of Tituba's excursions into the black arts—especially her abilities as a fortune-teller—spread to other girls in the Village. Her circle of admirers grew to include Thomas and Ann Putnam's 12-year-old daughter Ann Jr. and their 19-year-old servant Mercy Lewis; 17-year-old Elizabeth Hubbard; 16-year-old Mary Walcott; Elizabeth Booth and Susannah Sheldon, both 18 years old; and 20-year-old servants Sarah Churchill and Mary Warren.

These young women well knew the Puritan admonitions against what Boston minister Cotton Mather called "little sorceries." Occult deeds such as palm reading and conjuring with crude fortune-telling devices like sieves, scissors, and candles relied on the forces of the Devil. Ministers pounded from their pulpits the warnings that magick and sorcery usurped the authority of an all-knowing, all-powerful God.

Despite these cautions, the girls and young women persisted in their dalliances with Tituba and her divination skills. "Who shall be my husband?" one girl asked. "What shall be my husband's calling?" another posed. "Shall I be rich?" another wanted to know. For the answers, Tituba turned to a makeshift crystal ball.

She poured an egg white into a glass of water, and all eyes watched as the substance sank slowly to the bottom. But glimpses of future romance and fortune did not emerge. Instead, the image that formed looked like a coffin. Several girls gasped, and all were filled with fear. Betty wept and trembled. What evil had their play brought forth in Salem Village?

Throughout December, Betty erupted frequently into fits of weeping, and as the New Year of 1692 unfurled, Betty became more visibly disturbed. Unable to concentrate on the simplest chores, she sat alone staring blankly. When her mother attempted to rouse her, Betty reacted violently, hurling herself about the room, screaming, and babbling incoherently.

The malady then spread to Abigail. She, too, fell into trancelike stupors. She threw herself on the floor and ran around and under furniture like a dog, barking and howling like a mad creature.

Alarmed, the Reverend Parris ordered prayers for the girls, but these only worsened their conditions. Merely beginning the Lord's Prayer sent the girls into convulsions. Abigail screamed and covered her ears. Enraged as the prayer continued, she grabbed flaming pieces of wood from the fireplace and threw them around the parsonage. An agitated Betty hurled a Bible across the room then burst into tears, sobbing that she was damned.

The conditions of the girls deteriorated further as January slipped into February. Then the contagion spread beyond the walls of the parsonage. The next affected were Mary Walcott and Susannah Sheldon. Soon after, the malady visited the Putnam home, where both Ann Jr. and servant Mercy Lewis writhed in agony as convulsions racked their bodies. Then other young women throughout the Village became affected with the mysterious symptoms, and many of the citizens who witnessed the afflictions were near panic with terror.

The people of Salem Village drew parallels between the symptoms occurring in their households and the symptoms in the Goodwin household in Boston nearly four years earlier. Cotton Mather had written about the case of 13-year-old Martha Goodwin in his book, *Memorable Providences Relating to Witchcrafts and Possessions*.

In the summer of 1688, some of the Goodwin family linen disappeared, prompting Martha to accuse the laundry girl of theft. According to Mather, the laundry girl's mother, Mary Glover, "whose miserable husband before he died, had sometimes complained of her, that she was undoubtedly a witch . . . in her daughter's defense bestowed very bad language upon the girl . . . ; immediately upon which, the poor child became variously indisposed in her health, and visited with strange fits, beyond those that attend an epilepsy, or a catalepsy."

Mather further reported that one of Martha's sisters and two of her brothers "were seized . . . one after another, with affects like those that molested her." According to Mather:

Sometimes they would be deaf, sometimes dumb, and sometimes blind, and often, all this at once. One while their tongues would be drawn down their throats; another-while they would be pulled out upon their chins to a prodigious length. They would have their mouths opened unto such a wideness, that their jaws went out of joint; and anon they would clap together again with a force like that of a strong spring-lock. The same would happen to their shoulder-blades, and their elbows, and hand-wrists, and several of their joints. They would at times lie in a benumbed condition; and be drawn together as those that are tied neck and heels; and presently be stretched out, yea, drawn backwards, to such a degree that it was feared the very skin of their bellies would have cracked. They would make most piteous out-cries, that they were cut with knives, and struck with blows that they could not bear. Their necks would be broken, so that their neck-bone would seem dissolved unto them that felt after it; and yet on the sudden, it would become again so stiff that there was no stirring of their heads; yea, their heads would be twisted almost round; and if main Force at any time obstructed a dangerous motion when they seemed to be upon, they would roar exceedingly.

A number of physicians, including the locally prominent Dr. Thomas Oakes, examined the Goodwin children. He "concluded nothing but an hellish witchcraft could be the original of these maladies." After confessing that she was a witch, Mary Glover was tried, found guilty, and hanged in Boston.

Refusing to accede to the witchcraft rumors that swirled throughout Salem Village, Parris called upon Dr. William Griggs to diagnose the illness of his daughter and niece. The good doctor poked, prodded, and peered, ruling out this disease and that condition. He consulted his medical books then delivered the diagnosis that reverberated throughout Salem Village: "The evil hand is on them."

Immediately, Parris proclaimed a state of spiritual emergency in the Village, summoning help from nearby ministers. The Reverend Nicholas Noyes from Salem Town brought with him a reputation for being gentle and forgiving with sinners who repented while being fierce and unforgiving with those who denied their guilt. The Reverend John Hale arrived from Beverly. On two previous occasions, he had dealt with charges of witchcraft lodged against women in his own area. On those occasions, Hale was not convinced that evil was the precipitating factor, and he worked strenuously and successfully to clear the accused. However, as he assessed the situation in Salem Village, Hale wondered if he had erred. He observed:

> These children were bitten and pinched by invisible agents. Their arms, necks, and backs turned this way and that way, and returned back again, so as it was impossible for them to do so themselves, and beyond the power of any epileptic fits, or natural disease to effect. Sometime they were taken dumb, their mouths stopped, their throats choked, their limbs racked and tormented so as might move a heart of stone to sympathize with them, with the bowels of compassion for them. I will not enlarge in the description of their cruel sufferings, because they were in all things afflicted as bad as John Goodwin's children at Boston, in the year 1689.

The ministers began their emergency work by holding a public day of fasting. Then they conducted private, intense sessions of therapeutic prayer with the afflicted girls. Some of the girls sat trancelike, seemingly impervious to the Divine words. Others, like Abigail, shrieked, wailed, and sobbed piteously. Having failed to alleviate the torments, the ministers reached a dramatic decision: The girls must expose the witches who were at the root of the calamity.

"Who torments you?" the girls were asked. They remained silent as the ministers pounded the question into their brains. When that failed to elicit responses, the ministers suggested the names of women in the area suspected of being witches and watched the girls' reactions for hints about the identities of the perpetrators. Again, the young women remained silent.

As days went by without revelations, frustration grew palpable in Salem Village. Many agreed that the names of the witches had to be ferreted out by any means necessary. Taking matters into her own hands, Mary Sibley, aunt of Mary Walcott, visited the Reverend Parris's parsonage on February 25, 1692, and asked Tituba and John Indian to bake a witch's cake.

Traditional English folklore held that a witch's cake—a white-magick concoction of rye meal and the urine of those afflicted—baked in the hearth fire and fed to a dog would confirm the presence of witchcraft. Either the dog would behave as if tormented, or the dog would flee to the witch, revealing that the dog was the witch's familiar. The witch's cake was fed to the Parris family dog, but this animal's reaction is not known. However, the response from Parris was swift and vehement.

Reverend Parris was appalled when he learned what Sibley had done. He berated her privately for "going to the Devil for help against the Devil." In front of the whole congregation, he called her "to deep humiliation for what she has done." Sibley admitted her wrongdoing, but the deed could not be undone. "The Devil hath been raised among us," Parris told his congregation, "and his rage is vehement and terrible; and, when he shall be silenced, the Lord only knows."

Fear of the Devil's rage, the unrelenting images of hellfire and brimstone pouring forth from the pulpit, and the superstitious belief in the power of the witch's cake probably worked to loosen the lips of the afflicted girls. The youngest among them—Betty Parris—was the first to point an accusing finger. She named Tituba as her tormenter. Following Betty's lead, the other young women broke their silence as well. In addition to Tituba, they named two other suspects: Sarah Good and Sarah Osborne.

On February 29 (1692 being leap year), formal complaints were filed against the three suspected witches by Thomas Putnam, Edward Putnam, Joseph Hutchinson, and Thomas Preston. The charge was suspicion of witchcraft perpetrated against Elizabeth Parris, Abigail Williams, Ann Putnam, and Elizabeth Hubbard. Tituba, Sarah Good, and Sarah Osborne were arrested and thrown into Ipswich Prison.

How believable were these accusations? Tituba's exotic appearance, her Caribbean background, and her closeness to Abigail and Betty made her a likely suspect. Another strong suspect was Sarah Good, who has been described as "a proper hag of a witch if Salem Village had ever seen one."

At age 39, Sarah Good's hard life revealed itself in her appearance and comportment. Her gray hair, wrinkled face, and bent body made her look nearly 70, despite a pregnancy and a young daughter, Dorcas. Good's sharp tongue, abrasive personality, and slovenly habits had poisoned the community against her.

Good's downward spiral began in 1672 with the suicide of her father, wealthy innkeeper John Solart, an act that brought disgrace to the family. Thereafter, Good was denied her rightful portion of the inheritance by her mother's remarriage and subsequent death.

Good married Daniel Poole, a former indentured servant who later died, leaving her the burden of his debts. She next married laborer William Good. Unable to satisfy his wife's creditors, Good was jailed for a time, and the couple lost their land. Sarah was reduced to tramping through the streets of Salem Village, begging for handouts and shelter.

The residents of Salem Village wanted as little to do with her as possible. They blamed dirty, unkempt Sarah Good for the recent smallpox epidemic that had swept through the area. They resented her ungratefulness and insolence when they bestowed charity upon her and her scoldings and curses when they turned her away. They also feared that her foul-smelling pipe would set ablaze their barns if she were allowed to bed down among the hay bales. Clearly, for the people of Salem Village, Good was the epitome of the word "witch."

In direct contrast to Sarah Good was the third woman accused, Sarah Osborne. Sixty-year-old Osborne not only owned property but was fairly prosperous since her 1662 marriage to Robert Prince, who owned a 150-acre farm next to the land owned by Captain John Putnam Sr. After her husband died, Sarah invited a young immigrant, Alexander Osborne, to become the overseer of her property as well as her lover, which caused tongues to wag. Their subsequent marriage failed to quell the scandalous talk, and the rumor mongers spread additional innuendo that she had not attended church services for the last fourteen months. Osborne claimed that she was ill and confined to her bed, but her excuses fell on deaf ears.

Osborne was also involved in a long legal battle with John and Thomas Putnam, executors of her first husband's will. The will stated that Osborne's two sons from her first marriage would inherit the property when they reached legal age. The sons accused her of remarrying in order to move control of the property to Alexander Osborne and to deny them their rightful inheritance.

On March 1, Tituba, Sarah Good, and Sarah Osborne were marched to Salem Village to face magistrates John Hathorne and Jonathan Corwin. The gathering place could not accommodate the throng of spectators on hand to witness the unfolding events, so the proceedings were moved to the meetinghouse.

Members of the General Court of the colony of Massachusetts, Hathorne and Corwin were responsible for conducting a preliminary inquest to determine if enough evidence existed to hold the suspected witches for trial.

However, these men lacked formal legal training because, at the time, the professional practice of law was not permitted in the colony. In the absence of legal training, three things guided Hathorne and Corwin in the proceedings: God's will as contained in the Biblical admonition "Thou shalt not suffer a witch to live," the theological opinion of the day that the Devil possessed the power to influence the lives of human beings, and recognized scholarly texts that addressed witchcraft as a legal issue.

Hathorne and Corwin had synthesized this theological-legal thinking about witchcraft, placed their own interpretation on the collective wisdom, then agreed to specific understandings regarding rules of evidence. Allowable evidence supporting the charge of witchcraft included finding on the body of the accused a "witch's teat" or "witch's mark"—any scar, blemish, or birthmark thought to be a spot on which the witch's familiar suckled.

The magistrates also allowed into evidence testimony on the misfortunes befalling those with whom the accused had exchanged angry words or had had disagreements, reports of the accused having extraordinary strength or unusual abilities, face-to-face meetings of the accused and the afflicted during which the afflicted succumbed to fits and convulsions, and incidents of the accused being unable to recite a prayer or a passage from the Bible. A true witch was believed to be unable to speak holy words.

While agreeing with Increase Mather that the water test was unreliable as evidence, the magistrates retained the use and admissibility of the touch test. During a convulsion, the afflicted would be permitted to touch the accused. If the accused were a witch, the affliction would be transferred from the body of the accused to the body of the witch.

However, the most damaging proof that could be admitted to the inquest was spectral evidence. Hathorne and Corwin agreed that "the devil could not assume the shape of an innocent person in doing mischief to mankind." Therefore, evidence of physical harm done to an individual or to property by the specter of a person weighed heavily against the accused, and the illusionary nature of the evidence precluded the individual from offering a convincing defense.

The first person scheduled to face the magistrates was Sarah Good. She had proved a handful for the authorities. She had engaged in an altercation with one of the guards, had attempted suicide, and on the way from the jail to Salem Village on the morning of the inquest had thrown herself from her horse in three escape attempts. Two strong constables, each gripping one of her thin arms, escorted Good into the meetinghouse. She approached Hathorne and Corwin with an attitude of defiance.

Hathorne began the questioning, asking Good what evil spirits she knew, if she had made a contact with the Devil, and why she was hurting the children. Good denied any knowledge or involvement. He then asked what person or creature she employed to torment the girls, and again she denied the accusations. When Hathorne asked why she had departed muttering from Reverend Parris's house, she claimed that she had only thanked him for what he had given her child.

Among the sworn statements entered into evidence against Good were depositions from Ann Putnam Jr. and Elizabeth Hubbard. Ann swore that:

> On the 25th of February, I saw the apparition of Sarah Good which did torture me most grievously. But I did not know her name until the 27th of February, and then she told me her name was Sarah Good, and then did she prick me and pinch me most grievously and also since several times urging me vehemently to write in her book.

Elizabeth's statement told a similar story: "Sarah Good came to me barefoot and barelegged and did most grievously torment me by pricking and pinching me, and I verily believe that Sarah Good hath bewitched me."

Hathorne then asked Betty Parris, Abigail Williams, Ann Putnam Jr., and Elizabeth Hubbard to face Sarah to determine if she was "the person that had hurt them." The girls identified her. Then "they were all dreadfully tortured and tormented for a short space of time, and the affliction and tortures being over they charged Sarah Good again that she had then so tortured them."

Hathorne again turned to Good, pointing to the evidence of the girls' behavior and asking why she tormented them or who she employed to do so. She testified that she did neither, and when Hathorne asked her to explain how the girls came to be so tormented, Good deflected the blame.

"I do not know, but it was some you brought into the meetinghouse with you."

"We brought you into the meetinghouse."

"But you brought in two more."

"Who was it then that tormented the children?"

"It was Osborne."

Good's attempt to shift the blame away from herself and onto the other two accused, especially Sarah Osborne, proved unsuccessful. Her husband, William Good, testified that "he was afraid that she either was a witch or would be one very quickly." He shocked the spectators when he reported that recently he had seen "a teat a little below her right shoulder which he never saw before."

When Hathorne asked if he had observed Sarah doing evil deeds, William replied that she treated him badly and "I may say with tears that she is an enemy to all good." Sarah tried to demonstrate her innocence by reciting a psalm, but she managed to mutter only a few lines. As she was dismissed by the magistrates, Sarah called out, "It is Gammer Osborne that doth pinch and afflict the children," "gammer" being a term of address for elderly women.

Next, Sarah Osborne was led into chamber. Ill and weak, she approached the magistrates haltingly, supported by the strong grips of two constables. Hathorne's initial questions centered around her familiarity with evil spirits, whether she had a contract with the Devil, and why she had hurt the children. Osborne denied each accusation. Then Hathorne's questioning shifted to Osborne's relationship to Sarah Good.

"What familiarity have you with Sarah Good?" he asked.

"None. I have not seen her these two years," Osborne replied.

"Where did you see her then?"

"One day agoing to town."

"What communications had you with her?"

"I had none, only 'how do you do' or so."

"Sarah Good says that it was you that hurt the children."

"I do not know that the Devil goes about in my likeness to do any hurt."

Hoping to convince the magistrates of her innocence, Osborne attempted to align herself with the afflicted girls, explaining that "she was more likely to be bewitched than that she was a witch." Hathorne questioned her further, and "she answered that she was frightened one time in her sleep and either saw or dreamed that she saw a thing like an Indian all black which did pinch her in her neck and pulled her by the back part of her head to the door of the house."

Osborne also admitted that she had heard a spirit voice telling her that she should no longer go to Sabbath services. While she had agreed, she testified that she had gone to the next Sabbath services. Hathorne challenged her to explain why she had not been to services since the last time, apparently hoping to prove that she had yielded to the Devil. "Alas. I have been sick and not able to go," Osborne responded.

Throughout Osborne's testimony, the afflicted girls wailed and writhed in their seats. In their sworn statements, Elizabeth Hubbard and Ann Putnam Jr. stated that Osborne's apparition had tortured them grievously with pricks and pinches. Mercy Lewis swore that Osborne's apparition had urged her to "write in her book," referring to the belief that witches who joined Satan's service pledged their allegiance by signing their names or making their marks in the Devil's book. Abigail Williams testified that she had been afflicted "with pains in her head and other parts" by the apparitions of Sarah Osborne, Sarah Good, and Tituba.

A trembling Tituba was led into the room next, and her entrance caused the screams, cries, and convulsions of the afflicted girls to escalate. Had her appearance aroused the Devil within them, or did they fear the repercussions of her truthful testimony?

Since the incident of the witch's cake, Tituba most likely had been beaten by the Reverend Parris to get her to admit the truth. No doubt she discovered that the beatings ceased when she told him what he wanted to hear. Therefore, Tituba probably decided to appease the magistrates in the same way. While she initially denied being familiar with evil spirits and hurting the children, she finally admitted that "the Devil came to me and bid me serve him." That caused a hush to fall over the spectators, including the afflicted girls. So Tituba told those assembled what they wanted to hear, during three days of testimony.

Tituba revealed that "four women and one man they hurt the children." When Hathorne pressed her to identify the individuals, Tituba mentioned the names of Sarah Good and Sarah Osborne but confessed that she did not know the names of the other two women. She described the fifth person as a tall, white-haired man from Boston who dressed in black and who asked her to serve him.

"What service?" Hathorne asked.

"Hurt the children," Tituba said, "and last night there was an appearance that said 'Kill the children.' And if I would not go on hurting the children, they would do worse to me."

Tituba revealed that the man sometimes took the shape of a hog or a large black dog. He "had a yellow bird that kept with him, and he told me he had more pretty things that he would give me if I would serve him." She confessed that the man had forced her to pinch Elizabeth Hubbard that very morning and that the night before Good and Osborne had forced Tituba to go to the home of Thomas Putnam Jr. with the intention of killing Ann Putnam Jr. with a knife. Several witnesses confirmed that when tormenters afflicted Ann, "she did complain of a knife—that they would have cut her head off with a knife."

Tituba had more fantastic details to share with the stunned spectators. She claimed, "I ride upon a stick or pole and Good and Osborne behind me. We ride taking hold of one another." She told the magistrates that she had also seen two cats—one black and one red—and two rats—one black and one red—that told her to serve them. She revealed that Good kept a cat and a yellow bird as familiars and that rather than eating meat, the bird "did suck her between her [Good's] fingers."

One of Osborne's familiars was "a thing with a head like a woman with two legs and wings." The transcript commented that "Abigail Williams that lives with her uncle Mr. Parris said that she did see this same creature, and it turned into the shape of Goody Osborne." The other familiar belonging to Osborne was "a thing all over hairy, all the face hairy and a long nose. I don't know how to tell how the face looks. With two legs, it goes upright and is about two or three foot high and goes upright like a man. Last night it stood before the fire in Mr. Parris's hall."

The afflicted girls fell into convulsions again and raised consternation among those in the courtroom. Hathorne asked if Tituba could see who was tormenting them. "Yes," she answered, "it is Goody Good. She hurts them in her own shape."

Hathorne pressed Tituba to name others that she saw hurting the girls. "I am blind now. I cannot see," she told him and fell immediately onto the floor in convulsions. Hathorne and Corwin were unconvinced that Tituba's sudden blindness was due to her having renounced her calling as a witch—a common superstition of the time—but they were certain that she had more evidence.

When her testimony resumed the next day, Tituba regaled the courtroom with additional details about the tall, white-haired man from Boston. She revealed that the man had appeared to her in mid-January, telling her that he was God and promising her "many fine things," including "a little bird something like green and white" if she agreed to serve him for six years. Skeptical about his claims, Tituba attempted to go to the Reverend Parris for counsel, but the tall man stopped her. Only after she called him God did the tall man vanish.

The man returned to the parsonage five nights later in the company of the four witches and told Tituba to pinch Betty and Abigail. "I would not hurt

Betty. I loved Betty," Tituba testified. But the spectral visitors forced Tituba to pinch the girls, who were sitting in a room with the Reverend Parris. Parris had not seen Tituba in the act of pinching because "they would not let my Master see."

Two days later the tall man returned and compelled Tituba to make her mark in his book. As she did, she noticed that the pages contained the marks of nine other people. Hathorne asked if the tall man had told her the names of all those who had signed. No, Tituba replied, the tall man had mentioned only that the marks of Good and Osborne were in the book. When asked if the man had told her where the nine lived, she answered, "Yes. Some in Boston and some here in this town, but he would not tell me where they were."

A collective shudder went through the spectators at the thought that unidentified witches were still loose in Salem. When the testimony ended on March 5, Hathorne and Corwin determined that they had sufficient evidence against Tituba, Good, and Osborne. The women were returned to the Ipswich jail, and on March 7 they were transferred to a prison in Boston to await trial.

The magistrates temporarily adjourned the preliminary inquest so that Hathorne, Corwin, Parris, and others could confer with one another and the afflicted girls to determine the identity of the other witches in the Salem community. Betty Parris was spared this interrogation. Her mother convinced Parris to send their daughter to Salem Town, where she stayed in the home of Stephen Sewall in order to recuperate.

To aid in the witch quest, a day of fasting and prayer was declared for March 11. Before the day had ended, another specter appeared to the afflicted girls, and Ann Putnam Jr. revealed the name of this witch—Martha Corey.

The community reeled at the accusation. According to Marion L. Starkey, Corey was "a respectable matron, a member of the congregation in good standing and a tireless attendant of meeting." However, Corey also had a number of strikes against her. She had given birth years earlier to an illegitimate mulatto son which she and her second husband, Giles, had raised. She had a reputation for speaking her mind and for being intransigent in the belief that her point of view was always the right one. One of her views was that this witchcraft business was utter nonsense. Last, she had the annoying habit of anticipating what people were about to say.

Despite these deficits, Corey's status as someone who believed in God and belonged to the church accorded her special consideration. On March 12, the magistrates dispatched Edward Putnam—Ann's uncle—and Ezekiel Cheever—

clerk at the preliminary inquiry—to meet with Corey to discuss the charges lodged against her. Prior to their setting out, the men asked Ann to describe the clothing worn by Corey's specter. Perhaps the emissaries questioned Ann's reliability as a witness. Perhaps Ann saw herself getting backed into a corner. "I am blind now; I cannot see," Ann replied. She explained that Corey knew about the forthcoming interview and had taken away her vision with a spell.

Putnam and Cheever found Martha at the Corey home, working at the spinning wheel in the kitchen. She smiled at them and then said, "I know what you are come for. You are come to talk with me about being a witch, but I am none." The men were startled. But Corey's next comment condemned her in the eyes of her visitors, "Did she tell you what clothes I have on?"

Corey faced her accuser in the Putnam home on March 14. According to Edward Putnam, as soon as Corey entered the house, Ann "fell into grievous fits of choking, blinding, feet and hands twisted in a most grievous manner." Ann accused Corey of afflicting her and reported that Corey had allowed a yellow bird—her familiar—to suck on her hand between her middle and index fingers. Corey offered her hand to Ann to examine, and then Corey rubbed the spot. Immediately, Ann fell to the floor blinded. After she regained her vision, Ann screamed that she saw Corey's specter at the fireplace, turning a spit on which a man was impaled. Mercy Lewis, the Putnam's servant, attacked the specter with a stick but "cried out with a grievous pain in her arm as if one had struck her with a stick." Ann reported that Corey had struck Lewis with an iron rod. Corey was ordered out of the house.

That night Edward Putnam witnessed Mercy Lewis being "drawn toward the fire by unseen hands as she sat in a chair, and two men [had] hold of it. Yet she and [the] chair moved toward the fire though they labored to the contrary. Her feet going foremost, and I seeing it stepped to her feet and lifted with my strength together with the other two and all little enough to prevent her from going into the fire with her feet foremost, and this distress held until about eleven of the clock in the night."

Corey was blamed for this mayhem as well as for afflicting Abigail Williams and Ann Putnam Sr. A warrant was sworn out for Corey's arrest on Saturday, March 19, but the order could not be carried out until after the Sabbath. That meant that Corey could attend church services on Sunday as usual.

The guest minister that Sunday was Deodat Lawson, a former minister of Salem Village. He had arrived the day before and had been briefed on the recent happenings. As he mounted the pulpit for the service, Lawson was unsure what to expect but was soon shocked by the behavior of several of the afflicted girls: "They had several sore fits, in the time of public worship, which did something interrupt me in my first prayer; being so unusual."

He also reported that "in sermon time when Goodwife Corey was present in the meetinghouse, Abigail Williams called out, 'Look where Goodwife Corey sits on the beam suckling her yellow bird between her fingers!' Ann Putnam another girl afflicted said there was a yellow bird sat on my hat as it hung on the pin in the pulpit." The girls claimed that Corey's specter darted throughout the house of worship, pinching and choking them. Pandemonium ensued even as the adults tried to restore order.

Martha Corey ignored the girls' antics and the caustic stares of the worshippers. She would have her day in court soon enough, and she would open the eyes of both magistrates and ministers to the foolishness they had allowed to infect the Village.

On March 21, a defiant Corey faced the magistrates in the packed meetinghouse. Her requests to pray before the proceedings were rebuffed by a stern John Hathorne who wasted little time in setting the tone for the inquiry: "We do not send for you to go to prayer. But tell me why you hurt these?"

"I am an innocent person," Corey replied. "I never had to do with witchcraft since I was born. I am a gospel woman."

Hathorne peppered Corey with questions about the visit from Putnam and Cheever. He asked her to explain how she knew that they planned to visit her and how she knew that Ann Putnam had been asked to describe her clothes that day. At first, Corey answered that Cheever had told her, but Cheever interrupted her and "bid her not to begin with a lie." Next, Corey suggested that her husband had told her. When questioned, he denied it. Then, Corey offered, "I had heard speech that the children said I troubled them, and I thought they might come to examine." Finally, she admitted that no one had told her.

Throughout the questioning, the afflicted girls provided a backdrop of taunts, calling Corey a "gospel witch." When Corey bit her lip, the afflicted girls complained of being bitten. When Corey moved her hands, the afflicted girls complained of being pinched. Then one of the girls announced that "there is a man whispering in her ear."

"What did he say to you?" Hathorne asked.

"We must not believe all that these distracted children say," Corey answered.

"Cannot you tell what that man whispered?"

"I saw nobody."

"But did not you hear?"

"No."

The afflicted girls increased their fits, wails, and screams. Despite the din, Hathorne continued his questioning, asking Corey about a statement she had made that the Devil could not stand before her. She denied making the statement; however, several "sober witnesses confirmed it." Hathorne asked her about the accusation that she had turned a man on a spit. She denied doing so, saying, "I saw no spit." Corey denied striking Mercy Lewis on the arm and denied having a yellow bird as a familiar. Hathorne demanded that Corey confess to being a witch, and she replied, "So I would if I were guilty." When Hathorne asked Corey if she believed the children were bewitched, she replied: "They may for ought I know. I have no hand in it." Hathorne asked her to explain the afflictions of the young girls. "If you will all go hang me, how can I help it?" she answered.

One witness who brought Martha Corey closer to the noose was her husband, Giles. When called to the stand, he was unable to confirm his wife's testimony about the visit from Putnam and Cheever. He mentioned that she had removed the saddle from his horse on a day that he had planned to ride into the Village to attend the hearings. He wondered why she did that. He also related that for the last week praying had been difficult to do when she was close by. Once, after he had gone to bed, he found Martha kneeling at the hearth as if in prayer although he had heard nothing coming from her lips.

Giles also reported suspicious incidents with his animals. The week before, he had gone into the woods to retrieve an ox, but the animal "could not rise but dragged his hinder parts as if he had been hip shot." Giles also had a cat that acted strangely. "My wife bid me knock her in the head, but I did not, and since she is well."

The evidence presented against Corey convinced Hathorne and Corwin to hold her for trial. As she was led off, she cried out, "You can't prove me a witch!" Unfortunately, she couldn't prove that she wasn't a witch, so she joined the company of Sarah Good, Sarah Osborne, and Tituba, awaiting their fates in jail.

Two days after Martha Corey was jailed, an arrest warrant was issued for the fifth accused witch—Rebecca Nurse. The charge of "vehement suspicion of having committed sundry acts of witchcraft" sent shock waves through the

Salem community. Seventy-one-year-old Nurse was a respected member of the church and a pious, God-fearing matriarch who practiced charity to others. Certainly she had her human failings. Her partial deafness often caused her to ignore greetings and questions from neighbors, and she sometimes lost her temper. But to accuse this much loved, ailing woman of dealing in devilry was beyond comprehension.

The Reverend Deodat Lawson could hardly believe it either, but he had witnessed strange afflictions in Abigail Williams in the Parris parsonage, presumably caused by Goodwife Nurse. After his March 19 visit to Parris, Lawson reported that Abigail "was at first hurried with violence to and fro in the room, sometimes making as if she would fly, stretching up her arms as high as she could, and crying 'Whish, Whish, Whish!' several times; presently after she said there was Goodwife Nurse and said, 'Do you not see her? Why there she stands.' And then said Goodwife Nurse offered her The Book, but she was resolved she would not take it, saying often 'I won't, I won't, I won't, take it, I do not know what Book it is; I am sure it is none of God's Book. It is the Devil's Book, for ought I know.'"

On March 23, the Reverend Lawson paid a call to the home of Thomas Putnam Jr. Ann Sr. had been afflicted for several days by the bites, pinches, and pricks of witches. She asked Lawson to pray for her, and he recorded what happened next:

> At the first beginning she attended; but after a little time was taken with a fit: yet continued silent and seemed to be asleep. When prayer was done, her husband going to her found her in a fit. He took her off the bed to set her on his knees, but at first she was so stiff, she could not be bended. But she afterwards set down but quickly began to strive violently with her arms and legs. She then began to complain of and as it were to converse personally with Goodwife Nurse, saying 'Goodwife Nurse, be gone! Be gone! Be gone! Are you not ashamed, a woman of your profession, to afflict a poor creature so? What hurt did I ever do you in my life?'

Before Nurse was taken into custody, the magistrates dispatched Israel and Elizabeth Porter Sr., Hathorne's sister and brother-in-law, to Nurse's home to discuss the witchcraft claims with her. They found Nurse ill in her bedchamber where she had lain for the last eight or nine days. She greeted her visitors warmly then asked about the afflicted girls in the Village. "I go to God for them," Nurse said. "But I am troubled, oh I am troubled at some of their crying out. Some of the persons they have spoken of are, as I believe, as innocent as I."

When the Porters revealed the reason for their visit, Nurse sighed then said, "Well, if it be so, the will of the Lord be done." She sat trancelike for a moment then said, "As to this thing I am innocent as the child unborn. But surely, what sin hath God found in me unrepented of that He could lay such an affliction on me in my old age?"

Moved by her words and knowing that her arrest was certain, the Porters recorded their impressions of their meeting with Nurse and submitted it to the court as testimony on her behalf. In part they stated: "According to our best observation we could not discern that she knew what we came for before we told her."

On March 24, Essex County marshal George Herrick roused Nurse from her sickbed, placed her under arrest, and brought her to the meetinghouse. Frail and weak, Nurse strained to hear the testimony against her, but the screams and cries of the afflicted girls drowned out the words of the witnesses. Hathorne approached his questioning of Nurse more gently than he had with the others, perhaps recognizing the extent of her infirmities or perhaps being unsure of her guilt. To the charges, she answered, "I can say before my Eternal Father, I am innocent, and God will clear my innocency."

Then Henry Kenney entered a complaint, testifying that "since this Nurse came into the house, he was seized twice with an amazing condition." Edward Putnam next swore that Nurse had afflicted his niece, Ann Putnam Jr. To which Nurse declared, "I never afflicted no child never in my life."

Ann Putnam Sr. cried out from the spectator section, "Did you not bring the black man [the Devil] with you? Did you not bid me tempt God and die? How oft have you eat and drunk your own damnation?" After her outburst, Ann had to be led from the meetinghouse by her husband.

Ann's accusations in open court paled in comparison to the statements she included in her official deposition. Of all the witnesses, she had leveled the most serious charge against Nurse: murder.

Ann's deposition stated:

> Immediately there did appear to me six children in winding sheets which called me aunt which did most grievously affright me, and they told me that they were my sister's children of Boston and that Goody Nurse and Mistress

Cary of Charlestown and an old deaf woman at Boston had murdered them and charged me to go and tell these things to the magistrates or else they would tear me to pieces for their blood did cry for vengeance. Also there appeared to me my own sister Bayley and three of her children in winding sheets and told me that Goody Nurse had murdered them.

Distressed by the accusations and distracted by the noise and confusion surrounding her, Nurse uttered "Oh Lord, help me" then spread out her hands. Instantly, the afflicted girls were tormented by convulsions.

Hathorne noted the action and reaction and said, "Do you not see what a solemn condition these are in? When your hands are loose, the persons are afflicted." The afflicted girls mimicked Nurse's gestures and movements, then Mary Walcott and Elizabeth Hubbard accused Nurse of harming them.

"Here are these two grown persons now accuse you," Hathorne charged. "What do you say? Do not you see these afflicted persons and hear them accuse you?"

"The Lord knows I have not hurt them. I am an innocent person," Nurse answered.

"It is very awful to all to see these agonies and [to see] you an old professor thus charged with contracting with the Devil by the effects of it, and yet to see you stand with dry eyes when there are so many wet."

"You do not know my heart."

"You would do well if you are guilty to confess and give glory to God."

But Nurse clung to her defense of innocence, prompting Hathorne to ask if she thought the girls were truly bewitched.

"I do think they are."

Hathorne continued. "When this witchcraft came upon the stage there was no suspicion of Tituba. She professed much love to that child Betty Parris, but it was her apparition did the mischief, and why should not you also be guilty, for your apparition doth hurt also."

"The Devil may appear in my shape."

Nurse's speculation that the Devil could appear in human guise without the knowledge or permission of the individual was significant, but the magistrates ignored it. Nurse was sent to jail to await trial.

On the same day that elderly Rebecca Nurse was incarcerated, the youngest of the accused witches—4-year-old Dorcas Good—was taken into custody and charged with "suspicion of acts of witchcraft." Mercy Lewis, Mary

Walcott, and Ann Putnam Jr. accused the girl of sending her apparition to bite, pinch, and choke them in retaliation for their testimony against her mother, Sarah Good.

Confused and frightened, Dorcas attended a brief hearing. Whenever Dorcas looked at them, the afflicted girls screamed and cried out that her specter was about the room, biting and pinching them. She was jailed, and two days later Hathorne, Corwin, and John Higginson, a Salem Town minister, visited the child in her cell. She admitted that she owned a snake that sucked on her index finger—indeed she pointed to a dark red spot on the lowest joint of her finger where she claimed the snake suckled—and that the snake had been a gift from her mother.

Possession of a familiar and evidence of a witch's mark condemned Dorcas to imprisonment for witchcraft while awaiting trial. Her hands and feet were bound in child-sized chains that had to be made especially for her. She languished in prison until December 1692 when Samuel Ray of Salem posted a recognizance bond of £50 for her release on bail. No records exist indicating that she was brought to trial.

In 1710 her father, William Good, recollected that "Dorcas, a child of 4 or 5 years old, was in prison 7 or 8 months, and, being chained in the dungeon, was so hardly used and terrified that she has ever since been very changeable, having little or no reason to govern herself."

With the incarcerations of Rebecca Nurse and Dorcas Good, the citizens of Salem held their collective breaths, wondering who would be accused of witchcraft next. They did not have long to wait.

On Sunday, April 3, Sacrament Day, the Reverend Parris presented a sermon based on the Biblical verse "Have not I chosen you twelve, and one of you is a devil." Since Puritans believed that church members were elected or chosen by God, the meaning was clear to those attending the service: God had chosen the members of the Salem congregation, and two of them, Martha Corey and Rebecca Nurse, had defected to the Devil's side. Parris described such defectors as "sons and heirs of the Devil, the free-holders of hell; whereas other sinners are but tenants."

That was enough for the sister of Rebecca Nurse, Sarah Towne Cloyce. According to Deodat Lawson, "Goodwife Cloyce went immediately out of the meetinghouse, and flung the door after her violently, to the amazement of the congregation." To the stunned congregates, Parris proclaimed, "Christ knows how many devils there are in his church and who they are."

After the service, lips whispered about Cloyce's abrupt departure. Her defenders claimed that she had become ill suddenly and that she had not intended to slam the door; the strength of the wind had swept the door from her grasp. But others believed that Cloyce's behavior suggested an ominous portent.

The girls' convulsions began anew, and they pointed fingers to a horrible sight that only they could see: a coven of witches sharing the Devil's sacrament of "red bread and bloody wine." One of the girls cried out: "Oh Goody Cloyce, I did not think to see you here. Is this a time to receive the sacrament? You ran away on the Lord's Day and scorned to receive it in the meetinghouse. Is this a time to receive it?"

On April 4 complaints were issued against Cloyce "for high suspicion of sundry acts of witchcraft," and she was arrested on April 8. The hearing on April 11 was moved from Salem Village to Salem Town for the convenience of a group of dignitaries, including Deputy Governor Thomas Danforth and members of the General Court —Isaac Addington, Samuel Appleton, James Russell, and Samuel Sewall—whose concern for the witchcraft situation drew them to Salem for firsthand observations. Those in the community who had hoped that these officials would view the testimony more objectively and the behavior of the afflicted girls more skeptically were sorely disappointed.

Danforth led the inquiry, calling John Indian, Mary Walcott, Abigail Williams, Mercy Lewis, and Ann Putnam Jr. as witnesses against Cloyce. Indian testified that Cloyce had pinched, bit, and choked him "a great many times." Cloyce shouted at him, "Oh, you are a grievous liar." In response, Indian tumbled to the floor, writhing in pain.

The afflicted girls testified next. Mary Walcott swore that Cloyce had visited her with "the book," urging her to "touch it, and be well." Walcott revealed that Cloyce had been in the company of Rebecca Nurse, Martha Corey, and many others whom Walcott did not know. Similarly, Abigail Williams testified that she had seen a coven of forty witches at the Parris parsonage, celebrating the Devil's sacrament with Cloyce and Sarah Good serving as deacons.

The last revelation was too much for Cloyce. She asked for a cup of water then sat down. Immediately, the afflicted girls shouted that they saw the black man, the Devil, whispering in Cloyce's ear and saw a yellow bird flying around her head. This brought Cloyce to the brink of faint and prompted one of the girls to comment: "Oh, her spirit is gone to prison to her sister Nurse!"

As Sarah Cloyce was led off to jail, another accused witch, Elizabeth Proctor, took her place at the defendant's bar. She was the pregnant wife of well-respected, prosperous landowner and tavern proprietor, John Proctor, one of the early critics of the witchcraft inquests.

The witchcraft woes of the Proctors began with the spectral visions and convulsions of their servant, Mary Warren. John Proctor reportedly cured Warren by seating her at her spinning wheel and promising her a beating if she moved from the spot, whether afflicted or not. When the magistrates summoned Warren to testify in court, Proctor protested that the appearances kept her from her work, but he was overruled. He remarked, "She must have her fits forsooth."

In late March 1692, John Proctor traveled to Salem Village to pick up Warren after one of her court appearances. He was unafraid to make known his opinion about the afflicted girls: "They should rather be had to the whipping post. If they are let alone we should all be devils and witches." In his view, the real witches were not the women being accused but the ones doing the accusing. "Hang them! Hang them!" Proctor shouted to anyone who would listen. Unfortunately, some of those who listened were the afflicted girls.

On March 28, a few days after Proctor's public tirade against the afflicted girls, one of them fell into a trance in Ingersoll's ordinary and spoke out about Elizabeth Proctor: "There's Goody Proctor . . . Old Witch! I'll have her hang." Hearing the remark, Sarah Ingersoll, Daniel Elliot, and William Raymond looked about, saw nothing, and accused the girl of lying. The girl ended her trance suddenly, explaining, "It was for sport. I must have some sport."

The next day, the specter of Elizabeth Proctor was seen at the home of Thomas Putnam Jr., causing his wife and daughter and their servant Mercy Lewis to experience convulsions. Complaints were filed, and Proctor was subsequently arrested.

When Proctor's inquiry commenced on April 11, her husband stood beside her. Perhaps his presence served to inhibit the willingness of the afflicted girls to testify. When Mercy Lewis was questioned, "her mouth was stopped"; when Ann Putnam Jr. was addressed, "she could not speak"; and when Abigail Williams was asked "Does she hurt you?" the girl's "hand was thrust in her own mouth."

The first witness to speak against Elizabeth Proctor was John Indian, who swore, "This is the woman that came in her shift and choked me." The afflicted girls remained silent "by reason of dumbness or other fits." When Danforth asked Proctor to respond, she said, "I take God in heaven to be my witness, that I know nothing of it, no more than the child unborn."

That seemed to loosen the tongues of the afflicted girls, and they cried out that Proctor had hurt them. Abigail swore that Proctor had tried to entice her to sign her name in her book. Addressing Proctor directly, Abigail asked, "Did not you tell me that your maid [Mary Warren] had written?" Proctor replied, "Dear child, it is not so. There is another judgment, dear child." The girls then fell into fits. One of them shouted, "There is Goody Proctor upon the beam!" and pointed to Proctor's specter hovering near the ceiling.

Then Abigail and Ann Jr. turned on John Proctor. According to the transcript: "By and by, both of them cried out of Goodman Proctor himself, and said he was a wizard. Immediately, many, if not all of the bewitched, had grievous fits."

The girls accused him of afflicting one of the spectators, Mrs. Joseph Pope. "Afterwards some of the afflicted cried, 'There is Proctor going to take up Mrs. Pope's feet.' And her feet were immediately taken up."

Danforth turned to John Proctor. "What do you say, Goodman Proctor, to these things?"

"I know not," he replied. "I am innocent."

"You see, the Devil will deceive you. The children could see what you were going to do before the woman was hurt. I would advise you to repentance, for the Devil is bringing you out."

Proctor did not repent, but the parade of witnesses that subsequently testified against him assured him of a place in the Boston jail to which his wife was sent.

A curious postscript to the Proctor inquest was the fate of their servant, Mary Warren. She did not appear in court to testify against John or Elizabeth Proctor; and in fact, during Elizabeth's questioning, Abigail Williams had accused Warren of having written her name in the Devil's book. Thus, Warren made a unique transition from afflicted to accused.

According to historian Chadwick Hansen: "Lately [Warren] had taken to denying both her own testimony and that of others. The girls' evidence was false, she said; they 'did but dissemble.' By this she did not mean that they were simply lying. She meant that they were living in two different worlds of experience—that of their fits, and that of normal perception—and the world of their fits was false."

Warren was arrested on April 18, examined the following day, and subsequently imprisoned. While she was incarcerated, several jailed witches gave a deposition, attesting to statements that Warren had made discrediting the afflicted girls: "When we were in Salem Jail, we heard Mary Warren several times say that the magistrates might as well examine Keyser's daughter, who has been distracted many years, and take notice of what she said as well as any of the afflicted persons. Mary Warren said 'When I was afflicted I thought I saw the apparitions of a hundred persons.' She said her head was distempered; that she could not tell what she said. And Mary told us that when she was well again, she could not say that she saw any of [the] apparitions at the time aforesaid."

Warren was held in the Salem jail until early June. When she was released, she rejoined the inner circle of afflicted girls, who most likely regarded her with suspicion.

Suspicion crept into the nooks and crannies of Salem Village in 1692. Husbands and wives looked with distrust at each other; neighbors had misgivings about one another; people felt uncertain about friends. Unfortunately, for Salem Village, this contamination within the community was only just beginning.

FIVE

The Salem Witch Trials
⚘

S the spring months of 1692 blossomed, witchcraft accusations proliferated like dandelions in a green meadow. By June 2, seventy people had been accused. Twenty-five were from Salem Village and ten from Salem Town; the others came from Topsfield, Reading, Beverly, Billerica, Lynn, Charlestown, Malden, Woburn, and nine other towns in eastern Massachusetts. Notable among those accused were:

BRIDGET BISHOP. Thrice-married Bishop had had numerous run-ins with the authorities over marital difficulties and an accusation of thievery. She had been charged with witchcraft in 1680, but the official records do not contain the disposition of the case. When she was brought to her hearing in Salem on April 19, she told Hathorne, "I take all this people to witness that I am clear." Throughout questioning, she insisted, "I am innocent to a witch. I know not what a witch is." When asked "if she were not troubled to see the afflicted persons so tormented," Bishop answered, "No, I am not troubled for them." Her attitude and her habit of rolling her eyes during her interrogation contributed to the decision to have her jailed.

GEORGE BURROUGHS. Former minister of Salem Village, the Reverend George Burroughs resided in Maine, but he was not immune to the reach of witchcraft accusations in Salem. Ann Putnam Jr. accused him of being the "black minister," the one who officiated at Sabbath meetings of witches and wizards that were held in the Reverend Parris's pasture. She claimed that Burroughs celebrated communions of red bread and blood wine and that his sermons exhorted followers to persuade others to enter the Devil's service. Ann claimed that he had confessed to having bewitched to death his first two wives and having killed Deodat Lawson's wife and child. Abigail Williams confirmed Ann's claims.

The magistrates issued an arrest warrant for Burroughs, charging him with "suspected . . . confederacy with the Devil." The most damaging testimony was presented by Mercy Lewis, whom Burroughs had taken into his home after her parents had been murdered by Indians. Lewis reported that Burroughs confessed he could raise the Devil, his servant, and that Burroughs bewitched people at a distance by sending the Devil in his shape. The people of Salem Village reeled as these accusations assailed their former minister. Burroughs was thrown into prison, supposedly reunited with the very witches he had recruited for Satan.

GILES COREY. Husband of accused witch Martha Corey, Giles was known as a quarrelsome, quick-tempered man with a criminal record for various offenses, including theft. Some neighbors believed also that he dabbled in the occult. During an argument with neighbor Robert Moulton, Giles threatened that his "sawmill should saw no more." Later, that statement came to pass. Then God had "awakened him upon repentance," and Giles confessed his transgressions and became a member of the church. This did little to help him when on April 19 he faced the magistrates and his accusers. The afflicted girls condemned Giles with testimony of his beating, pinching, and choking them.

MARY TOWNE EASTY. The sister of accused witches Rebecca Nurse and Sarah Cloyce, Easty entered her April 22 hearing with "such grace, courage and good sense that Hathorne gave way to one of those moments of doubt." Several times Hathorne asked the afflicted girls, "Are you certain this is the woman?" Easty maintained her innocence, and when Hathorne asked what she thought caused the action of the girls, Easty replied, "It is an evil spirit, but whether it be witchcraft I do not know."

Easty joined her sisters in jail, but her gentle manner impressed the guards, who spoke to the magistrates on her behalf. The magistrates questioned the afflicted girls again, and they testified that Easty's specter no longer tormented them. She was released from prison on May 18. But two days later when Mercy Lewis was taken ill with convulsions and comas, Mary Walcott identified the tormenting specter as that of Easty. Constables roused Easty from sleep, placed her in custody, and carted her off to jail again. Reportedly, at the same time that Easty was imprisoned, the convulsions that had plagued Mercy Lewis ceased.

DORCAS HOAR. Hoar had been accused of witchcraft previously in Beverly, and belief in her innocence had prompted the Reverend John Hale to speak out in her defense. Hale would not make that mistake twice; this time he allowed Hoar to face her Salem accusers without the benefit of his support. She approached her hearing with defiance. Hathorne asked why she had afflicted the girls, and Hoar replied that she had not hurt a child anytime in her life. When Hathorne suggested that her "appearance" had done the harm, Hoar answered, "How can I help it?" Several girls announced that the black man was whispering in her ear, and Hoar declared, "Oh, you are liars, and God will stop the mouths of liars!" The magistrates castigated Hoar for her outburst and ordered her to refrain from speaking in that manner again. In response, she shouted, "I will speak the truth as long as I live." Hoar was jailed.

GEORGE JACOBS SR. Irascible, 80-year-old George Jacobs had referred to the afflicted girls as "bitch witches" and was accused of witchcraft by his servant, Sarah Churchill, and his granddaughter, Margaret Jacobs. George Jacobs was arrested on May 10, and authorities discovered a witch's mark near his right shoulder. Jacobs hobbled into the hearing using two canes and responded to the magistrates in a no-nonsense manner: "I never wronged no man in word nor deed. You tax me for a wizard, you may as well tax me for a buzzard. I have done no harm."

The magistrates asked him to explain how his specter could afflict Churchill. Jacobs suggested that "The devil can go in any shape . . . can take any likeness." Hathorne disagreed, stating that the person would have to give his or her consent. Jacobs was asked to repeat the Lord's Prayer, but he failed to recite it correctly. He lashed out at the magistrates: "Well burn me or hang me! I'll stand in the truth of Christ. I know nothing of it."

After Jacobs was jailed, both Sarah Churchill and Margaret Jacobs recanted their testimony against him. Churchill explained that she had lied "because they threatened her, and told her they would put her into the dungeon . . . along with Mr. Burroughs." Margaret Jacobs explained that she had been intimidated by the magistrates and fearful that she would be hanged if she did not accuse her grandfather. She wrote: "What I said was altogether false against my grandfather." The magistrates ignored both recantations, and Jacobs remained in jail.

SUSANNAH MARTIN. "Susannah Martin was every inch a witch," according to historian Marion L. Starkey, "bright of eye, salty of tongue, and the central figure of every marvelous event that had happened in Amesbury for going on three decades." In 1669, after having been accused of bewitching a neighbor, Martin admitted her deeds, somehow escaped trial, and thereafter went about her spectral doings in the community with impunity.

When Martin appeared in Salem Village for her trial on May 2, the afflicted girls commenced their convulsions. Martin laughed, and the magistrates scolded her. "Well I may [laugh] at such folly," she responded, setting the tone for her inquest. Hathorne asked her what ailed the girls. "Do not you think they are bewitched?" he inquired.

"No. I do not think they are," Martin replied.

"Tell me your thoughts about them."

"Why, my thoughts are my own, when they are in, but when they are out, they are another's."

"Who do you think is their Master?"

"If they be dealing in the black art, you may know as well as I."

When Hathorne asked Martin to explain her spectral appearances to torment the girls, she replied with an allusion to the Biblical Witch of Endor: "He that appeared in Samuel's shape, a glorified saint, can appear in anyone's shape."

The magistrates heard testimony from Martin's neighbors about the mischief her "shape" had caused them over the decades. John Allen testified that, after he refused to do her a favor, Martin bewitched his oxen so that they drove themselves into the ocean. John Kimball testified that, after arguing with Martin, she sent phantom puppies to plague him, nipping at his heels, darting between his feet, and then vanishing as he raised his ax against them. Robert Downer testified that, after having words with Martin, she threatened that "some she devil would fetch him away." That night a cat jumped through his window, pounced on his bed, and held him fast by his throat "a considerable while and was like to throttle him." Based on the testimony of her neighbors and unwilling to engage further in a battle of wits with the saucy Martin, the magistrates sent her to jail.

These and others accused of witchcraft faced a special Court of Oyer and Terminer ("to hear and determine") that was convened by new governor Sir William Phips on June 2, 1692. Phips appointed as judges men "of the best prudence," all members of the Governor's Council: presiding chief justice Deputy Governor William Stoughton, a man with an unquenchable desire to eradicate witchcraft; Salem physician Bartholomew Gedney; Boston merchant John Richards; Essex County judge Nathaniel Saltonstall; Wait Winthrop, grandson of the colony's first governor; Samuel Sewall, future Chief Justice of the Massachusetts Superior Court; and Boston merchant Peter Sergeant.

The judges not only consulted the legal wisdom contained in standard books on witchcraft law, they also appealed to the religious wisdom of Cotton Mather. In a letter to Judge John Richards, Mather blamed Salem's troubles on a "horrible witchcraft." Yet he urged caution with the use of spectral evidence: "It is very certain that the devils have sometimes represented the shapes of persons not only innocent, but also very virtuous." He suggested guidelines for the court: rely on spectral evidence only as "presumption" of guilt and obtain reliable confessions, not those wrought from "a delirious brain, or a discontented heart," through "cross and swift questions." If confessions were not forthcoming, Mather recommended other methods of gathering evidence: having the accused recite the Lord's Prayer, locating a witch's mark, and uncovering among the accused's personal property artifacts of witchcraft such as charms and "poppets," dolls fashioned to resemble the afflicted.

Despite Mather's recommendation, the Court of Oyer and Terminer assigned more weight to spectral evidence than mere signs of presumptive guilt. They accepted as fact and entered into evidence the testimony of witnesses obtained during the preliminary hearings. The only new evidence allowed consisted of depositions gathered since the preliminary hearing and the testimony of witnesses who had further information. However, little of this evidence benefited the accused, who stood before the court without defense.

The trials began immediately, and Bridget Bishop was the first to face the

Court of Oyer and Terminer. She was accused of a range of crimes: pinching and choking, coercing others to sign the Devil's book, and murder. Samuel Gray testified that Bishop's specter had made nocturnal visits to him. After Gray had rejected her advances, he reported that his infant son in a nearby cradle "gave a great screech, and the woman disappeared. It was long before the child could be quieted; and though it were a very likely thriving child, yet from this time it pined away, and after . . . months died in a sad condition."

William Stacey testified that he had experienced a series of misfortunes that he blamed on Bishop, including having money disappear from his pockets and being "hoisted from the ground and thrown against a stone wall."

John Bly and William Bly testified that "being employed by Bridget Bishop, to help take down the cellar wall of the old house, wherein she formerly lived, they did in holes of the said old wall find several poppets, made up of rags and hogs bristles, with headless pins in them, the points being outward. Whereof she could give no account unto the Court, that was reasonable or tolerable."

The most damning evidence was discovered by a jury of women who "found a preternatural teat upon her body, but upon a second search, within three or four hours, there was no such thing to be seen."

The jury found Bishop guilty and the judges sentenced her to be hanged, but this created a legal conundrum. At that time, Massachusetts law had no provision for the death penalty in witchcraft cases. On June 8, the General Court revived a colonial law, making witchcraft a capital crime punishable by death. Bishop's sentence was reinstated, and her execution was scheduled for June 10, on which day Sheriff George Corwin brought her to Gallows Hill. There she was hanged "from the branches of a great oak tree" and afterwards her body was flung into a shallow, unmarked grave.

After Bishop's execution, Judge Nathaniel Saltonstall voiced his distress with the reliance on spectral evidence in the Bishop case. This brought the trials to a temporary halt until the issue of spectral evidence could be decided. Governor Phips turned to the twelve leading ministers of the colony for their advice on the matter.

The ministers recommended that the proceedings "be managed with an exceeding tenderness towards those that may be complained of, especially if they have been persons formerly of an unblemished reputation." They warned about the adverse effects of the outbursts from the afflicted and the questionable worth of spectral evidence "inasmuch as . . . a Demon may, by God's permission, appear, even to ill purposes, in the shape of an innocent, yea, and a virtuous man." They went as far as suggesting that refusing to accept spectral evidence and the confessions of accused witches might "put a period" to the "dreadful calamity" and to the accusations.

They recommended that evidence for convictions "be more considerable than barely the accused person being represented by a specter unto the afflicted." They also cautioned against the use of various tests to confirm guilt, indicating that a change in the afflicted caused by "a look or touch of the accused" was not to be taken as "infallible evidence of guilt." In fact, the ministers stated, such changes were "liable to be abused by the Devil's legerdemains." They concluded their response by recommending that the government proceed with "the speedy and vigorous prosecution of such as have rendered themselves obnoxious, according to the direction given in the laws of God, and the wholesome statutes of the English nation, for the detection of witchcrafts."

Chief Justice William Stoughton believed that the ministers had confirmed the correctness of the court's previous policies and procedures, and most of the other judges fell into step behind him. Nathaniel Saltonstall, the only dissenter, resigned from the court and was replaced by Jonathan Corwin.

When the court reconvened on June 30, five women were tried, convicted, and condemned to die: Sarah Good, Rebecca Nurse, Susannah Martin, Elizabeth How, and Sarah Wildes.

During Good's trial, one witness accused her of stabbing her with a knife and presented as evidence a portion of the knife blade that she said was used in the attack. The judges were about to accept this evidence when a young man stepped from the spectator's section and identified the partial blade as belonging to a knife he had broken the day before. He testified that he had discarded the piece and that the girl had seen him throw it away. He brought out a knife haft and the other portion of the blade. The judges found that the two pieces matched, reprimanded the girl for lying, and then allowed her to continue testifying.

At the trial of Rebecca Nurse, most of the evidence presented was spectral. This was countered by a petition signed by thirty-nine Village residents attesting to Nurse's exemplary life and by testimony from her daughter, Sarah. Sarah swore that: "I saw Goody Bibber pull pins out of her clothes and held them between her fingers and clasped her hands round her knees and then she cried out and said Goody Nurse pinched her. This I can testify."

After deliberating on the evidence, the jury returned their verdict: Not guilty. Bedlam erupted. "Out of the throats of the girls issued a howling and roaring that was both more and less than human," according to Starkey. "Their bodies jerked and snapped in the unearthly choreography of their convulsions."

Chief Justice Stoughton regained control of the courtroom. In an unusual move, he addressed the jury foreman, Thomas Fisk, stating: "I will not impose on the jury, but I must ask you if you considered one statement made by the prisoner."

The statement was one that Nurse had made when confessed witches Deliverance Hobbs and her daughter entered the court to testify. Nurse had said, "What, do these persons give in evidence against me now? They used to come among us."

Fisk admitted that the jury "could not tell how to take her words . . . till she had a further opportunity to put her sense upon them." Stoughton questioned Nurse about her previous statement, but the old woman who was "hard of hearing and full of grief" stared blankly at him and made no response. The jury returned to their deliberations and reversed their verdict to guilty. They interpreted "They used to come among us" as meaning that Hobbs and her daughter had participated in gatherings of witches along with Nurse.

Following Nurse's guilty verdict, the Salem Town church of which she was a member publicly excommunicated her on July 3. Nurse was present in the church, but mercifully, her deafness spared her the knowledge of this action which assured eternal damnation for her soul. She was then taken from the church and brought back to prison to await her certain fate.

Despite the condemnation of the court and the church, Nurse's outraged family appealed to Governor Phips, asking him to review a dossier of materials about Nurse's case. Phips studied the documents, considered the jury's unusual reversal, and pondered Nurse's explanation that deafness caused her silence when she was requestioned. He authorized a reprieve for Nurse and ordered her to be released from prison.

Nurse's freedom was short-lived. A great wailing and crying arose from the afflicted girls when they learned of Nurse's release; many of them claimed to be dying. Would the governor accept responsibility for their deaths? Phips expeditiously rescinded the reprieve.

On July 19, Sarah Good, Rebecca Nurse, Susannah Martin, Elizabeth How, and Sarah Wildes were hanged at Gallows Hill.

As Sarah Good approached the gallows, the Reverend Nicholas Noyes commanded her to confess that she was a witch. After all, he stated to those assembled, she knew that she was a witch. She replied, "You are a liar. I am no more a witch than you are a wizard, and if you take away my life God will give you blood to drink."

An eerie epilogue to this event occurred twenty-five years later. As Noyes lay dying, he choked on blood that hemorrhaged from his mouth. The memory of Sarah Good's curse haunted those who had been present when she uttered her final earthly words.

The bodies of the dead women were tossed into a shallow grave on Gallows Hill. The executions spread fear and panic among the other accused witches. Rebecca Nurse's death proved that even righteousness of character and support of the community failed to allow one to escape the hangman's noose. Individuals of means took flight from the law, including Philip and Mary English, John Alden, Nathaniel and Elizabeth Carey, and others.

On August 5, six more defendants faced the Court of Oyer and Terminer: George Burroughs, John and Elizabeth Proctor, George Jacobs Sr., John Willard, and Martha Carrier. Only Burroughs and John Proctor challenged the court, but they were unsuccessful. The six were found guilty, and all but the pregnant Elizabeth Proctor were sentenced to be hanged on August 19.

Two petitions were submitted to the court on behalf of the Proctors, one signed by thirty-one residents of Ipswich, and the other signed by twenty other area residents, confirming the exemplary conduct of the couple. John Proctor also took pen in hand to defend himself and the others accused.

On July 23, he wrote to five Boston ministers, explaining "the innocency of our case" and the "enmity of our accusers and our judges and jury" who had "condemned us already before our trials." His letter also mentioned that torture had been used to compel confessions: "My son, William Proctor, when he was examined, because he would not confess that he was guilty when he was innocent, they tied him neck and heels till the blood gushed out at his nose, and would have kept him so twenty-four hours if one more merciful than the rest had not taken pity on him and caused him to be unbound." Proctor begged the ministers to use their power with Governor Phips either to move the trials from Salem to Boston or to have the judges replaced. He also beseeched that they "would be pleased to be here . . . hoping thereby you may be the means of saving the shedding of our innocent blood."

Proctor's pleas persuaded the ministers to consider the issue of prejudgment as it related to the means of prejudgment: spectral evidence. On August 1, Increase Mather and seven other ministers met in Cambridge and determined: "That the Devil may sometimes have a permission to represent an innocent person as tormenting such as are under diabolical molestations, but that such things are rare and extraordinary, especially when such matters come before civil judicatures."

Mather traveled to Salem to attend the trials, as Proctor had begged him to do. Unfortunately, Mather did not attend the trial of the Proctors; he attended the trial of George Burroughs. John Proctor was found guilty and condemned. Because of her pregnancy, Elizabeth was allowed to "plead her belly" and received a stay of execution until the birth of her child.

Like Proctor, George Burroughs attempted to sway the court with a written statement that read, in part: "There neither are nor ever were witches that having a compact with the Devil can send a devil to torment other people at a distance." The jury remained unmoved.

The afflicted girls then testified that Burroughs's specter had bitten them the night before, and they had the bite marks to prove it. The judges ordered an examination of Burroughs's teeth. When he objected, his mouth was pried open, and his bite pattern was compared to the bite marks on the girls. The judges also compared the teeth of others in the courtroom to the bite marks on the girls, but only Burroughs's bite pattern matched. The jury condemned Burroughs. Even Increase Mather agreed with the decision, writing: "Had I been one of his judges, I could not have acquitted him."

The five condemned witches faced their deaths on August 19 at Gallows Hill. Boston merchant Thomas Brattle recorded his impressions:

> They protested their innocency as in the presence of the great God whom forthwith they were to appear before. They wished, and declared their wish, that their blood might be the last innocent blood shed upon that account. With great affection [emotion] they entreated Mr. C[otton] M[ather] to pray with them. They prayed that God would discover what witchcrafts were among us. They forgave their accusers. They spake without reflection on jury and judges for bringing them in guilty and condemning them. They prayed earnestly for pardon for all other sins and for an interest in the precious blood of our dear Redeemer, and seemed to be very sincere, upright, and sensible of their circumstances on all accounts, especially Proctor and Willard, whose whole management of themselves from the jail to the gallows and whilst at the gallows was very affecting and melting to the hearts of some considerable spectators . . .

Boston merchant Robert Calef reported:

> Mr. Burroughs was carried in a cart with the others through the streets of Salem
> to execution. When he was upon the ladder he made a speech for the clearing
> of his innocency, with such solemn and serious expressions as were to the ad-
> miration of all present. His prayer (which he concluded by repeating the Lord's
> Prayer) was so well worded, and uttered with such composedness, and such (at
> least seeming) fervency of spirit as was very affection and drew tears from many
> (so that it seemed to some that the spectators would hinder the execution).

The crowd was astounded. They believed that servants of Satan were unable to recite the Lord's Prayer as Burroughs had done. The spectators cried
out for mercy for their former minister. According to Calef, Cotton Mather on
horseback stood in his stirrups to respond to the crowd, telling them that "the
Devil has often been transformed into an angel of light." That appeased the
crowd, and the execution was carried out.

On September 9, six more witches were tried and found guilty: Mary
Bradbury, Martha Corey, Mary Easty, Dorcas Hoar, Alice Parker, and Ann
Pudeator. On September 17, nine more had their fates sealed at the hands of
the jury: Rebecca Eames, Abigail Faulkner, Ann Foster, Abigail Hobbs, Mary
Lacy, Mary Parker, Wilmot Redd, Margaret Scott, and Samuel Wardwell.

Eight of the condemned were scheduled to be hanged on September 22:
Corey, Easty, Alice Parker, Pudeator, Scott, Redd, Wardwell, and Mary Parker.
Five confessed and gained reprieves: Eames, Hobbs, Lacy, Foster, and Hoar.
Two avoided execution: Faulkner's pregnancy enabled her to "plead her belly,"
and Bradbury escaped with the help of friends.

After receiving her sentence, Mary Easty shared farewells with her husband and children, then made a final appeal to the governor and the judges:

> I petition to your honors not for my own life, for I know I must die . . . that
> no more innocent blood be shed, which undoubtedly cannot be avoided in the
> way and course you go in. I question not, but your honors do to the utmost
> of your powers, in the discovery and detecting of witchcraft and witches, and
> would not be guilty of innocent blood for the world; but by my own inno-
> cency I know you are in the wrong way. . . . I would humbly beg of you, that
> your honors would be pleased to examine some of those confessing witches, I
> being confident there are several of them have belied themselves . . . They say

myself and others have made a league with the Devil . . . I know and the Lord He knows . . . they belie me, and so I question not but they do others.

After Martha Corey was condemned, she was excommunicated from the church in absentia. Parris and two deacons delivered the news to Corey in prison and found her "justifying herself, and condemning all that had done anything to her just discovery or condemnation . . . After prayer—which she was willing to decline—the dreadful sentence of excommunication was pronounced upon her."

Far worse was the fate of Martha Corey's husband, Giles. Although the records of his case no longer exist, historians believe that he was called to the Court of Oyer and Terminer after September 9. Corey may have felt contempt for the court, or he may have believed that his property would be safeguarded if he avoided conviction on witchcraft charges. At his appearance, Corey either pleaded not guilty and refused to stand trial, or he remained silent, refusing to enter a plea. So that the trial could proceed, the judges ordered the old, but seldom-invoked, English practice of "peine forte et dure" to convince him to cooperate.

On September 17, Corey was taken from his prison cell to a field next to the Ipswich jail where he was staked to the ground and had a wooden plank positioned on top of him. Sheriff George Corwin then placed large rocks one by one on the plank, pressing the life out of Corey's body. As each rock was added, Corey had the chance to stop the torture. Legend holds that his only utterance was "More weight."

Corey's agony continued for two days, during which he received only "three morsels" of bread and "three draughts" of water. Robert Calef recorded the last ignominy of Corey's ordeal: ". . . his tongue being pressed out of his mouth, the Sheriff with his cane forced it in again, when he was dying." Corey expired on September 19, and after his death, it was reported that Ann Putnam Jr. had experienced a spectral assault with eerie similarities.

According to her father, Thomas Putnam Jr., a group of witches laid on Ann's chest, crushing her and promising her that she would die before Corey. The witches were driven away by a shrouded apparition who revealed to Ann that he had been pressed to death years before by Giles Corey. Corey had avoided conviction for the crime by making a pact with the Devil, but now it was time for him to pay for his transgression. The specter told Ann: "It must be done to him as he has done to me."

On September 22, the eight condemned individuals were taken by cart to Gallows Hill and executed. Looking on, the Reverend Nicholas Noyes remarked: "What a sad thing it is to see eight firebrands of hell hanging there."

That same day, in nearby Wenham, Massachusetts, the specter of Mary Easty appeared to 17-year-old Mary Herrick. Easty told Herrick: "I am going upon the ladder to be hanged for a witch, but I am innocent and before a twelfth-month be past you shall believe it." Although the girl knew of Easty's reputation as a witch and believed that she was guilty, Herrick decided to remain silent about the ghostly visitation.

Not long after, Herrick began experiencing pains for which no physical cause could be found. Her discomfort increased when another specter materialized, and Herrick recognized the apparition as the wife of the Reverend John Hale. Yet, Sarah Hale was alive, well, and leading a pious life in Beverly. Why would Mrs. Hale's apparition appear to afflict a young woman?

The silent specter returned regularly to choke and pinch her. After two months, it finally spoke: "Do you think I am a witch?" Herrick replied, "No! You be the Devil!" At that moment, Easty reappeared, explaining that she was innocent, had been wrongly executed, and that she had returned "to vindicate her cause." Easty called for "Vengeance! Vengeance!" and directed Herrick to reveal all to the Reverend Hale and to Herrick's pastor, the Reverend Joseph Gerrish. If Herrick did so, she was promised, neither Easty nor Mrs. Hale would afflict the young woman again.

Herrick revealed this "delusion of the Devil" to Gerrish, who called for Hale. After hearing about Herrick's spectral visitations, Hale was shaken to the core, realizing that the Devil had used the shape of his innocent wife to deceive. This convinced Hale that the use of spectral evidence to convict accused witches was wrong.

Hale was not the only one to reverse his thinking about the witchcraft claims. As the witch hunts spread to Andover and to Gloucester, the accusations of the afflicted girls became more outrageous and increasingly unbelievable. When the Lady Mary Phips, wife of Governor Phips, and Margaret Thatcher, the mother-in-law of Judge Jonathan Corwin and one of the wealthiest women in the colony, were accused of being witches, citizens began to suspect that the girls were agents rather than victims of the Devil. The Reverend Samuel Willard of Boston who had initially supported the witch trials was now vocal in his opposition. He characterized the accusers as "scandalous persons, liars, and loose in their conversation." He asserted that their spectral sight provided evidence not of bewitchment but of possession.

As the tide of opinion turned against them, several of the afflicted recanted their testimony, and Tituba confessed that she had lied. Petitions in support of the accused poured into the court, and members of the community criticized openly the court's procedures. Twenty-four residents of Andover sent a petition to Governor Phips, calling the afflicted girls "distempered persons." Their letter also stated: "We know not who can think himself safe if the accusations of children and others who are under a diabolical influence shall be received against persons of good fame."

In an open letter, Thomas Brattle acknowledged the dilemma of the court: "I am very sensible that it is irksome and disagreeable to go back, when a man's doing so is an implication that he has been walking in a wrong path; however, nothing is more honorable than, upon due conviction, to retract and undo (so far as may be) what has been amiss and irregular."

Authorities could not avoid taking action. On October 3, Increase Mather delivered a paper, titled "Cases of Conscience Concerning Evil Spirits Personating Men," to a conference of ministers in Cambridge. Containing a preface signed by fourteen prominent ministers, the document questioned seriously the validity of spectral evidence. Mather admonished, "It were better that ten suspected witches should escape, than that one innocent person should be condemned."

On October 12, Governor Phips declared a moratorium on the witch trials, and on October 29, he officially dissolved the Court of Oyer and Terminer.

Beginning on December 16, special sessions of the Superior Court of Judicature completed the trials with significant procedural changes in place, specifically: changes of venue, jurors not chosen exclusively from Puritan church membership rolls, and strict limits to spectral evidence beyond presumptive proof of guilt. William Stoughton presided. The Superior Court considered cases for four months, and an overwhelming majority of the trials ended in acquittal or dismissal. For example, the case against Sarah Cloyce was dismissed, her husband paid her prison fees, and eventually the couple moved from Salem Village.

At the end of January 1693, Chief Justice Stoughton considered the fates of those who had been temporarily reprieved. Elizabeth Proctor had given birth to her baby and could face execution. Most of the others were confessed witches. Although the preponderance of evidence was spectral, Stoughton reversed the court's practice of sparing the lives of those who had confessed and signed their death warrants. Governor Phips interceded and issued reprieves for all of them.

When he learned about the governor's decision, Stoughton took it as a rebuke of his judicial conduct throughout the trials. Stoughton walked off the bench and did not return until April 25. By that time, the remaining justices and the jury had broken with Stoughton's hardline view and had cleared the cases of all those brought before the court.

In May 1693, Phips issued a general pardon of all accused witches still in prison and ordered their release, upon payment of their incarceration costs. The epicenter of the infamous witch hunt, Tituba, was sold as a slave to pay her jail fee of £7.

The toll from the witch trials was significant: More than 150 individuals from twenty-four towns and villages had been formally charged and imprisoned. Nineteen persons had been hanged, and one man had been pressed to death. At least five other individuals died in jail: Lydia Dustin, Ann Foster, Sarah Osborne, Roger Toothaker, and the unnamed infant of Sarah Good.

In the aftermath of the trials, Salem and its surrounds continued to suffer. The ordeal had erupted early in 1692 and ended the following spring of 1693. Thus, energies that should have been put toward working the land were shifted to dealing with the accusations, trials, and executions. For example, Marshal George Herrick complained to Governor Phips that constant work in connection with the witch hunt had kept him from his "poor farm" so much that he hardly had any provisions for the forthcoming winter.

The costs of incarcerations strapped many families who mortgaged their homes in order to free their loved ones. Upon release, accused witches often found that their belongings and properties had been confiscated. Those who had been condemned, reprieved, and pardoned found that they had no legal existence. Elizabeth Proctor's husband, John, before his execution had written a will that disinherited his wife. Following her release from prison, Elizabeth was unable to contest the will.

Since money was in short supply for residents, Salem Village decided to "make void" the salary of the Reverend Parris. Parris refused to stand for that and took legal action against his parishioners. In court, representatives of the parishioners—Joseph Putnam and three relatives of Rebecca Nurse—stated that "Mr. Parris . . . has been the beginner and procurer of the sorest affliction not to the village only but to the whole country."

Parris attempted unsuccessfully to placate his flock through his sermons, but they had hardened their hearts against him. In November 1693, he struck back by charging them with "factious and seditious libel" and stating that they were guilty of "disturbing the peace of this church and many other good people amongst us, sadly exposing all to ruin."

Animosity grew to such levels that in April 1695, an assembly of ministers met in Salem to arbitrate the dispute. They agreed that Parris had taken "unwarranted and uncomfortable steps" during the "dark time of confusion" and recommended that members of the flock extend Christian reconciliation to their minister. The majority of parishioners refused. Parris moved his family away from Salem Village, and the parishioners replaced him with a newly ordained, 22-year-old minister, Joseph Green.

To heal the wounds, a day of fasting, prayer, and repentance was declared throughout Massachusetts for January 14, 1697, so that "all God's people may offer up fervent supplications unto him . . . ; that all iniquity may be put away which hath stirred God's holy jealousy against this land; that he would show us what we know not, and help us wherein we have done amiss to do so no more."

A former member of the Court of Oyer and Terminer, Judge Samuel Sewall offered his public acknowledgment of guilt in a statement that was read from the pulpit by the Reverend Samuel Willard while Sewall stood humbled before the congregation. The twelve jurors also asked for forgiveness in a written apology, noting:

> We fear we have been instrumental with others, though ignorantly and unwittingly, to bring upon ourselves and this people of the Lord the guilt of innocent blood. . . .
>
> We do therefore hereby signify to all in general (and to the surviving sufferers in especial) our deep sense of and sorrow for our errors in acting on such evidence to the condemning of any person, and do hereby declare that we justly fear that we were sadly deluded and mistaken, for which we are much disquieted and distressed in our minds, and do therefore humbly beg forgiveness.

The Reverend John Hale wrote his confession in *A Modest Enquiry Into the Nature of Witchcraft and How Persons Guilty of That Crime May Be Convicted*:

. . . such was the darkness of that day, the tortures and lamentations of the af-flicted, and the power of former [precedents], that we walked in clouds and could not see our way. And we have most cause to be humbled for error on the hand, which cannot be retrieved. So that we must beseech the Lord, that if any innocent blood hath been shed, in the hour of temptation, the Lord will not lay it to our charge, but be merciful to his people whom he hath redeemed.

Cotton Mather noted in his diary for January 15 that he was "afflicted last night with discouraging thoughts, as if unavoidable marks of the Divine dis-pleasure might overtake my family for not appearing with vigor to stop the proceedings of the judges when the inexplicable storm from the invisible world assaulted the country."

The only afflicted girl who publicly confessed her guilt was Ann Putnam Jr., and she did so in August 1706 when she was 27 years old. Ann's parents had died in 1699, and she sought as an extended family the community of the church. However, before she could be admitted to communion, the Reverend Joseph Green stipulated that Ann had to confess her great sin to the Salem Village congregation. She stood in the church with eyes bowed as Green read her confession:

I desire to be humbled before God for that sad and humbling Providence that befell my father's family in the year about '92, that I, then being in my child-hood, should by such a providence of God be made an instrument for the ac-cusing of several persons of a grievous crime, whereby their lives were taken away from them, whom now I have just grounds and good reason to believe they were innocent persons; and that it was a great delusion of Satan that de-ceived me in that sad time, whereby I justly fear I have been instrumental with others, though ignorantly and unwittingly, to bring upon myself and this land the guilt of innocent blood; though what was said or done by me against any person I can truly and uprightly say before God and man, I did it not out of any anger, malice, or ill-will to any person, for I had no such thing against any of them; but what I did was ignorantly, being deluded by Satan.

The congregation forgave Ann for "being deluded by Satan" and wel-comed her into the community. She enjoyed the family of the church until her death in 1716.

One person not so willing to forgive was Philip English. The wealthiest man in Essex County, English and his wife Mary had been accused of witch-craft in the spring of 1692. Mary was jailed, but the couple managed to escape to New York. When the trials ended, English and his wife returned to Salem to find their good names and their way of life in ruins. Soon after, Mary English died, and Philip attributed her early demise to her arrest, imprisonment, and flight from execution.

After the couple had fled to New York, Sheriff George Corwin had seized their property and holdings worth nearly £1,200. English sued for compensa-tion, and the court battle dragged on for years. The case was settled finally af-ter English's death when his estate received an award of £200.

Following Corwin's death in 1697, English seized the corpse and refused to relinquish it to the family until he received payment of a £60 debt. In 1722, the Reverend Nicholas Noyes sued English for calling him a murderer for his actions during the Salem witch hunt. English remained a broken, bitter man until his death in 1736.

On his deathbed, English met his Christian duty by forgiving those who had sinned against him. When he thought of Judge John Hathorne, his neigh-bor and one of the magistrates who had presided at Mary English's prelimi-nary inquest, Philip English absolved him, too. Then he added: "[But] if I get well, I'll be damned if I forgive him!"

Dark clouds of sorrow, anger, and animosity hovered over Salem for years after the devastating witchcraft trials. Even today, the infamy of that terrible time haunts historians, psychologists, scholars, and others who ponder the dy-namics of the circumstances. What were the precipitating factors? How did events escalate? Why was the peace of Salem disturbed?

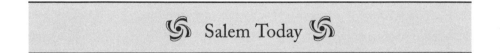

🌀 Salem Today 🌀

Today Salem, Massachusetts, offers visitors various educational experiences about witches, witchcraft, and the witch trials, including:

THE WITCH HOUSE: At the corner of North and Essex Streets is the only home still standing in Salem with a direct link to the Witch Trials of 1692. The Witch House was the residence of Jonathan Corwin, one of the judges who presided at the Witch Trials. Corwin is buried in the nearby Broad Street Cemetery. Tours through the

Witch House are led by guides dressed in period costumes who share information about the lifestyles, furnishings, and architecture of seventeenth-century New England and who provide insights into the witch hysteria that unfolded in 1692, with emphasis on the role that the Corwin family played in witch trial history.

THE OLD BURYING POINT: The oldest burying ground in the city of Salem is the resting place of John Hathorne, one of the judges who presided at the Witch Trials and an ancestor of author Nathaniel Hawthorne. Embarrassed by his family history, Hawthorne added the "w" to his name to distance himself from his famous ancestor.

THE HOUSE OF THE SEVEN GABLES HISTORIC SITE: This site is a national historic district, comprising a collection of six houses listed on the National Register of Historic Places. One of the oldest surviving seventeenth-century wooden mansions in New England, the Turner-Ingersoll Mansion was Nathaniel Hawthorne's inspiration for his novel, *The House of the Seven Gables*. Hawthorne's modest birthplace is part of the site, and the restored house offers a glimpse of what it might have looked like during the author's childhood.

PEABODY ESSEX MUSEUM: The preeminent collections of the Peabody Essex Museum offer more than one million objects, exploring two hundred years of art, architecture, and culture from New England and the world. The Phillips Library houses 552 original court documents related to the Salem Witch Trials. Visitors can also find Witch Trial memorabilia such as "witch pins" that were used to examine suspected witches plus a small bottle supposedly containing the finger bones of executed witch George Jacobs Sr.

THE SALEM WITCH TRIALS TERCENTENARY MEMORIAL: The Salem Witch Trials Tercentenary Memorial was designed by architect James Cutler and artist Maggie Smith and was selected from among 242 entries in an international competition. Located adjacent to the Old Burying Point, the memorial was dedicated in August 1992 by Nobel Laureate Elie Wiesel and provides thought-provoking symbolism to visitors. The inscribed stone reads: "The memorial is surrounded on three sides by a granite wall. Inscribed on the threshold are the victims' protests of innocence. This testimony is interrupted mid-sentence by the wall, symbolizing society's indifference to oppression. Locust trees represent the stark injustice of the trials. At the rear of the memorial, tombstones in the adjacent cemetery represent all who stood in mute witness to this tragedy. Stone benches within the memorial perimeter bear the names and execution dates of the victims."

THE SALEM WITCH MUSEUM: In an imposing, stone Romanesque building is Salem's most visited museum. The Salem Witch Museum offers a thoroughly researched and powerfully presented historical overview of the Witch Trials of 1692, using theatrical sets, life-sized figures, dramatic lighting, and multi-lingual narration. The presentation is offered in English, Japanese, French, German, Italian, and Spanish.

THE SALEM WITCH VILLAGE: Salem's Witch community assisted in creating and developing the Salem Witch Village, an experience that takes visitors back in time to reveal the myths and the facts about witches and witchcraft. Visitors discover the realities of witch superstition, hysteria, and tortures and learn the truth behind witchcraft legends and traditions.

SALEM WAX MUSEUM OF WITCHES & SEAFARERS: Realistic, London-made wax figures and dramatic, multimedia presentations re-create the sights and sounds of the Witch Trials of 1692. A hands-on activity area allows visitors the chance to experience how accused witches were confined in their jail cells.

THE WITCH DUNGEON MUSEUM: Visitors experience the live reenactment of the trial of beggar-woman Sarah Good, adapted from the 1692 trial transcript. Guided tours of the dungeon reveal the actual size of the cells in which accused witches were held and the horrible conditions in which they lived while awaiting their trials. The Witch Dungeon Museum also offers a re-created village and Gallows Hill.

Throughout the history of witchcraft, many beliefs have emerged about witches' appearance and activities. Their image as old crones who fly through the night on broomsticks has remained a staple of folklore for centuries. The Spanish artist Francisco Goya rendered witches many times in his works, often in satirical drawings such as this one from *Los Caprichos.*

ᏽᎲᏽ

This 1693 concept of the witch's sabbat shows many of the common activities described by accused witches: flying, reveling with demons, the "kiss of shame" on the Devil's hindquarters, and concocting potions. The print appears in the German translation of Nicholas Remy's *Demonolatreiae. Rare Books Collection, Carl A. Kroch Library, Cornell University*

ᏽᎲᏽ

Die dem Bock ehrende Hexen

Concepts of witchcraft appear in cultures around the world. In Africa, many still believe in the power of witch doctors. This soapstone sculpture and carved wood panel depicting medicine men were crafted by artists from Zimbabwe and Nigeria, respectively. *Harmon Foundation, Contemporary African Art Collection, National Archives & Records Administration*

In Native American civilizations, shamans practice an earth-based religion to commune with the spirit world, cure illness, and guide people toward prosperity. These photos of early twentieth-century shamans from the North Pacific Coast come from the Sir Henry S. Wellcome Collection. *National Archives & Records Administration, Pacific Alaska Region (Anchorage)*

Accused witches withstood many tortures and trials. In the
swimming trial, the accused was bound and thrown into water.
Supposedly, witches would float and the innocent would sink.
Of course, an innocent person might well drown before family
and friends could rescue her. This engraving, from a 1613
pamphlet entitled *Witches Apprehended, Examined, and Executed,*
depicts the swimming of Mary Sutton. *Rare Books Collection,*
Carl A. Kroch Library, Cornell University

From the frontispiece of Matthew
Hopkins's *Discovery of Witches* (1647),
this engraving shows Hopkins in the
company of two witches and their
familiars. Hopkins extracted the names
of the familiars by torture. One of his
first victims testified that she owned five
familiars: a kitten; a legless spaniel; a
black rabbit; a polecat; and a magickal
creature named Vinegar Tom, a
greyhound with the head of an ox. *Rare
Books Collection, Carl A. Kroch Library,
Cornell University*

This stereotypical image of a colonial American witch bearing away children on her broomstick conforms to the portrayal of witches as old, malicious crones. In Salem in the 1690s, elderly, outcast women were among the first to be accused of witchcraft, but the hysteria soon engulfed other members of the community. *Peabody Essex Museum*

This 1853 painting by T. H. Matteson recreates a scene from the Salem Witchcraft Trials. It shows an accused witch being examined for "witch's marks," unusual outgrowths or discolorations of the skin thought to indicate the place from which familiars fed on the witch's blood.
Peabody Essex Museum

This December 1892 illustration from *Harpers New Monthly Magazine* shows an accused witch in Salem being confronted by one of the afflicted girls. The accuser claims, "There is a flock of yellow birds around her head." The court routinely accepted such unseen evidence of guilt.
Peabody Essex Museum

The Trial of George Jacobs, August 5, 1692, by T. H. Matteson, imagines a scene from the trial of the eighty-year-old accused witch. Jacobs's accusers both later recanted their testimony against him; however, the court ignored them and let Jacobs remain in jail. Later, he was hanged.
Peabody Essex Museum

The Wicked Witch of the West (Margaret Hamilton) in 1939's *The Wizard of Oz* reinforced the image of the frightening, evil witch. However, the film did provide a counterpoint in Glinda, The Good Witch of the North.
Eddie Brandt's Saturday Matinee

Television audiences found a new, benign concept of witches with the premier of "Bewitched" (1964–72). In the series, Samantha Stevens (Elizabeth Montgomery) is a lovely young witch who chooses to live as a middle-class housewife when she marries a mortal.
Eddie Brandt's Saturday Matinee

In film, witches and witchcraft remain favorite topics, and their portrayal receives a variety of treatments. In 1987's *The Witches of Eastwick*, a group of lonely women (Susan Sarandon, Cher, and Michelle Pfeiffer) becomes a modern coven of witches. *Warner Bros.*

☾〜☾

The Witches (1990) adapts Roald Dahl's children's book about the plan of the Grand High Witch (Anjelica Huston) to turn all of England's children into mice. *Warner Bros.*

☾〜☾

Turning to historical events, the film version of Arthur Miller's *The Crucible* (1996) uses the basic facts of the Salem Witchcraft Trials to create an allegory of accusations gone awry. An adulterous John Proctor (Daniel Day-Lewis) finds himself and his wife accused of witchcraft by his young mistress' jealous revenge. *Twentieth Century Fox*

☾〜☾

SIX

Why the Peace of Salem Was Disturbed

OR more than three hundred years, countless theories have been advanced to explain why the peace of Salem was disturbed, including fraud, political factionalism, conspiracy, hysteria, misogyny, and others. Scholars from various disciplines carry on lively debates even today, and the definitive answer may never be known.

THE "AFFLICTED" WERE FRAUDS

Firsthand observer of the events in Salem, Boston merchant Robert Calef shared his opinions of the Salem proceedings in *More Wonders of the Invisible World*, published in 1700. He called the afflicted girls "pretended sufferers," "actors in these tragedies," and "pretended afflicted."

To support his view, he called attention to a blatant falsehood that went unchallenged by the court. At Sarah Good's trial, when one of the afflicted presented a piece of knife blade and accused Good of having stabbed her, a young man produced the rest of knife. He explained that he had earlier broken it and that the girl had seen him throw the piece of blade away. Rather than dismiss the evidence of the afflicted girl, the court merely chided her, telling her not to tell lies, and allowed her to continue her testimony.

Calef also noted that the bites the girls claimed came from spectral tormenters were often compared with the teeth of the accused. Sardonically, Calef referred to "bewitched eyes" or eyes that "can see more than others." Such bewitched eyes saw a match between the teeth and the bite mark. However, "such as had not such bewitched eyes have seen the accusers bite themselves, and then complain of the accused." He further stated: "It has also been seen when the accused, instead of having just such a set of teeth, had not had one in his head."

Calef also commented on two incidents that occurred in Gloucester in late 1692. Some of the afflicted girls traveled there when a soldier suspected that his ailing sister was bewitched. On their way to visit the sister, "they met with an old woman, and instantly fell into their fits. But by this time the validity of such accusations being much questioned, they found not that encouragement they had done elsewhere, and soon withdrew." When the girls arrived at the house, they "swore that they saw three persons sitting upon Lieutenant Stephens's sister till she died." Although the girls' statements were accepted, the accused persons were granted a bail bond and avoided incarceration.

Calef summarized the proceedings as ". . . a biggoted zeal, stirring up a blind and most bloody rage, not against enemies, or irreligious proffligate persons, but . . . against as virtuous and religious as any they have left behind them in this country." He characterized the afflicted girls as "vile varlets" and accused them of engaging in whoredom and incest both before and after the witchcraft trials. He scolded the magistrates and ministers for their reliance on spectral evidence and castigated them for upholding the accusations "so long as they apprehended themselves in no danger."

Another eyewitness, Boston merchant Thomas Brattle, drafted a letter on October 8, 1692. He stressed his belief that the charges made by the afflicted girls were false and that in certain cases the girls had been coached to name specific individuals: "Several persons have been apprehended purely upon the complaints of these afflicted, to whom the afflicted were perfect strangers, and had not the least knowledge of imaginable, before they were apprehended."

He questioned the veracity of the girls' tormented states, noting that "many of these afflicted persons, who have scores of strange fits in a day, yet in the intervals of time are hale and hearty, robust and lusty, as though nothing had afflicted them."

Brattle also questioned the ability of the girls to see specters even when their eyes were closed. "I am sure they lie, at least speak falsely, if they say so; for the thing, in nature, is an utter impossibility." He wrote also that the girls' testimony about the Devil's book, witches' meetings, and mock sacraments "are nothing else but the effect of their fancy, depraved and deluded by the Devil, and not a reality to be regarded or minded by any wise man."

Former minister and mayor of Salem, the Reverend Charles Wentworth Upham published *Lectures on Witchcraft* in 1831 and a two-volume work, *Salem Witchcraft*, in 1867. He was convinced that the behavior of the afflicted had shown "deliberate cunning and cool malice." Upham wrote in an essay:

> It was perhaps their original design to gratify a love of notoriety or of mischief by creating a sensation and excitement in their neighborhood, or, at the worst, to wreak their vengeance upon one or two individuals who had offended them. They soon, however, became intoxicated by the terrible success of their imposture, and were swept along by the frenzy they had occasioned.

In his book, *Witchcraft at Salem*, historian Chadwick Hansen refers to two incidents in the trial documents that suggest fraud on the part of the afflicted girls. The first is the broken-knife incident during the Sarah Good trial; the second incident occurred before the examination of Elizabeth Proctor.

Daniel Elliot testified: "I being at the house of Lieutenant Ingersoll on the 18th of March in the year 1692, there being present one of the afflicted persons, which cried out and said, 'There's Goody Proctor.' William Raymond being there present told the girl he believed she lied, for he saw nothing. Goody Ingersoll told the girl she told a lie. Then the girl said that she did it for sport—they must have some sport." Raymond's testimony was similar, but concludes, "Goody Ingersoll sharply reproved them. Then they seemed to make a joke of it."

According to Hansen: "If all that happened was that the girls 'seemed to make a joke of it' then we may be dealing simply with hysterical laughter. But if one of them actually said 'she did it for sport' then it is clearly fraud."

FEAR OF WITCHCRAFT CREATED HYSTERIA

Despite the suggestions of fraud, however, Hansen credits fear with causing the events in Salem. He claims that "witchcraft actually did exist and was widely practiced in seventeenth-century New England." According to Hansen, the power of witchcraft is real in a society that believes in witchcraft, and he frames a hypothetical example:

If you believe in witchcraft and you discover that someone has been melting your wax image over a slow fire or muttering charms over your nail-pairings, the probability is that you will get extremely sick. To be sure, your symptoms will be psychosomatic rather than organic. But the fact that they are obviously not organic will make them only more terrible, since they will seem the result of malefic and demonic power.

He provides a litany of the afflicted girls' symptoms: convulsive movements; distorted body positions; memory loss; temporary loss of hearing, speech, and sight; a choking sensation in the throat (called globus hystericus); hallucinations; and feelings of being pinched and bitten. Hansen attributes the behavior of the girls to the psychological condition known as hysteria.

Hansen does not fault Dr. William Griggs, who declared that "The evil hand is on them." In Hansen's view, many physicians of the time believed in witchcraft and ascribed it as the basis of some diseases. But he believes that "the cause of these hysterical symptoms . . . was not witchcraft itself but the victim's fear of it."

He notes the three degrees of witchcraft: first is white magick, practiced for benevolent purposes; second is black magick, practiced for malicious purposes; third is a pact with the Devil. In the third degree, according to Hansen, "the witch is no longer merely invoking the Devil's aid through her charms and spells, but actually believes she has made a contract to serve him." He demonstrates that "all three degrees of witchcraft were practiced there [in New England] during the latter seventeenth century: white magic commonly, black magic not uncommonly, and pact on at least one occasion."

So-called white magick was afoot within Tituba's circle of girls, as they used the egg-and-glass method to divine their futures. When, instead of an image of the future, they believed they saw a coffin, Betty Parris and Abigail Williams were among the first to be affected with hysteria. According to Hansen, "It was anything but innocent for the two seventeenth-century girls who believed that they had conjured up a specter in the shape of a coffin."

White magick was also used to try to identify those who tormented the girls. Tituba and John Indian prepared a witch's cake which was fed to the Parris family dog. The outcry from the Reverend Parris over this incident alerted all to the possibility that the Devil had been raised among them. Belief in the power of the witch's cake and guilt over dabbling in the occult probably prompted Betty Parris to make the first of the accusations, naming Tituba as a witch.

When the magistrates examined Tituba, she identified Sarah Good and Sarah Osborne as two of four women who hurt the children; and she described a fifth person as a tall, white-haired man from Boston clad in black. Tituba testified that he sometimes took the shape of a hog or a large black dog and that a yellow bird accompanied him. She revealed that the man had ordered her to pinch one of the girls and that she, together with Good and Osborne, had flown to the Putnam home on broomsticks to kill Ann Putnam Jr. When the magistrates pressed Tituba to name others, she claimed to be blind and fell onto the floor in convulsions.

According to Hansen:

> Tituba's confession is in general similar to witchcraft confessions from other times and places. Part of it may have been suggested to her. But not all. It is far too detailed and far too original in some of its details to have been merely the product of the magistrates' leading questions. . . . The most likely conclusion is that her confession was the product both of experience with the occult and of hysterical hallucinations as vivid and as terrifying as those of the afflicted girls.

The afflicted girls also suffered in the presence of the accused. Hansen offers an explanation as to why the magistrates were convinced of the validity of such evidence: "Here were girls afflicted with violent physical symptoms which had no known physical cause, but which a physician had attributed to witchcraft. There was a malicious old woman accused of causing them. When the sufferers accused her they were immediately thrown into convulsions. What could be more plausible than that the convulsions were inflicted as revenge for the accusation?"

Another typical hysterical behavior occurred during the examination of Martha Corey. When Corey bit her lip, the afflicted girls complained of being bitten, and when she moved her hands, the afflicted girls complained of being pinched. According to Hansen:

> From Martha Corey's examination on, any motion on the part of the accused was apt to produce a corresponding effect in the afflicted children. It must have been a most convincing spectacle, as though black magic were being worked before the very eyes of the beholders. And as the effects produced on the children were obviously painful they were that much more convincing. In some cases there were seen to be marks of bites or pinches on the children's flesh; on other occasions there were pins literally stuck in their flesh.

Hansen provides three explanations for this behavior. First, hysterics are highly suggestible. "For hysterics familiar with the idea of image magic it would be easy to assume that an accused person biting her lip was trying to bite them." Second, hysterics often harm themselves. "Some of the bites and pinches, too, were probably self-inflicted, but it is also probable that some were not." Third, hysteria is contagious. "Not only were the fits increasing in violence, but the longer the court sat, the more people were afflicted."

Another defendant against whom image or sympathetic magick weighed heavily was Bridget Bishop. Hansen believes that "Bishop was in all probability a practicing witch." Two men testified that they had found poppets used for image magick in holes of an old wall in her house. Hansen comments: "If fits were occasioned by fear of someone like Bridget Bishop, who was actually practicing witchcraft, they might also be occasioned by fear of someone who was only suspected of practicing it."

When pious Rebecca Nurse was tried, convicted, and thrown into prison, her family appealed to Governor Phips. He authorized a reprieve for Nurse, but then the afflicted girls complained of renewed torments, and Phips rescinded his reprieve. According to Hansen: "One must never forget the hysteric's susceptibility to suggestion. . . . Expecting to be tormented at the time the reprieve would be granted, they were tormented."

Hansen bolsters his view by citing a passage from John Hale's 1702 book *A Modest Enquiry Into the Nature of Witchcraft*: "Probably the cause may be that

Satan . . . may inflict his mischief on the person . . . suiting hereby his design to man's faith about it." Thus, Hale, who had observed the afflicted girls first-hand, accepted the reality of witchcraft and subscribed to the belief that the behavior of the afflicted girls was psychosomatic.

FACTIONALISM FED THE CRISIS

In 1682, a full decade before the witchcraft trials, Salem Village resident Jeremiah Watts described the community as one in which "brother is against brother and neighbors [are] against neighbors, all quarreling and smiting one another." According to historians Paul Boyer and Stephen Nissenbaum in *Salem Possessed: The Social Origins of Witchcraft,* various strata of factionalism— Salem Village versus Salem Town, supporters of the Reverend Samuel Parris versus his opponents, the Putnam family versus the Porter family, even Thomas Putnam Jr. versus his half brother Joseph Putnam—plagued Salem Village and fed the witchcraft crisis.

After its founding, Salem Town prospered, outgrowing the land that was the original settlement. Land grants created a new western settlement known informally as "Salem Farms," the lands used for growing food to feed Salem Town. Tethered legally to Salem Town, "Salem Farms" sought independence during the 1660s. Fearful of losing tax revenues, Salem Town opposed its in-dependence.

The Town did grant the farmers' request to build a meetinghouse and to hire a minister, releasing the farmers from paying church taxes in Salem Town. The farmers agreed to select annually a committee to calculate the tax that each household would contribute to support the minister. They met in No-vember 1672, elected a committee, and made plans for erecting a meeting-house and hiring a minister for the area, now referred to as Salem Village.

Villagers still paid Salem Town civil taxes, had constables appointed by Salem Town, were represented in the General Court by Salem Town, and had most important decisions about Village matters decided by Salem Town se-lectmen.

Salem Town also had an ecclesiastical hold on Salem Village, which was merely a parish of Salem Town. A parish was comprised of church members—who could take communion—and the congregation—who could not take communion. Church members had to participate in the rite of communion at the meetinghouse in Salem Town.

Controversies and grievances between Salem Village and Salem Town erupted over the years. In 1690, Salem Town rejected a committee request that Salem Village be granted full independence as a township. Boyer and Nissenbaum note that such tensions grew over the years "within the Village itself: while some residents strove to define the political and religious power of the Village ever more broadly, others continued to identify themselves primarily with Salem Town."

This split was particularly evident in the calling of ministers. Under the law, only church members could call a minister or vote for those who served on the Village Committee. Since the Village was not yet a church, the General Court declared that the "inhabitants" of the Village had the power to call a minister.

James Bayley began his ministry in 1672, but a vocal minority in Salem Village turned against him. Following his departure in 1680, George Burroughs was called. He quickly fell out of favor, had his salary withheld, and was arrested and jailed on a complaint filed by Captain John Putnam. Driven in disgrace from the Village, Burroughs was brought back in 1692. Then he was charged with witchcraft and executed for being a wizard.

Deodat Lawson became minister in 1684. However, controversy erupted two years later when a group of villagers led by Captain John Putnam and his nephew, Thomas Putnam Jr., urged the establishment of an official church and the ordination of Lawson as its minister. This was opposed by a number of individuals, including Joseph Porter and his brother-in-law Daniel Andrew. The dispute became so explosive that arbitrators from Salem Town were asked to intervene. They ruled in favor of the anti-ordination faction but provided no recommendations to resolve the difficulties. However, they noted that the tenor of the dispute suggested "the effects of settled prejudice and resolved animosity." They predicted that such behaviors "have a tendency to make such a gap as we fear, if not timely prevented, will let out peace and order and let in confusion and every evil work."

Lawson left in 1688, but according to Boyer and Nissenbaum, "the basic lines of factional divisions in Salem Village were hardening year by year."

The proponents of ordination desired the separation from Salem Town. They were served in that purpose by the next minister, Samuel Parris, who was called in June 1689. Four months later, the "inhabitants" of Salem Village voted to give to Parris "and his heirs" the parsonage, its barns, and two acres of land. A transfer of this kind had been expressly forbidden by a resolution passed in 1681, but this resolution was "made void and of no effect" by the 1689 vote.

In November 1689, Parris was ordained as a Christian minister by the associate pastor of the church in Salem Town, Reverend Nicholas Noyes. Then Parris, his wife, and twenty-five Salem Village residents signed a covenant that declared them a Church of Christ. By the summer of 1690, twenty-six additional villagers signed a covenant and joined the church, then representing almost one-quarter of the Village's adult population.

With an established church in Salem Village, the political power in the community would shift from the "inhabitants" to the church members. According to Boyer and Nissenbaum, "The one firm result of the year's maneuverings was the emergence of a church which, if it went unchallenged, could become the single most powerful force for political autonomy in the Village."

With his first sermon in 1689, Parris publicly characterized those who opposed political autonomy as enemies of the church and by extension his enemies as well. Those men moved against Parris slowly but deliberately.

On October 16, 1691, the Village Committee of Parris supporters was voted out in favor of Parris opponents: Joseph Porter, Joseph Hutchinson, Joseph Putnam, Daniel Andrew, and Francis Nurse. The new committeemen voted not to assess a tax that year for payment of the minister's salary.

In retaliation, the elders of the church asked Salem Village to impose a tax to pay his salary. When no action was taken, the elders agreed to file suit against the Village Committee in county court. Write Boyer and Nissenbaum: "The flames of Village factionalism, smoldering away for years, now burst spectacularly into the open." In addition to these legal and religious factors, other points of contention, including economic and geographic factors, wracked Salem Village and fed the witchcraft crisis.

Salem Town grew to be a wealthy mercantile area from 1661 to 1681, while Salem Village's agrarian prosperity declined. Salem Village also experienced diminishment of available land, many of its men owning little or no land by the 1690s. Additionally, Boyer and Nissenbaum estimate that by 1690 average landholding had dropped significantly as tracts were divided among successive generations. They write: "The diminishing availability of land . . . was felt here with particular intensity, for Salem Village . . . could neither expand nor easily generate new settlements in contiguous open lands."

The quality and location of the land also determined whether Salem Village farmers would exist at a subsistence level or rise to profitability. The better lands lay in the east, nearer the coast and the roads and waterways to Salem Town's markets. Lands in the western part of Salem Village contained more hills and marshy areas.

These various circumstances fed the flames of factionalism in Salem Village and exploded in witchcraft accusations in 1692. At the center of the conflagration were two main factions: The pro-Parris group led by the Putnam family became the primary witch accusers, while the anti-Parris group led by the Porter family became the opponents of the witch hunt.

Parris's supporters included the majority of Salem Village church members, poorer villagers, and those in the western section of Salem Village. Villagers who belonged to other churches, wealthier residents, and those in the east and in Salem Town opposed him. Many of the afflicted girls resided in the western part of Salem Village while many of the accused resided in the eastern part.

Although the factions' leaders shared many of the same socioeconomic traits, Boyer and Nissenbaum point to a number of factors that highlight the divergence of the Putnam and Porter families. The Putnams pursued mainly agrarian interests on their northwestern lands, some distance from the markets. An ill-fated ironworks business soured them on manufacturing and commerce. They dominated the Village Committee for years but enjoyed only the fringes of power in Salem Town.

The Porters pursued more diversified interests, farming from the eastern section of the village into Salem Town and operating a sugar business and sawmills. Their lands afforded easy access to both the Village and the Town. One of the figures in the witchcraft crisis, Israel Porter, maintained political power in Salem Town almost continually from 1679 to the end of the century.

The sharp contrast in these families' fortunes grew into a bitter rivalry, feeding into the witchcraft crisis as the Putnams sought to lash out at their perceived enemies. Boyer and Nissenbaum reveal "the almost monotonous frequency with which the Putnam name occurs on complaints, warrants, and accusatory testimony." Indeed, 12-year-old Ann Putnam, daughter of Thomas Putnam Jr., rose from the circle of afflicted girls as the one most vocal in making witchcraft accusations. The authors note that eight members of the Putnam family, "drawn from all three of its branches, were involved in the prosecution of no fewer than forty-six accused witches."

By contrast, the Porters acted to undermine the promoters of the witch trials. Israel Porter circulated a petition on behalf of accused witch Rebecca

Nurse with the intention of not only saving Nurse but energizing opposition to the trials. He and his wife, Elizabeth, also visited Nurse prior to her arrest and attested that she was not only blameless of witchcraft but that she was a paragon of Christian piety.

The last stratum of factionalism explored by Boyer and Nissenbaum was within the Putnam family itself—Thomas Putnam Jr. versus his half brother Joseph Putnam.

Thomas was the eldest son of the wealthiest man in Salem Village. His father's estate would be shared in dowries for his sisters and the land divided between Thomas and his brother, Edward. As the eldest son, Thomas expected to receive the family homestead and about three hundred acres of land.

What he didn't expect was his father's remarriage in 1666 to a Salem Town widow, Mary Veren, who had been married to a ship captain and whose brothers and son-in-law were successful Salem Town merchants. Veren's daughter from her first marriage was married to a Salem Town merchant who was also a town selectman. Thomas's father and stepmother also welcomed a new child, Joseph, in 1669.

Thomas Jr. had other misfortunes. He married the daughter of a wealthy Salisbury resident George Carr, but when Carr died, the estate and commercial interests fell under the control of his widow and two of her sons as executors. Despite a court protest by Thomas Jr. and others in the Carr family, the bulk of the estate went to the widow and her sons.

Thomas Putnam Sr. died in 1686, his will leaving much of the estate and the best land to his new wife and youngest son. The will also specified that Joseph would inherit at 18 rather than at the customary age of 21, that Mary and Joseph would be joint executors, and that Israel Porter would also serve as an overseer of the estate.

The document was challenged by a petition signed by Thomas, his brother, and their brothers-in-law Jonathan Walcott and William Trask. It stated that they were "extremely wronged" by the will and requested the court to name Thomas as executor "so that each of us may have that proportion of our deceased father's estate which by the law of God and man rightly belongs to us." The petition failed.

One year later 18-year-old Joseph Putnam came into his inheritance, making him one of the wealthiest men in Salem Village. Two years later, Joseph married Elizabeth Porter Jr., daughter of Israel Porter.

According to Boyer and Nissenbaum, "By joining the Porter clan Joseph

Putnam had managed to break free of the narrow agrarian constraints which held the rest of the Putnams down, and to strengthen his links (already strong through his mother) to the social, commercial, and political life of Salem Town. And he had achieved all this—and here was the most galling part of the business [for the Putnams]—through no real effort of his own."

In Salem Town, Joseph served seven terms as a selectman, but he also had a strong political position in Salem Village. He served on the Village Committee in October 1691 with his in-laws Joseph Porter and Daniel Andrew, and with the two other anti-Parris committeemen, Joseph Hutchinson and Francis Nurse. He called the 1691 meetings in which Salem Villagers agreed to investigate the "fraudulent" conveyance of the parsonage and its land to Samuel Parris. Additionally, he was the only Putnam to sign the anti-Parris petition of 1695.

Boyer and Nissenbaum build a strong case for Thomas Putnam Jr.'s resentment of his stepmother and half brother. The authors believe that by 1692 Thomas and his family "were prepared to believe that witchcraft lay at the root of their troubles." They review the role the Putnams played in the witchcraft crisis: The afflicted persons include Ann Putnam Sr., Ann Putnam Jr., and Mercy Lewis, a servant in the Thomas Putnam Jr. household. Thomas signed complaints against twenty-four persons and testified against twelve. Other testimony includes that of Ann Putnam Jr., who testified against at least twenty-one individuals; Edward Putnam, who testified in thirteen cases; and Thomas's brother-in-law, Jonathan Walcott, who testified in seven. Additionally, Jonathan's daughter Mary, who lived in the Thomas Putnam Jr. household, claimed to have been tortured by sixteen specters.

Boyer and Nissenbaum note, however, that the Putnams never directly attacked Mary Veren Putnam or Joseph Putnam. Instead, they "projected their bitterness onto persons who were, politically or psychologically, less threatening targets: notably older women of Mary Veren Putnam's generation. Against such persons they vented their rage and bitterness which they were forced to deny (or to channel through such stylized outlets as legal petitions) in their relations with Mary and Joseph."

Although the initial afflictions occurred in the Parris household, the symptoms soon spread to the Thomas Putnam Jr. household. After the first accused witches were imprisoned, Ann Sr. and Ann Jr. complained of being tormented by Martha Corey, a covenating member of the Salem Village church, and her husband, Giles, a prosperous farmer. According to Boyer and Nissenbaum, the accusation "betrayed the fact that witchcraft accusations against the powerless, the outcast, or the already victimized were not sufficiently cathartic for them. They were driven to lash out at persons . . . who reminded them of the individuals actually responsible (so they believed) for their own reduced fortunes and prospects."

Boyer and Nissenbaum believe that the Putnams "moved further up the social and economic ladder" with the accusations by the two Anns against Rebecca Nurse, the wife of Francis Nurse, the Village Committee member who had a property dispute with Nathaniel Putnam in the 1670s. "Rebecca Nurse appears the inevitable victim, since she was an ideal 'substitute' for Mary Veren Putnam: both were women of advanced years, both were prosperous and respected, both were in failing health, and both were members of the Salem Town church."

A detractor of this particular argument is author Frances Hill. In *A Delusion of Satan: The Full Story of the Salem Witch Trials,* Hill agrees that the Putnams tended to seek revenge on perceived enemies and that their social group looked with envy on thriving, well-connected Salem merchants. "But," Hill states, "the authors' lateral jump to viewing the Putnams' victims as psychological projections of the woman who had helped cheat them out of their inheritance seems more imaginative than convincing." In the view of Boyer and Nissenbaum, however, the Putnams believed that "It was Mary Veren and her son Joseph who were the serpents in Eden, and if they, or their psychological equivalents, could only be eliminated, all might again be well."

Additionally, at the heart of all the other disputes was "a moral conflict involving the very nature of the community itself . . . what its essential character was to be." Those in the east identified themselves with Salem Town and saw on the horizon the growth of preindustrial capitalism. Those in the west identified themselves with Salem Village and saw an erosion of the stability and continuity of farm life. In essence, the western residents went to war in the witchcraft crisis against the eastern residents in a futile attempt to preserve the status quo.

CONSPIRACY GRIPPED THE COMMUNITY

Historian Enders A. Robinson suggests that a conspiracy was at the heart of the Salem witch trials. In his book *The Devil Discovered,* Robinson states: "The Salem witch hunt was driven by conspiracies of envious men intent on destroying their enemies. Their maneuvers were sanctioned by the old guard of Puritan leaders acting in tacit collusion." One of the contributing factors was the threat to the theocratic government of Massachusetts by a new royal charter.

The Massachusetts Bay Colony charter established Massachusetts as a Puritan commonwealth, under which only male members of the Puritan or Congregational church could vote. Since the clergy influenced church membership, they could control elected government, including the positions of governor, magistrates, deputies, and justices of the peace.

In 1684, King Charles II annulled the charter, making illegal the existing government in Massachusetts, and royal authorities began writing a new charter for New England. The Reverend Increase Mather left for England in May 1688 to ensure that the proposed new charter preserved the spirit of the old one. When instituted on October 7, 1691, the new charter granted freedom of religion and extended the right to vote to all citizens who owned property. To appease Mather, the ministers of the crown allowed him to make key nominations. He chose Sir William Phips as the new royal governor, William Stoughton as the lieutenant governor, and individuals of the Puritan old guard as members of the Council.

According to Robinson, the charter threatened the rule of the Puritans. "Now for the first time, they would be faced with a situation where the common rabble could vote in political elections. Their Puritan church would no longer hold exclusive control over the lives of the people."

Coupled with the external threat of the new charter was the internal threat of witchcraft erupting in Salem Village. Since witchcraft was a "crime of the vilest sort," the crisis entered the legal realm, and ten men then realized that they could use these events to destroy their enemies. According to Robinson, the founding members of the conspiracy were Thomas Putnam Jr., the Reverend Samuel Parris, and Dr. William Griggs.

THOMAS PUTNAM JR. "saw a way to retaliate against those with whom the Putnam family had longstanding and often justifiable grudges." He represented the Putnam contingent which included Jonathan Walcott, Edward Putnam, Nathaniel Ingersoll, Nathaniel Putnam, John Putnam Jr., Jonathan Putnam, and John Putnam Sr. For years, the Putnams had engaged in a land dispute with the Towne, How, Easty, Hobbs, and Wildes families of Topsfield. Believing that they could regain the land and assume political control of Salem

Village, the Putnams targeted numerous individuals, including Rebecca Towne Nurse, Mary Towne Easty, Sarah Towne Cloyce, Elizabeth Jackson How, William Hobbs, Deliverance Hobbs, Abigail Hobbs, and Sarah Wildes.

REVEREND SAMUEL PARRIS recognized witchcraft as "a powerful weapon with which to defeat his enemies, those who questioned his demands in Salem Village. With his opponents eliminated, Parris knew that his tenure in the ministry would be secure."

DR. WILLIAM GRIGGS "practiced his own brand of folk magic in conjunction with his medical treatments, and now glimpsed a golden opportunity to do away with the midwives and other rivals."

Robinson theorizes that Parris used Tituba to set off the witch hunts and that the "inner circle" of afflicted girls had connections with the Putnam, Parris, and Griggs households. Elizabeth Parris and Abigail Williams were the daughter and niece, respectively, of the Reverend Samuel Parris. Ann Putnam Jr., Mary Walcott, and Mercy Lewis were the daughter, niece, and servant, respectively, of Thomas Putnam Jr. Elizabeth Hubbard was the great-niece of Dr. William Griggs. The conspirators used "manipulation and stealth" to suggest to the afflicted girls the persons they should name as witches. Then the conspirators filed legal complaints so that arrest warrants could be issued.

According to Robinson, the conspirators had no idea how far they could go. They expected support from some in the community against certain undesirables, and they expected John Hathorne to champion the hunt. They did not guess, however, that "the highest level of government, the ruling, old-guard Puritans, would not only act in collusion to support their cause of destroying the 'enemies of the church,' but would give them a free hand in determining who those enemies were."

Robinson believes that the conspirators chose as their first victims Sarah Good because she was widely disliked and Sarah Osborne because "she seemed about to prevail in a legal case against the Putnam family." They next chose Martha Corey and Rebecca Nurse because "they were strong women of high standing." The accusations escalated from there.

Robinson asserts that the witch hunt "was primarily directed . . . at mothers, wives, and daughters in the upper echelons of society, at rich widows and respectable matrons, at army officers and sea captains, at wealthy merchants and large landholders, and at ministers and church members."

He outlines a "hierarchy of the witch hunt," showing its sponsors as the clergy and the old-guard Puritans. The clergy saw the witch hunt as a way to intimidate their congregations and to retain their power. The old-guard Puritans were members of the upper legislative body who feared the new charter and sought to control the population. The agents of the witch hunt were the accusers, who used the afflictions of the girls as a way to destroy their enemies, and the afflicted, who were immersed in the hysteria sanctioned by the accusers. The victims were the members of families that threatened the old guard or drew the envy or wrath of the accusers. The remaining population merely observed the unfolding drama "until they saw that anyone was fair game."

One individual who observed the drama was the half brother of Thomas Putnam Jr., Joseph Putnam, who was hated by the Putnam family. When he learned that his sister-in-law, Ann Putnam Sr., was among the afflicted and was making accusations, he warned that if her "foul lies" touched anyone in his household, she would "answer for it." Thomas Putnam must have respected Joseph's admonition because the conspiracy never approached his threshold.

Robinson claims the conspiracy reached to the highest levels of government. When Sir William Phips assumed the royal governorship, he was persuaded by William Stoughton to establish a court in which to try the accused witches. "Stoughton recommended the establishment of a flagrantly illegal tribunal, by means of a special executive commission." That tribunal was the Court of Oyer and Terminer. According to Robinson: "Phips unwittingly had created a kangaroo court, a tool giving arbitrary power to the Puritan old guard; its use would not go wanting."

Under the new charter, witchcraft was no longer a capital crime. However, on June 8 the General Court in Boston reestablished the death penalty for witchcraft. On June 10, Bridget Bishop became the first to face the hangman's noose. Her execution disturbed some ministers; and Cotton Mather, fearing that his witchcraft war would be halted, addressed their concerns about the use of spectral evidence in a document called *The Return of Several Ministers Consulted*: "Nevertheless, we cannot but humbly recommend unto the government, the speedy and vigorous prosecution of such as have rendered themselves obnoxious, according to the direction given in the laws of God, and the wholesome statutes of the English nation, for the detection of witchcrafts."

Robinson credits Thomas Brattle, Robert Calef, and Increase Mather with the vision to see through Cotton Mather's feigned objectivity. Their writings provided Sir William Phips with the ethical and moral basis he needed to dissolve the Court of Oyer and Terminer and to have the remaining cases decided by a Superior Court of Judicature.

Robinson concludes: "The Salem episode can be explained only as a delusion, born of deceit. It can be labeled the last of the religious witch hunts. Furthermore, it marks the first of the series of political and criminal witch hunts that have plagued society ever since."

FEAR OF WOMEN PROPELLED THE CRISIS

Historian Carol Karlsen believes that "witchcraft confronts us with ideas about women, with fears about women, with the place of women in society, and with women themselves. It confronts us too with systematic violence against women. . . . [W]itches were generally thought of as women and most of those who died in the name of witchcraft were women." In her book, *The Devil in the Shape of a Woman: Witchcraft in Colonial New England,* Karlsen examines the tensions that gave birth to the fears about women that led to the witch hunt.

When the Puritans sailed for New England, they brought with them their views about the types of people who were witches, their practices, the origins of their powers, and the means of ferreting out and ridding themselves of witches. The societal view was that witches inflicted harm on people and property, while the clergy believed that witches were in partnership with the Devil to win men's souls. The Devil granted a witch's powers through a diabolical covenant. He offered powers and the satisfaction of worldly desires, while she offered allegiance and support for the destruction of God's kingdom.

The Puritan belief that a witch was likely to be a woman was derived from the *Malleus Maleficarum* published in Germany in 1486. The book established that "more women than men are ministers of the Devil." The authors argued that women were intellectually, morally, and physically inferior to men; that women had insatiable appetites and passions; and that women yielded easily to temptation by the Devil, as did Eve. To overcome their limitations and to exact revenge on the more favored, women turned to witchcraft.

In New England, according to Karlsen, "the single most salient characteristic of witches was their sex." Between 1620 and 1725, 344 individuals were accused of witchcraft. Of the 342 identified by gender, females numbered 267, males only 75. Of the males accused, 36 were suspected by association as relatives or supporters of female witches.

Those women most susceptible to witchcraft accusations were over 40 and without husbands. According to Karlsen, "In the eyes of her community, the woman alone in early New England was an aberration: the fundamental female role of procreation was at best irrelevant to her. At worst, of course, she might be performing this function outside the institution of marriage. Moreover, women alone . . . were not the 'helpmeets' to men Puritans thought women should be."

Women alone also posed a concern in a society whose inheritance customs favored men. Inheritances could provide good lives for widows but made them and their daughters vulnerable to witchcraft accusations. Karlsen notes that in many cases women from families without male heirs were accused of witchcraft either right before or just after they came into their inheritances and that women from families without male heirs "account for most of New England's female witches." At the heart of the matter was the fear of independent women.

Women were also viewed as aberrations if they refused to accept their position in the social order: under the authority of a man. A woman's show of discontent, anger, envy, malice, seduction, dishonesty, and pride defined her as one who viewed herself above her place—a place ordained by God—and were signs that she had aligned herself with the Devil.

Karlsen provides an exhaustive exploration of the factors contributing to the fears about women that led to the witch hunt. She believes that "Only by understanding that the history of witchcraft is primarily a history of women . . . can we confront the deeply embedded feelings about women . . . among our witch-ridden ancestors."

ERGOTISM PRECIPITATED THE CRISIS

In an April 1976 issue of *Science,* graduate student in psychology Linnda R. Caporael offered a physiological explanation for the Salem witchcraft crisis: convulsive ergotism. Little known in 1692, ergotism results from eating grain contaminated with a parasitic fungus.

"The possibility that the girls' behavior had a physiological basis has rarely arisen, although the villagers themselves first proposed physical illness as an explanation," Caporael speculates. "However, because the Puritans identified no physiological cause, later historians have failed to investigate such a possibility."

Caporael notes the various theories for the crisis in Salem and acknowledges that "no single explanation can ever account for the delusion; an inter-action of them all must be assumed." However, she seeks "some reasonable jus-tification for the initially afflicted girls' behavior."

She discounts purposeful fraud as an explanation because of "the gravity of the girls' symptoms: all the eyewitness accounts agree to the severity of the affliction." She discounts clinical hysteria because "previous witchcraft accusa-tions in other Puritan communities in New England had never brought on mass hysteria." She discounts factionalism as an explanation because "support-ers of Parris were also prosecuted while some non-supporters were among the most vociferous accusers." While affirming that some of the official records of-fer evidence of fraud, hysteria, and factionalism, Caporael believes that "not all the records are thus accountable."

The "reasonable justification" Caporael offers is convulsive ergot poison-ing, which she believes affected not only the girls but other members of the community as well.

Today ergotism is recognized as a disease caused by the parasitic fungus, *Claviceps purpurea,* that grows on a variety of cereal grains, particularly rye. The fungus forms on the heads of rye dark purple structures called ergots. Resem-bling rye seeds, ergots contain active substances—alkaloids—that are powerful pharmacologic agents. Some are used today as drugs such as ergotamine, used to treat migraine headaches, and ergonovine, which stops postpartum uterine bleeding. However, other alkaloids are poisonous. One of the most potent is isoergine (lysergic acid amide), a substance which is 10 percent as active as the hallucinogenic LSD (lysergic acid diethylamide).

Ergot was not recognized as a fungus until the mid-nineteenth century. Prior to that, farmers thought that ergots were merely sunbaked kernels. Fa-vorable conditions for ergot infestation include warm, damp, rainy springs and summers. Rye grown in low, wet ground breeds abundant ergot. Summer rye is more susceptible than winter rye, and crop contamination can occur in var-ious concentrations. Ergot affects animals that graze on wild rye grass as well as humans who consume rye grains.

If the ergot-contaminated grains are harvested, threshed, and made into bread, ergot poisoning can become epidemic. Long-term ergot poisoning, er-gotism, seems to affect children and women to a greater degree than men. Er-gotism occurs in two forms: gangrenous and convulsive. Gangrenous ergotism attacks the extremities and causes the limbs to waste away. This was epidemic during the Middle Ages.

Convulsive ergotism, according to Caporael, has numerous symptoms:

> These include crawling sensations in the skin, tingling in the fingertips, vertigo, tinnitus aurium, headaches, disturbances in sensation, hallucination, painful muscular contractions leading to epilepiform [i.e., resembling epilepsy] convulsions, vomiting and diarrhea. The involuntary muscular fibers such as the myocardium and gastric and intestinal muscular coat are stimulated. There are mental disturbances such as mania, melancholia, psychosis, and delirium. All of these symptoms are alluded to in the Salem witchcraft records.

Caporael examines the growing conditions, the timing of events in Salem, the localization of the contamination, and the symptoms of those afflicted to paint a picture of "a community stricken with an unrecognized physiological disorder affecting their minds as well as their bodies."

By the 1640s, rye was a well-established crop in New England that was sowed in April, harvested in August, and stored in barns until the colder months when the grain was threshed. From 1691 to 1692, the weather pattern offered favorable conditions for fungal infestation. Entries in Samuel Sewall's diary mention a warm, rainy spring leading to a hot, stormy summer in 1691. A drought the following year made infestation unlikely.

Caporael believes that the timing of the events in Salem dovetails with this pattern. The Puritans probably threshed the grain before their only holiday, Thanksgiving, and the girls' symptoms first occurred in December 1691. By fall 1692, "the witchcraft crisis ended abruptly and there is no further mention of the girls or anyone else in Salem being afflicted."

According to Caporael:

> To some degree or another all rye was probably infected with ergot. It is a matter of the extent of infection and the period of time over which the ergot is consumed rather than the mere existence of ergot that determines the potential for ergotism . . . In all probability, the infestation of the 1691 summer rye crop was fairly light; not everyone in the village or even in the same families showed symptoms.

Caporael believes that the most likely site for the infestation was in the western part of Salem Village, including the farm of Thomas Putnam, an area of swampy meadows. She correlates this contention with the residency pattern of the accusers, the accused, and the defenders of the accused within the confines of Salem Village. Caporael finds that thirty of thirty-two adult accusers lived in the western section, while twelve of the fourteen accused and twenty-four of the twenty-nine defenders lived in the eastern section. "The general pattern of residence, in combination with the well-documented factionalism of the eastern and western sectors, contributed to the progress of the witchcraft cases," according to Caporael.

The residency pattern of the afflicted girls varies slightly, but Caporael provides rationales for ergot contamination in the cases of Ann Putnam Jr., Mercy Lewis, Mary Walcott, Betty Parris, Abigail Williams, Elizabeth Hubbard, and Mary Warren. Putnam, Lewis, and Walcott resided on the Thomas Putnam farm, the seeming center of the infestation. Caporael notes that Ann Putnam Sr. also evidenced symptoms of ergotism.

Betty Parris and Abigail Williams, the daughter and niece of the Reverend Samuel Parris, resided in the parsonage in the middle of the village. Caporael believes that their exposure to the contaminated rye occurred because a portion of Parris's salary was paid in provisions. "The villagers were taxed proportionately to their landholdings. Since Putnam was one of the largest landholders . . . an ample store of ergotized grain would be anticipated in Parris's larder."

Elizabeth Hubbard, the great-niece of local physician William Griggs, resided with the doctor and his wife east of the Village in Salem Town. Caporael speculates that Griggs, who was not a farmer, may have obtained Putnam grain either by purchasing the supplies or by bartering his medical services for it. Ann Putnam Sr. was probably a frequent patient because of the physical and mental disorders from which she suffered.

Mary Warren, a servant in the John Proctor household, resided with the Proctors on their farm southeast of the Village in Salem Town. Caporael is hard pressed to link Warren with the contaminated grain, because the Proctors raised their own food and no one else in the household exhibited any symptoms of ergotism. Proctor doubted the afflicted girls' claims, and he and his wife, Elizabeth, were eventually tried and convicted for witchcraft. According to Caporael: "One document offered as evidence against Proctor indicates that Mary stayed overnight in the village. How often she stayed or with whom is unknown."

Caporael points out that at first Warren was one of the afflicted girls and then she became one of the accused. During Warren's appearance before the magistrates, "four witnesses attested that she believed she had been 'distempered' and during the time of her affliction had thought she had seen numerous apparitions. However, when Mary was well again, she could not say that she had seen any specters." Caporael suggests that these behaviors were the result of ergot poisoning.

Caporael then correlates the symptoms evident in the trial records—sensations of being choked, pinched, bitten, and pricked with pins; visions of specters; violent fits—with the known symptoms of ergotism: "The choking suggests the involvement of the involuntary muscular fibers that is typical of ergot poisoning; the biting, pinching, and pricking may allude to the crawling and tingling sensations under the skin experienced by ergotism victims." She attributes the visions of specters to hallucinations and other perceptual disturbances, and she attributes the violent fits to epileptiform convulsions. "The physical symptoms of the afflicted and many of the other accusers are those induced by convulsive ergot poisoning."

While admitting that her theory relies on circumstantial evidence and acknowledging the influences of political, social, and religious factors, Caporael believes that convulsive ergotism was the true Devil raised among the people of Salem. "Without knowledge of ergotism and confronted by convulsions, mental disturbances, and perceptual distortions, the New England Puritans seized upon witchcraft as the best explanation for the phenomena."

In a December 1976 article in *Science,* Dr. Nicholas P. Spanos, an assistant professor, and Jack Gottlieb, a doctoral candidate in the Department of Psychology at Carleton University in Ottawa, Canada, countered Caporael's arguments, demonstrating that the evidence did not support ergot poisoning as a hypothesis, that the features of the Salem crisis did not resemble an ergotism epidemic, and that the symptoms of those afflicted were not those of convulsive ergotism. They suggest, instead, that "the afflicted girls were enacting the roles that would sustain their definition of themselves as bewitched and that would lead to the conviction of the accused."

ENCEPHALITIS LETHARGICA CAUSED THE CRISIS

Another theory focusing on a physiological cause is offered by independent scholar Laurie Winn Carlson in *A Fever in Salem: A New Interpretation of the New England Witch Trials.* Carlson parallels the physical symptoms of possession—convulsions, hallucinations, distorted language, and paralysis—with the symptoms of encephalitis lethargica, an inflammation of the brain. She offers a number of explanations for the transmission of the illness and supports her theory by citing the trial records; histories of witchcraft; and scientific studies of plagues, especially the 1916–1930 encephalitis lethargica pandemic. According to Carlson, "It is difficult to find anything in the record at Salem that *doesn't* support the idea that the symptoms were caused by that very disease."

The afflicted included not only girls and women but boys and men. Even the animals of Salem Village were not immune. Carlson states: "The colonists reported symptoms in their animals that were eerily like those of the 'bewitched' people: bruised flesh similar to the 'bites' on the girls' arms, animals jumping and running in circles like hypermanic children, and animals with their necks twisted out of place."

After their animals began acting in peculiar ways, neighbors of Martha Carrier accused her of witchcraft. Benjamin Abbott testified that some of his cattle had died "suddenly and strangely." Cows had aborted calves, and a number of cattle staggered out of the woods with their tongues hanging out. Carrier's nephew lost a 3-year-old heifer, two yearlings, and a cow to unnatural causes, and another neighbor complained that although his cow appeared "very lusty," the animal had died on its back with its legs thrust into the air. Another cow in excellent health "pined and quickly lay down as if she was asleep and died." Martha Carrier was arrested, convicted, and hanged for witchcraft.

One case of human illness that Carlson cites is the mysterious death of Daniel Wilkins, 17-year-old grandson of Bray Wilkins of the large Wilkins family that lived in the western part of Salem Village. After he was "taken speechless" in May 1692, Daniel grew seriously ill, unable to speak or to eat. A doctor was called who declared "it was not a natural cause but absolutely witchcraft." At the same time, Bray Wilkins was suffering, too, and feeling much "like a man on a rack." He blamed an in-law, John Willard, for his torment.

The Wilkins family summoned the Reverend Samuel Parris, who brought with him two of the afflicted girls, Mercy Lewis and Mary Walcott. When the girls entered Daniel's room, they screamed that they saw the specter of John Willard crushing Daniel's throat and chest. When they entered Bray's room, they screamed that they saw Willard's specter sitting on Bray's belly. Although Bray eventually recovered, Daniel died three hours later.

When Daniel's body was examined, bruises were discovered on his back, and "many places of the greatest part of his back seemed to be pricked with an instrument about the bigness of an awl." When they turned the body over, blood hemorrhaged from the nose and mouth. John Willard was arrested, convicted, and hanged for witchcraft.

Carlson posits that the mysterious afflictions of Salem Village in the late 1600s can be understood when compared to an epidemic in the early part of the 1900s. Beginning in 1916, Europeans were felled with convulsions, hyperactivity alternating with spells of catatonic stupor, and extreme eye-muscle disorders. Other symptoms included confusion, hallucinations, partial paralysis, memory loss, difficulty speaking, drowsiness, epileptic seizures, loss of hearing, sensitivity to light, double vision, and personality changes. Some sufferers complained of twitches on the skin surface (sensations similar to being pinched), while others complained of red marks on the skin called erythemata (marks similar to witches' bites). According to Carlson, "Sometimes behaviors were grotesque: a patient would open his mouth wide, twist his trunk and arms backward in the most extreme fashion, stamp at the same time with his feet, and utter a snorting sound."

Encephalitis lethargica was first identified as a distinct form of encephalitis and named during the 1916 epidemic. Encephalitis occurs when a virus, bacteria, or spirochete enters the bloodstream and travels to the brain, causing inflammation. White blood cells attack the invader, and the brain tissue swells. Nerve cells can destruct, and the brain can hemorrhage.

Known by a variety of names—"sleeping sickness," encephalitis lethargica, or epidemic encephalitis—the mysterious illness had infected five million people worldwide within a decade. Most of the epidemics started at the beginning of winter, and the largest proportion of acute cases occurred from January through March. The disorder struck people in all age groups, but those from 10 to 21 were most vulnerable; most of the victims were women. The outbreak appeared mostly in small towns and rural communities.

From 1918 to 1920, encephalitis lethargica killed more than half a million people. Those who survived were often left neurologically impaired, some with Parkinson's-like symptoms that lasted for forty years. Domestic livestock seemed to be affected as well. In a single season in California, more than six thousand horses died after a virus attacked their brains and spinal cords. Then, just as mysteriously as it had started, the pandemic of encephalitis lethargica both in humans and in animals ended in 1930.

What caused the 1916 to 1930 pandemic of encephalitis lethargica? Unlike colds and influenza, which are spread through person-to-person contact, encephalitis lethargica spreads via an arboviral transmission chain. Host animals such as wild birds harbor the virus. Blood-sucking insects such as mosquitoes or ticks acquire the virus by feeding on the birds. The mosquitoes or ticks then transmit the virus to domestic animals and to humans.

Carlson cites other epidemics of encephalitis lethargica as far back as the days of ancient Greece. Epidemics hit Germany in the 1500s, from 1672 to 1675, and from 1824 to 1826; Italy in 1597; England from 1673 to 1675; Sweden from 1754 to 1757; Hungary in 1889; and northern Italy from 1889 to 1891. The epidemics affected not only humans but domestic animals as well. In the early 1800s in Norfolk, England, reports surfaced of animals suffering sudden attacks and dying. One calf was "taken so strangely as if the back were broken, and much swollen and within the space of three or four days it died."

Carlson suggests that the areas of Europe most affected by epidemics of encephalitis lethargica were also the areas where the witchcraft persecutions were centered: western France, eastern England, Austria, Switzerland, northeastern Italy. She also notes that the migratory patterns of birds closely match those areas. According to Carlson, "Migratory birds may have brought disease from western Africa to Europe, where a virus in their blood was extracted by arboviral mosquitoes who then fed on peasants and villagers. Just as viral encephalitis is spread by mosquitoes today, a unique form may have been spread by warm-blooded wild birds who passed it on to mammals and humans."

She suggests a number of channels for the conveyance of a similar virus to North America. "Migratory birds on the east coast of North America travel north from the Guiana highlands and Venezuelan river bottoms, passing through Barbados and the West Indies on their way to Massachusetts and points north," according to Carlson. Flocks of migrating birds perhaps gathered at Martha's Vineyard and Plum Island—nearby to Salem—much as they do today.

Another channel of conveyance could be the ships that sailed from England to North America. One scenario suggests that the colonists could have been immune carriers with their own bodies containing the virus, or the virus could have been within the domestic animals that the colonists brought with them. A second scenario suggests that, like the spread of malaria, encephalitis lethargica could have been spread by infected female mosquitoes laying their eggs in the buckets and barrels of water on board for the voyage to New England. By the end of the voyage, the mosquitoes could have infected the entire shipboard of passengers and livestock.

Carlson points out that the terrain and geography of Salem and the regional weather patterns during the crisis period provided the ideal environment for mosquitoes. The western part of Salem Village where most of the afflicted resided was close to the forest and contained rocky, swampy land. According to Carlson, "The climate was favorable in the region, with an unusually warm and wet summer in 1691, followed in 1692 by an early spring and dry summer. This fits the weather pattern conducive to most epidemics of arboviral encephalitis in North America today."

This ideal environment increased the risk of mosquito bites, especially for the young female population in Salem Village. According to Carlson, "Young unmarried women and girls would have been given tasks such as milking cows and gathering eggs (early morning and evening tasks that occur just when mosquito activity increases), tending plants in the garden (mosquitoes are frequently found in grasses and vegetation; a garden would have fostered them), and going for water from the well, which meant water in buckets and barrels that would have attracted egg-laying mosquitoes."

Why did the complaints of afflictions end in Salem in the autumn of 1692? Carlson explains that "an arboviral encephalitis epidemic would have receded in the fall, when the air and water grew too cold for mosquitoes' survival."

Carlson also suggests that ticks could have been the transmitters of encephalitis. In the 1950s woodcutters who worked in the forests of Russia were victims of a tick-borne encephalitis epidemic. In the 1600s in Salem, the Putnam family had a logging and woodcutting operation and supplied firewood for their own use as well as for the use of the Reverend Parris's household as part of his salary.

According to Carlson, "Firewood, in the form of large logs used in colonial fireplaces, might have harbored wood ticks that had gone into winter hibernation but came out of the bark when logs were stored beside the hearth in a warm New England house." The Puritans were at risk for tick infestations because they rarely bathed and because laundry could not be washed during the winter months.

In conclusion, Carlson acknowledges that "many avenues must be explored, much research must be done. Perhaps we will never know what caused encephalitis lethargica."

Perhaps, too, we will never know the ultimate factor that ignited the witch-craft firestorm and disturbed the peace of Salem. The answer may be a convergence of factors, interlocking with one another in the same place and time to create an inevitable, tragic tableau.

SEVEN

Witches and the Craft Today

৶৶

HEN the last antiwitchcraft law was repealed in Great Britain in 1951, covens of Witches blossomed throughout the land like daffodils trumpeting spring after a long winter's slumber. One of those who cultivated the English soil from which the revival germinated was Gerald B. Gardner, known as the father of modern Witchcraft.

In the late 1930s, Gardner's interest in spirituality and the occult led to his association with a secret sect in the New Forest region of England. Sect members believed themselves to be Hereditary Witches descended from those who had practiced witchcraft since the Middle Ages.

150

Bolstering this perspective was a witchcraft theory that had been advanced by British anthropologist Margaret A. Murray during the 1920s. Following her evaluation of the trial records from the Inquisition, Murray concluded that witchcraft could be traced to "pre-Christian times and appears to be the ancient religion of Western Europe."

She argued that this ancient religion was an organized fertility cult that worshipped a deity whose birth, death, and rebirth were commemorated throughout the cycle of the seasons. Murray maintained that the male form of the deity was the two-faced horned god Janus and that the female form of the deity was the goddess Diana. The witches in this "Dianic cult," according to Murray, included both peasants and nobles who celebrated eight major festivals (sabbats), came together regularly for gatherings (esbats), and organized themselves into thirteen-member covens. Murray posited that the accusations made against witches during the Inquisition had an historical basis and that the Inquisitors had transformed the god of the witches into the Devil.

Another individual who contended that witchcraft was an ancient religion was American folklorist and author Charles Godfrey Leland. While traveling through Italy in 1886, Leland met a woman he called "Maddalena" who claimed to be a Hereditary Witch who worshipped Aradia, daughter of the moon goddess Diana.

Tuscany-born Maddalena purportedly revealed to Leland that she had been schooled in witchcraft by her grandmother, her aunt, and her stepmother. She also claimed that the family's witchcraft roots stretched back to the days of the ancient Etruscans. Through Maddalena, Leland met other Hereditary Witches; learned many witchcraft beliefs, spells, and incantations; and revealed those secrets in a series of books. His best known work, *Aradia, or the Gospel of the Witches,* related the Tuscan myth of Aradia. The fruit of the union between Diana, Queen of the Witches, and Lucifer the sun, Aradia was the messiah of Witches sent to earth by her mother to teach the arts of Witchcraft to the troubled human race. According to Leland, the legend of Aradia was a holy gospel of *la Vecchia Religione* or the Old Religion which was the prevailing theology in the northern part of Italy.

Scholars have since discounted Leland's tale of Hereditary Witches as fanciful and Murray's theory of organized pagan religious cults as undocumented. Three modern theories about the origins of witchcraft hold that European witchcraft was (1) a delusion that the Inquisition encouraged, (2) an invention that the Inquisition devised for political and social purposes, or (3) the remnants of ancient Pagan traditions.

However, at the time of Gardner's 1939 initiation, he accepted the belief that Witchcraft was a religion with roots in ancient times; a religion that began as rituals associated with the hunt, animal fertility, and plant propagation; a religion that recognized a Goddess of fertility and a God of the hunt. He believed that the religion went underground in times of persecution, surviving the invasions of the Romans, Saxons, and Normans and the Church's suppression of heretics. He believed that the religion was fading in the 1950s with isolated covens unaware of each other and much of the ritual lost.

According to Margot Adler in *Drawing Down the Moon:* "To him, Witchcraft was a peaceful, happy nature religion. Witches met in covens, led by a priestess. They worshipped two principal deities, the god of forests and what lies beyond, and the great Triple Goddess of fertility and rebirth. They met in the nude in a nine-foot circle and raised power from their bodies through dancing and chanting and meditative techniques. They focused primarily on the Goddess; they celebrated the eight ancient Pagan festivals of Europe and sought to attune themselves to nature."

Gardner and the coveners practiced in secret because Witchcraft was still against the law in Britain. Since many in his coven were elderly, Gardner feared that unless like-minded individuals knew of its continuing existence, the Craft of the Wise would eventually disappear completely. To foster this awareness, Gardner wrote a novel, *High Magic's Aid*, in 1949 that incorporated many of the rituals and beliefs that he had learned from his coven.

After Witchcraft was no longer illegal, Gardner formed his own coven and created new rituals by incorporating elements from folklore, mythology, literature, ancient pagan rites, and ceremonial magick. He and Doreen Valiente collaborated on ritual and nonritual material that formed the Book of Shadows for the tradition of Witchcraft that would eventually bear Gardner's name. His first nonfiction book, *Witchcraft Today*, generated intense interest in Witchcraft, thrusting Gardner into the media spotlight and prompting new covens to sprout up throughout England and the world.

In the succeeding decades, interest in Witchcraft surged. Margot Adler attributes the resurgence in Witchcraft and in Neo-Paganism to six primary factors that emerged from research she conducted in the mid-1970s:

1. *Beauty, vision, and imagination.* Adler's respondents stated that "their religious views were part of a general visionary quest that included

involvement with poetry, art, drama, music, science fiction, and fantasy."

2. *Intellectual satisfaction.*

3. *Personal growth.*

4. *Feminism.* "Many who wanted to find a spiritual side to their feminism entered the Craft because of its emphasis on goddess worship."

5. *Environmental response.*

6. *Freedom.* According to Adler, "Many people said that they had become Pagans because they could be themselves and act as they chose, without what they felt were medieval notions of sin and guilt. Others wanted to participate in rituals rather than observe them."

John K. Simmons, a professor of religious studies at Western Illinois University, believes that the rituals and the focus on nature resonate with individuals in their 30s and 40s who view Witchcraft as far different from the religions of their youth. "I think it feels familiar particularly to those of us who went through the '60s," Simmons says. "And when you add feminism and environmentalism, it feels like home to people."

However, was the Witchcraft that blossomed at the hand of Gerald Gardner authentic? Did he revive or did he reform an ancient religion? Did he establish a new religion? Disagreement has swirled around these questions for decades, and definitive answers may never emerge from the continuing debate.

According to Adler, "Today most revivalist Witches in North America accept the universal Old Religion more as metaphor than as literal reality—a spiritual truth more than a geographic one." That shift in thinking occurred over time, following the introduction of Witchcraft to the United States and as Witches considered the debate over the origins of their religion. By 1975, according to Adler, "Many Witches no longer accepted the Murrayite thesis totally. While some still talked of 'unbroken traditions,' few of them thought Gardner—or anyone else—had a direct line to the paleolithic. And people in the Craft were beginning to regard the question of origin as unimportant."

More important than the question of the origin is the issue of identity. The nature religion practiced today calls itself Neo-Pagan Witchcraft, Witchcraft, Wicca, the Craft, or the Old Religion. According to Adler, "Some Witches will tell you that they prefer the word *Craft* because it places emphasis on a way of practicing magick, an occult technology. And there are Witches . . . who define Witchcraft not as a religion at all, but simply as a craft. Others will say they are of the 'Old Religion,' because they wish to link themselves with Europe's pre-Christian past, and some prefer to say they are 'of the Wicca,' in order to emphasize a family or tribe with special ties. Still others speak of their practices as 'the revival of the ancient mystery traditions.'"

Practitioners identify themselves as Neo-Pagan Witches, Witches, or Wiccans. According to Adler, "Among the Wicca, there is a division over this word *witch*. Some regard it as a badge of pride, a word to be reclaimed, much as militant lesbians have reclaimed the word *dyke*. But others dislike the word."

Many prefer the terms Wicca and Wiccan since these words do not bear the negative associations of the words Witchcraft and Witch. The terms Wicca and Wiccan also differentiate those who practice Neo-Pagan Witchcraft from those who practice folk magick and other forms of witchcraft.

Wicca exists as a self-governing religion that does not look toward a central authority or share a common liturgy. Rather, each of the various traditions offers a distinct philosophy and set of beliefs as well as specific rites and rituals. Most of the traditions are derived from the Gardnerian tradition.

The commonalities among the traditions include a reverence for nature and a respect for all living creatures. Most modern Wiccans embrace a pantheistic philosophy, maintaining that the Divine Force is present in all of nature. Most espouse a polytheistic belief system, maintaining that the Divine Force manifests in a plurality of Pagan deities, chiefly the Goddess and the Horned God. Rites and rituals to honor the gods are based on the seasons and the phases of the moon and can include magickal rites performed for benevolent, not malevolent, purposes.

Most traditions induct new members during formal initiation ceremonies. Initiates swear an oath to "ever keep secret and never reveal the secrets of the Art except it be to a proper person, properly prepared..." According to Derek and Julia Parker in *The Power of Magic*, "Secrecy is considered extremely important: some American Wiccas reinforce the power of the spoken oath with a signed document in which the initiate promises 'to keep the secrets of the Craft of the Wise; never to reveal the rank or identity of any Witch . . . never to reveal the location of the covenstead, methods of working, or the manufacture or consecration of the tools,' never to 'misrepresent the Craft as being a parody of Christianity or any other religion [or] in any way connected with Satanism' on pain of 'the power of just retribution'—which in effect means losing their good name and standing among their peers."

The various traditions include:

GARDNERIAN. Followers of this tradition recognize the male/female polarity of all things in the universe, acknowledge the cycle of birth-death-rebirth, and honor the Goddess and the Horned God, who are represented by the high priestess and the high priest of the coven. While some covens regard the Goddess as supreme above the Horned God, other covens revere the female and male aspects of the Divine equally.

Some Gardnerians worship while dressed in robes; many others worship naked, or skyclad, because they believe that nakedness protects them from evil and brings them closer to nature. Gardnerians raise power for magick through various means, including the Great Rite, which is ritual sexual intercourse between the high priestess and the high priest, who are usually spouses or lovers. The Great Rite can be performed "in true," in private, but is more commonly performed "in token" within a magick circle. When performed symbolically, the high priest thrusts a ritual knife—representing the male element—into a cup—representing the female element. The cup is usually filled with wine and held by the high priestess.

Other means of raising power include meditation, dancing, chants, spells, invocations, and astral projection. Magick is performed with the help of benevolent elementals (i.e., nature spirits who exist in the elements of earth, air, fire, and water); with the sentinels of the four quarters, called the Guardians of the Watchtowers; and with the Pagan deities.

New members are usually welcomed into the coven in "perfect love and perfect trust" during a formal initiation ceremony. A woman is initiated by a man, and a man is initiated by a woman. Coveners move through three degrees of advancement, each degree spanning a minimum of a year and a day.

ALEXANDRIAN. Founded by Alexander Sanders, who crowned himself "King of the Witches," the Alexandrian Tradition was the second main branch of Neo-Pagan Witchcraft to blossom in England. This tradition borrowed extensively from the Gardnerian tradition but uses cord magick and ceremonial magick more extensively. Cord magick involves binding parts of the body with cords to facilitate clairvoyance and astral projection. Ceremonial magick includes elaborate, rigorous rituals in which the practitioner invokes spirits as a conduit for communing with the Divine Force.

HEREDITARY AND TRADITIONAL. Two types of Witchcraft that predate the Gardnerian revival are Hereditary and Traditional. Hereditary Witches claim an ancestral link with an initiated Witch, practice ancient rites and rituals, and often possess psychic abilities. Traditional Witches practice the ancient rites and rituals of a specific country. Both Hereditary and Traditional

Witches usually worship robed, and their covens are usually headed by the high priest.

WITCHCRAFT AS A SCIENCE. "The Official Witch of Salem," Laurie Cabot established the Witchcraft As A Science tradition in 1955 based on the belief that Witchcraft is a combination of religion, art, and science. Followers believe that Witchcraft can be used to increase psychic abilities by harnessing the power of light energy and by controlling alpha waves. Cabot believes that alpha waves contain the accumulated knowledge of the universe and that entering an alpha trance allows an individual to access this vast repository.

To draw light energy more readily and thus enhance psychic power, practitioners of Witchcraft As A Science garb themselves in black, a color that absorbs light. They favor gold jewelry because of the metal's association with Divine light, and they include at least one piece of silver jewelry in their ensembles as another means of heightening psychic abilities.

Initiates to the tradition adhere to the Wiccan Rede, but Cabot extends the creed by prohibiting practitioners from retaliating against malevolent energy or psychic assault. Rather than returning the attack to the perpetrator, which is acceptable in some other traditions, Witchcraft As A Science practitioners are trained to raise a psychic shield. This barrier affords protection, permitting the individual either to convert the negative energy into a positive force or to disintegrate the energy so that no one is harmed. Other training includes the study of parapsychology; astrology; meditation; aura reading, balancing, and healing; the art and science of using crystals; past-life regression; physiology; sociology; and anthropology.

DIANIC. Those who follow the Dianic tradition focus almost exclusively on worship of the Goddess. One branch of Dianic worship includes the feminist Craft whose orientation is matriarchal and whose members align themselves with the feminist movement and the women's spirituality movement. Members view Witchcraft as "womin's religion," and men are excluded from covens. Generally, this branch emphasizes creativity, psychic skills, and political action and is less concerned with structure and formal rituals.

Another branch of Dianic worship has a feminist focus but admits men as coven members. In this branch, according to Adler, "The Goddess is seen as having three aspects: Maiden-Creatrix, Great Mother, and Old Crone, who holds the door to death and rebirth. It is in her second aspect that the Goddess takes a male consort, who is as Osiris to Isis . . . Thus there is a place for the God, but the female as Creatrix is primary."

CELTIC. The rites and rituals of this collection of traditions are based on ancient Celtic myth, magick, and belief. The deities honored bear Celtic names.

FAERY TRADITION. Spelled "Faery," "Faerie," and "Fairy," this secret tradition was founded and developed by Victor Anderson and Gwydion Pendderwen and became well known through the writings of Starhawk, especially her book *The Spiral Dance*. The tradition is polytheistic but keeps secret the names of the deities. Initiates drawn to the Faery Tradition tend to possess a flair for the arts; and they often blend their prose, poetry, and music into the rituals, offering gifts of beauty to the gods. Followers tap into various currents of universal energy in the performance of magick. Two meditational tools used to create inner balance with the universe and to assist in self-development are the iron pentagram (points representing Sex, Self, Passion, Pride, and Power) and the pearl pentagram (points representing Love, Wisdom, Knowledge, Law, and Power).

NROOGD. The New Reformed Orthodox Order of the Golden Dawn takes its name from the nineteenth-century ceremonial magick fraternity, Order of the Golden Dawn, but NROOGD has no connection with the original. In fact, NROOGD is a Witchcraft tradition with no lineage other than its 1967 origins as an assignment in a ritual course at San Francisco State College. The student taking the course gathered a few close friends, including Aidan Kelly and Glenna Turner, to develop and conduct a Witches' sabbat. The troupe performed the ritual for the class in January 1968. Intrigued by the experience, the friends continued to meet as an informal occult study group. They modified the ritual and conducted it on Lammas, August 1, 1968, in a grove of redwood trees. The more than forty individuals participating felt changed by the experience, and by the end of 1969 members of the group realized that they had developed a new religion. They initiated each other as Witches and evolved into a coven by the end of 1971, recognizing the Triple Goddess.

SEAX-WICA. By 1973, Raymond Buckland, who had introduced the Gardnerian tradition to the United States in the 1960s, had become dissatisfied with the tradition. The rituals no longer fulfilled his spiritual needs. He saw internal conflicts perpetuated within some Gardnerian covens, and he believed that the three degrees of rank only encouraged egotism and the self-serving entrenchment of power. This prompted Buckland to develop a new tradition, Seax-Wica, that introduced a democratic atmosphere to the Craft and removed the inequities that he saw running rampant in the Gardnerian tradition.

The Seax-Wica tradition established only one degree of rank, the periodical election of a high priestess and/or high priest to lead the coven, and majority rule within covens about worshipping robed or skyclad. The Goddess and the Horned God shared levels of equal importance and reverence. The tradition allows self-initiation and solitary practice as well as initiation and practice by a coven.

By publishing the book of Craft rituals, *The Tree: The Complete Book of Saxon Witchcraft,* Buckland offered accessibility to the tradition to anyone, especially to those who were frustrated in trying to gain entry to the other traditions. Knowing that most Wiccans valued a tradition with an historical heritage, Buckland blessed Seax-Wica with a Saxon background. However, he declared in the Yule 1973 issue of *Earth Religion News* that: "By this I most emphatically do *not* mean that there is any claim to its liturgy being of direct descent from Saxon origins! . . . It is brand new." In fact, Buckland boasted in the same article: "While others fight over which is the oldest tradition, I claim mine as the youngest!"

Today Witchcraft traditions remain vibrant through change, and this evolution is driven by the contemporary religious needs of Witches. Some traditions incorporate elements from the Eastern world, from the belief systems of indigenous peoples, and from shamanistic ritual. Other traditions fuse together political activism for environmental causes with the quest for spiritual development. Rituals are revised or are supplanted by ones that hold more meaning. New songs, chants, and invocations are brought into being regularly. From the perspective of Witches, such mutability reflects the pliancy of Witchcraft as a religion, one that will always be meaningful for its followers. From the perspective of its critics, Witchcraft's adaptability is perceived as instability.

How many people practice the religion of Witchcraft today? No one knows. Because the religion has no central authority, because many Witches are solitary practitioners, and because much secrecy surrounds Wicca, even estimated numbers are questionable. Here is a sampling:

   ß The Witches' Voice Web site estimates that three million Witches, Wiccans, and Pagans practice worldwide with about one million in the

United States. The Institute for the Study of American Religion states that Witchcraft is the fastest growing religion in the United States.

ṣ In 1990 the United States Army in its handbook for chaplains estimated the Wiccan population in the United States to be fifty thousand.

ṣ In 1995, Julia Phillips, cofounder of the Pan Pacific Pagan Alliance which is Australia's largest organization for Pagans, stated: "In Australia today, there are many hundreds of professed pagans, and likely to be several thousand who are pagan in thought, if not in deed."

ṣ In 1998, the Web site of the Covenant of the Goddess stated that "Conservative reckonings estimate 200,000 Witches and/or Neo-Pagans in the US alone."

ṣ Phyllis Curott, author of 1998's *Book of Shadows,* estimates that between five and ten million Wiccans practice in the United States.

ṣ A British Broadcasting Company (BBC) news story in 1999 cited a 1997 study indicating that a hundred thousand Neo-Pagans practiced in the United Kingdom.

ṣ The Web site for Ontario Consultants on Religious Tolerance estimates that half a million Wiccans practice in the United States and thirty thousand in Canada.

In Canada, Witchcraft achieved legal recognition as a religion in 1987 after a yearlong, highly publicized religious discrimination case launched by Charles Arnold, a second-degree Wiccan high priest from Toronto.

In the United States, Witchcraft and other religious Neo-Pagan organizations are afforded protection under the Constitution. Several court decisions have recognized Wicca as a religion. In 1985, the District Court of Virginia declared that Wicca is "clearly a religion for First Amendment purposes." In 1986, the Fourth Circuit Federal Appeals Court confirmed that decision: "We agree with the District Court that the doctrine taught by the Church of Wicca is a religion."

Those who follow Witchcraft today face fear, hate, and prejudice from a public that does not understand Witchcraft, its practitioners, or practices. Members of the public believe that Witches do not believe in God. While they do not worship Christianity's monotheistic God, Witches honor the Goddess and the Horned God who are seen by many as the female and male aspects of the Divine Force. Members of the public confuse Witches with Satanists, although Witches do not recognize the Devil of Christianity. Many Witches declare that their religion predates Christianity and the Church's concept of Satan. Members of the public believe that Witches perform evil spells. However, Witches assert that their magick promotes harmony and that their ethical code—the Wiccan Rede—forbids them from doing harm.

"For centuries, Witchcraft has been the garbage heap upon which all moral refuse of other people has been dumped," according to Dr. Leo Louis Martello, author of *Witchcraft: The Old Religion*. "The Old Religion has been vilified, perjured about, twisted, persecuted and prosecuted, not because of what it was (and is) but because of what the Church said it was."

As a result and despite legal recognition and protection, Witches face employment discrimination because of religious preferences, prohibitions against wearing their religious symbols in public schools, the banning of books that feature witches as characters, and other assaults against their religious preferences. Ontario Consultants on Religious Tolerance tracks worldwide news of religious intolerance on their Web site (http://www.religioustolerance.org). For example:

- ॐ In October 1999, in the United Kingdom, the bones of a man who lived nearly 3,000 years ago were discovered at Abercrave in South Wales. When plans were announced to provide a Christian burial for the Bronze-Age man, a member of the local Celtic Neo-Pagan group protested: "I would hate to think that someone who found my remains in 3,000 years time would take it upon themselves to bury me as a Christian." The local minister did not agree: "We live in a Christian culture and at the end of the day we all believe in a God."
- ॐ In November 1999, the United Kingdom invalidated the charitable status of Pagan groups, including Witches, Druids, and followers of Odin, after the Charity Commission declared that Paganism is not a religion "in the charitable sense."
- ॐ In December 1999, the Anglican Archbishop of Cape Town advised limiting participation in the Parliament of the World's Religions to representatives from mainstream religions and excluding those who practice Paganism.
- ॐ In January 2000, in the United States, an eleventh-grade English teacher—and Wiccan priestess—in Scotland County, North Carolina, was suspended from her job allegedly because she practices Wicca. Following a formal protest, the teacher left the school district.

🖐 In February 2000, in the United States, a middle-school science teacher in Niles, Michigan, received a three-day suspension from the school board for lending a copy of Scott Cunningham's book, *Wicca: A Guide For the Solitary Practitioner,* to one of her students who was preparing a report on herbal healing.

In addition to tracking news of worldwide religious intolerance, Ontario Consultants on Religious Tolerance bestows periodically the "Burning Times Award," with the objective of recognizing "the North American political figure whose behavior most closely exemplifies the spirit of the Witch burning times." On May 20, 1999, the "Burning Times Award" was awarded to United States Representative Bob Barr, a Republican representing the 7th Congressional District of the State of Georgia. A member of the House Judiciary, Government Reform, and Banking committees, Barr was offended when the United States Army extended religious freedom to Wiccans serving as soldiers on the Fort Hood, Texas, Army base. Barr pressured the Army to terminate religious freedoms at Fort Hood. When this failed, he inspired a coalition of conservative Christian groups to launch a boycott against Army recruitment until that branch of the U.S. Armed Forces capitulated to his wishes.

The controversy began in 1997 when a group of enlisted personnel and officers stationed at Fort Hood –America's largest military post—near Killeen, Texas, outgrew their meeting area in private quarters. They requested permission from the United States Army to hold meetings and outdoor rituals on the grounds of the military base. Wicca has been included in the Chaplains Handbook for the Armed Services for more than two decades, so the Fort Hood group was officially sanctioned. Thus, Fort Hood became the first United States military installation to provide space for Wiccan rites and rituals. The Wiccans selected the legally incorporated church Sacred Well Congregation of San Antonio as their off-base sponsor and chose as their high priestess a six-year veteran of the military police and a soldier-of-the-year award recipient.

For two years, the Fort Hood Open Circle held twice-weekly evening study classes and celebrated full-moon and sabbat rituals. In March 1999, the Wiccans invited a photographer from the *American-Statesman* to observe their Spring Equinox rite. When the Austin newspaper published the photographs several weeks later, Christian groups bombarded the base with telephone calls, threatening to stage a march and disrupt the rituals.

Two months later, U.S. Representative Bob Barr learned about the Fort

Hood sabbat ritual and demanded an "end to taxpayer-funded witchcraft on American military bases." He fired off letters to congressional and military leaders, protesting chaplains at Fort Hood and other bases "sanctioning, if not supporting, the practice of witchcraft as a 'religion' by soldiers on military bases."

The responses to Barr's statements were swift. The executive director of the Armed Forces Chaplains Board at the Pentagon, Navy Captain Russell Gunter, asserted the military's obligation to respect and to provide for the religious needs of service members without judging those beliefs.

U.S. Representative Chet Edwards, a Democrat representing Waco, the district that includes the Fort Hood military installation, stated: "As a Christian, I have serious differences with the philosophy and practices of Wicca. But it would be terrible policy to require each installation commander to define what is a religion and decide which religions can be practiced by American citizens."

An apology was demanded by Major David Oringderff, a psychologist and sociologist who served twenty-two years in the Army. Founder of the Sacred Well Congregation, the sponsor of the Wiccan coven at Fort Hood, Oringderff wrote to Barr: "I am painfully aware that, despite constitutional guarantees and protection under law, intellectual and spiritual bigotry is alive and well in this country . . . Witches are quite accustomed to naïve notions and caustic rhetoric from zealots . . . [but not] coming from a man of your stature . . . Minority faith groups have been supported by chaplains for 20 to 30 years, and we follow the same regulations and follow the same rules as Jehovah's Witnesses, Buddhists, Mormons and any other minority faith groups. I find it ridiculous that we as a group are singled out for who we are and what we do and that we choose to express our faith in ways other than what the dominate culture chooses to express theirs."

In June 1999, the controversy escalated into a larger First Amendment conflict when nearly a dozen religious and conservative groups joined Barr in his campaign, pledging to boycott joining or reenlisting in the Army until Witchcraft rituals are prohibited on Army bases.

The Wiccan community mounted a strong defense in the face of the controversy. The Pagan Educational Network, Inc. coordinated the issuance of a joint statement supported by thirty Pagan and Wiccan organizations:

> Pagan leaders are calling for interfaith dialogue and support for First Amendment freedoms:

Members of other faiths need not fear working, training, fighting, or even dying alongside Wiccans and other Pagans. We respect all Americans' right to worship as they choose. We do not proselytize or in any way seek converts. We welcome and support interfaith dialogue, exploring our similarities and differences. Pagans are proud to serve alongside members of all faiths, upholding a Constitution which supports all our rights.

Paganism is a collection of diverse contemporary religions which are rooted in or inspired by indigenous traditions worldwide. Pagan religions are characterized by belief in the interconnection of all life, personal autonomy, and immanent divinities. These faiths are often nature-centered and supportive of gender equity. Contemporary Pagan culture values diversity, respect, good works, living lightly on the earth, individual freedom, and personal responsibility. We cherish our children, our elders, and our communities, and believe that religious liberty is an inalienable human right which must not be abridged.

Among those that supported the joint statement are organizations that believe in educating members of the public about Wicca and Witchcraft and in defending Paganism from attacks. Some of those organizations include:

- *Covenant of the Goddess*, an international organization founded in 1975 "to increase cooperation among Witches and to secure for Witches and covens the legal protections enjoyed by members of other religions." (http://www.cog.org)
- *Covenant of Unitarian Universalist Pagans, Inc.*, an independent affiliate organization of the Unitarian Universalist Association, is "dedicated to networking among Pagan-identified Unitarian Universalists, educating people about Paganism, promoting interfaith dialogue, developing Pagan liturgies and theologies and supporting Pagan-identified Unitarian Universalist religious professionals." (http:www.cuups.org)
- *Lady Liberty League*, a "National and Global referral and information exchange network of Pagan religious freedom activists," operating within the Circle Network, which is part of Circle Sanctuary. Founded in 1974 by Selena Fox, Circle Sanctuary "is dedicated to research, spiritual healing, counseling, and education." (http://www.circlesanctuary.org/liberty)
- *Witches' Anti-Discrimination League*, an Indiana-based organization whose mission is to "take a Proactive stance in matters affecting the well-

being and welfare of The Pagan Community. We shall respond to those in need of counseling, assistance in Discrimination matters and education of the General Public as to the Nature and True History of Witchcraft. Our main Goal, however, shall be, working toward Fair, Equal Administration of First Amendment Rights for all."

S *Witches' League for Public Awareness (WLPA)*, based in Salem, Massachusetts and with a presence on the World Wide Web (http://www.celtic-crow.com). The organization's mission is to be "a proactive educational network dedicated to correcting misinformation about Witches and Witchcraft. The work of the League springs from a shared vision of a world free from all religious persecution." Founded in May 1986 by Laurie Cabot, the League works with major Witch groups worldwide and with the American Civil Liberties Union to combat prejudice and bigotry against Witches and Witchcraft.

S *The Witches' Voice, Inc.*, "a non-commercial, community driven website, featuring daily craft news updates & powerful networking for the modern pagan community." Created by Wren Walker and Fritz Jung, the Witches' Voice site is one of the Internet's most popular Pagan sites. (http://www.witchvox.com)

Organizations such as these are committed not only to educating the public about Wicca but to educating those who desire to follow the Wiccan way. According to Margo Adler, "The feeling persists that those who practice Witchcraft or occultism are engaged in something fearful, pernicious, illegal, and immoral. This image has a long history. It is nourished by the media because it sells. But more important, this image encourages a fear of the unknown that blunts most people's curiosity and adventurousness."

For the curious and the adventurous, the basics of Witchcraft are explored next.

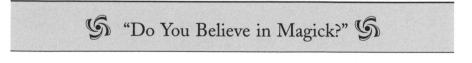

S "Do You Believe in Magick?" S

On August 8, 1990, a 76-year-old woman was found stabbed and bludgeoned to death in her vacation trailer at a Methodist campground in upstate New York. The initial state police investigation turned up few leads, prompting the victim's grandson to contact a local Hereditary Witch, Antonia "Tita" Jones, for help.

Tita visited the murder scene. "It was a scorchingly hot day, but I was so cold," Tita remembers. "I had chills because there was a soul wandering around who was not at rest." Through her clairvoyant powers, Tita sensed that the murderer was close by, watching the unfolding events. Tita also sensed that the murdered woman's cat had witnessed the crime.

Tita knew that cats were considered sacred by the ancient Egyptians. She approached the frightened animal and whispered in its ear an Egyptian incantation that the cat seemed to understand. Suddenly, Tita received visions of the murderer: a teenage girl close to the victim. "The images came from the cat," Tita recalls. She shared the information with the state police who, although skeptical, followed up the lead.

Two weeks later, Tita telephoned the state police and was told that they did not have sufficient evidence against the teen to make an arrest. Tita thought about the restless spirit of the murdered woman and the trauma the cat had experienced in witnessing the crime. She decided to perform a magickal ritual.

"I believe in the Egyptian pantheon," Tita says, "and King Solomon did as well. So I evoked him, and I evoked a certain entity that he used to consult." The result was the dispatching of "some disruptive entities" to the person who had committed the crime.

Within a week, the 18-year-old girl who lived next door to the victim went to state police headquarters and confessed to the crime. She admitted that she had liked her neighbor and that the victim had been kind to her. She had knifed and beaten the woman to death because the teen wanted to know what it felt like to murder someone.

But what had prompted her to confess? The teen said that she couldn't stand the weird feeling she'd had for the last few days that something eerie was hovering around her. The magickal ritual had worked.

The teen pled guilty at her trial, was convicted of second-degree murder, and received a sentence of twenty-two years to life.

EIGHT

The Basics of Witchcraft

N late December, nineteen men and women mingle in a meeting room at a Unitarian Universalist Church in upstate New York. A small table near the door holds the offerings they have brought: moon-shaped cookies, powdered doughnuts, sliced fruit, chips and dip, cheese and crackers, and bottles of soda and juice. Among the members of this diverse group are a physician, a teacher, a baker, a secretary, a writer, an engineer, a nurse, a computer programmer, a librarian, a minister, a bus driver, a business executive, and a chemist. They are practitioners of Druidism, Neo-Paganism, Shamanism, Irish Celtic Paganism, Odinism, Wicca, and other permuta-

tions of Paganism. They have gathered together to celebrate the return of the sun.

They talk among themselves about what they wish to accomplish during this Winter Solstice Sabbat. Do they want to simply honor the Goddess? Do they want to work for prosperity in the year ahead? Do they want to raise power for healing energy? Their varied wishes pose an impasse until the chemist proposes using petition magick, a cauldron, and a candle. In that way, each person can contribute a personal wish. They agree.

In the center of the room is a low rectangular table covered with a silk scarf colored in earth tones. On the scarf the altar is arranged: illuminator candles, a bowl of salt in the North, a feather in the East, a red ball in the South, a bowl of water in the West. A cauldron graces the center of the altar. On the floor near the altar are drums and rattles. On the floor underneath the altar is a silver tray bearing macaroons and a bottle of grape juice. Quarter candles stand at the ready in their appropriate places around the room: green in the North, yellow in the East, red in the South, blue in the West.

Signaling the start of the festival, the High Priest and the High Priestess welcome everyone to the celebration and solicit ideas for the evening's ritual. The High Priest writes each suggestion—drumming, a spiral dance, chanting, recitations, etc.—on a sticky-backed note that he posts on the wall for everyone to see. The group decides the best order for the various ritual components, and the High Priestess arranges and rearranges the sticky-backed notes into the proper sequence. She then calls for the participants to write down their personal petitions on slips of paper that are passed around and then placed on the altar. As the participants form a large circle around the altar, the ritual begins.

The High Priest asks for a volunteer to cleanse and consecrate the four representations of the elements that are on the altar: the bowl of salt represents the Earth, the feather represents the Air, the red ball represents Fire, and the bowl of water represents Water. The bus driver holds his hands over the bowl of salt and asks the Spirit of the North to cleanse, consecrate, and regenerate the salt in the name of the Spirit. He repeats this ritual with each of the elements and concludes the cleansing and consecration by taking three pinches of the salt, adding them to the water, then stirring the water three times in a clockwise direction with the index finger of his right or dominant hand. He then places his hands over the bowl, repeats a prayer for blessings upon the water, and visualizes the liquid glowing with white light.

The High Priestess next draws the circle, the sacred space that will confine the energy raised within the circle until it is released. Beginning in the North, she moves around the altar in a clockwise circle, sprinkling grains of salt while intoning words of cleansing, consecrating, and empowering. She ends with the words "So mote it be!" which like the Christian word "Amen" signify that the blessing is completed. She repeats this process with each of the other three elements—carrying the red ball and the feather and sprinkling the water—then ends the ritual by holding her hands above her head with palms facing upward and intoning a prayer to the Goddess and the God. "So mote it be!"

The High Priestess then casts the circle. She walks clockwise in a circular pattern, creating a bubble of invisible energy that encompasses all of the participants in the group. While she does so, the participants repeat a blessing in the form of a circle-casting rhyme.

Then, the High Priestess asks for four volunteers to call the quarters. Calling the quarters or the Watchtowers invites the elements, power animals, angels, or other positive energies into the circle for aid or protection during the magickal workings.

The librarian volunteers to call the North. She moves from the ring of participants to that quadrant of the altar; faces North; and requests that the powers of the earth join the circle, witness the rite, and guard the sacred space. She visualizes the earth and becomes that element. The participants echo the conclusion of the call: "So mote it be!" The minister, the business executive, and the chemist in turn call the remaining quarters.

Once the quarters have been called, the invocation takes place, and the teacher volunteers to conduct the practice. She assumes the Goddess Position—arms out and her feet spread apart—and invites the Goddess and the God to enter the circle.

After the Lady and the Lord have been asked to join the ritual, the participants check the order of the sticky-backed notes, knowing that the magickal work is next. Each person moves to the altar to retrieve the paper on which is written his or her personal petition then returns to his or her place in the circle, visualizing the success of the petition. The High Priestess calls upon the Goddess and the God to help in manifesting the petitions.

Raising power is next. The secretary, the engineer, and the nurse in turn recite poems, speak incantations, and read aloud personal essays in honor of the returning light. Then each participant moves forward, takes a drum or rattle from near the altar, and drops the personal petition paper into the cauldron at the center of the altar.

Since she has selected the largest drum, the physician starts the beat slowly with all of the group members joining in. The tempo increases with all of the participants pounding the drums and shaking the rattles faster and faster. Spontaneous chanting bursts forth. The drumming, rattling, and chanting reach a crescendo, and the physician concludes the ritual with final beats.

The participants put their instruments aside, and the baker leads the group in a song to honor the Goddess and the God and to welcome the return of the sun. While singing, the participants hold hands and dance in a circle, weaving themselves in spiral lines within the sacred space. Collectively feeling the rise of energy, participants laugh and shout joyously.

The dancing slows, and the circle reforms. The computer programmer steps forward and ignites the petition papers in the cauldron, chanting the words of a spell to bring the words on the papers to fruition. Everyone meditates on his or her intentions.

Communion is next with the High Priest and the High Priestess removing the plate of cookies and the bottle of juice from beneath the altar, blessing the food, and sharing it with the participants. The High Priest and the High Priestess thank the Lady and the Lord for their presence and release the divine energies. Those who called the quarters now close the quarters in reverse order. "Go if you must, stay if you like. Hail and farewell!"

Since she cast the circle, the High Priestess releases the circle. With the index finger of her dominant hand pointed out and downward, she walks counterclockwise around the circle, collecting energy in her hand then sends the energy into the ground. She stomps the floor with her foot and says, "This circle is open, but never broken." The participants chant together, ending with "Merry meet, merry part, merry meet again! So mote it be!"

Hugs, laughter, and chatter follow as the circle disbands and the participants feast on the moon-shaped cookies, powdered doughnuts, sliced fruit, chips and dip, cheese and crackers, and bottles of soda and juice. So mote it be!

This Winter Solstice Sabbat brought together practitioners of various pagan religions, including Witches. Witches are fond of saying that "all witches are pagans but not all pagans are witches." (Similarly, in traditional religions, "all Catholics are Christians but not all Christians are Catholics.")

Witches acknowledge a dual Deity, use magick to create harmony in the world and to empower themselves and others, adhere to a simple moral creed, and honor nature through seasonal cycles. The personally structured, Neo-Pagan religion that Witches follow is known as Wicca, Witchcraft, or the Craft. Practitioners refer to themselves as Wiccans, preferring that over the term Witch, a word that still bears negative connotations even today.

All religions acknowledge a Divine Force, the energy from which the universe was created. Unlike practitioners of Judeo-Christian religions who focus only on the masculine aspect, Wiccans recognize both the feminine and the masculine aspects of the Deity. The Goddess and the God are equal and complementary, representing the religious ideal of perfect, natural balance. Wiccans see the Divine Force everywhere around them as well as within them.

The Goddess is known by names such as the Great Mother, the Universal Mother, Mother Nature, Mother of the Gods that Made the Gods, the Queen of Heaven, etc. The womb of the Goddess is associated with the cauldron, and from the cauldron abundance pours forth. The gift of the Goddess is life, but life is given with the promise of death. Rather than viewing death as the end of existence, Wiccans believe that the end of life bestows rest from physical toils and existence in a spiritual plane between incarnations.

Wiccans recognize three aspects of the Goddess which are symbolized by the cyclical phases of the moon. These phases also correspond to the stages in a woman's life:

- the Maiden is represented by the new or waxing moon. The Goddess is young, symbolizing freshness, initiative, and adventure. The Greek goddess Artemis is associated with the new or waxing moon, but she is usually called by her Roman name, Diana. Virgin and huntress, Diana rules the earth, and depictions of the Maiden often show her as a huntress running with her hounds.
- the Mother is represented by the full moon. The Goddess is mature, symbolizing fulfillment, bounty, and balance. The Greek goddess Selene, who rules the sky, is associated with the full moon. Depictions of the Mother show her heavy with child.
- the Crone is represented by the waning moon. The Goddess is old, symbolizing wisdom, secrets, and death. The Greek goddess Hecate, who rules the underworld, is associated with the waning moon.

*   *   *

The phases of the moon are important for spellwork. From new moon to full moon, Wiccans accomplish attracting spells that pull desires such as love or abundance toward them. From the end of the full moon to the last quarter of the waning moon, Wiccans accomplish banishing spells that push obstacles, illness, negativity, or problems away from them.

While the moon is associated with the Goddess, the sun is associated with the God. The God represents sexuality, vitality, and power, and he rules with the Goddess in the endless cycle of birth, death, and rebirth. When depicted with horns on his head, he is known as the Horned God, lord of the woodlands and the tender of animals. The horns symbolize the crescent moon—also the symbol of the Goddess—and connote fertility and increase.

৩ "Oh My Love, Come To Me" ৩

In her book *Notions and Potions: A Safe, Practical Guide to Creating Magic & Miracles*, author Susan Bowes shares a spell for drawing in a loving relationship:

"This needs to be done preferably on a Friday night during the new moon phase . . [C]hoose a time when you will not be disturbed. Lower the lights and make the room comfortable and restful.

"Anoint either two or six pink candles with essential oils, such as patchouli and sandalwood, score them with your initials and then create your altar. Place representations of each of the four elements—air, earth, fire, and water—in the four corners, together with fresh flowers and any crystals or personal love tokens that you feel may enhance your ritual.

"Taking paper and colored pens, draw a picture of your heart. What does it have to offer you and your partner? How big is it? Is it afraid? Would you want it, if it was offered to you? Then take a second piece of paper and make a list of all the attributes you want in your prospective partner. Be specific. Make sure you ask for someone who is the right age, free of other emotional ties, and, above all, ready to enter into a committed relationship.

"Place your list and drawing on your altar, then light your candles, saying the following incantation:

> *Draw to me my perfect mate*
> *That I may love dear and true*
> *Let him/her my twin soul be*

And let our union bring infinite blessings
On all we do and on all we meet
So mote it be.

"Repeat this three times, absorbing it into your heart, body, and soul. As you meditate on the candle flame, ask your mind's eye to give you an image of the person you are drawing to you. Then take a few moments to give thanks to your guardian angels for being with you throughout this time. You can now ceremonially burn the list and drawing, bury them, or keep them in a safe place.

"Your ritual is now complete. The only thing left for you to do is to trust. Of course, it may take a little while before your perfect partner appears but if you open yourself up to signs and portents, the Universe has a funny habit of sending out little teasers just as your life is about to change."

The deities associated with the Horned God include Pan, the Greek god of the woodlands; Cernunnos, the Celtic god of fertility, animals, and the underworld; and Janus, the Roman god of good beginnings. The Horned God has no association with Christianity's god of evil, Satan. Although the public often assumes incorrectly that the Horned God is Satan, Witches neither believe in nor worship the Devil.

The ceremonies that Wiccans conduct and the ritual tools they employ honor the Earth and celebrate and strengthen their connection with the Goddess and the God, the creative energies of the universe. By drawing from this universal energy, Wiccans are empowered to work magick.

Magick can be thought of as the harmonious manipulation of natural energies to create desired transformations. Scholars often differentiate between energy manipulation—magick—and illusionary manipulation—magic—with these respective spelling variations. Pulling a rabbit out of a hat or sawing a person in two are examples of illusionary manipulation performed by stage magicians. Magick is a real and powerful religious practice.

All religions have practiced various forms of magick for thousands of years and continue to do so today. Saying a prayer is the simplest form of magick in which the petitioner speaks directly to the Divine Force in order to effect change. Catholics observe their priests performing higher-level ceremonial magick when consecrated bread and wine are transformed into the body and blood of Jesus Christ. Since Wiccans have direct links to the Divine Force, intermediaries such as priests, ministers, or shamans are not needed.

Wiccans create magick through a myriad of magickal systems that incorporate elements such as meditation, visualization, trance, chants, singing, playing musical instruments, invocations, spells, and rituals. The process of making magick involves first arousing personal power by having both the need and the intention to manifest magick. In the words of Aleister Crowley, "every intentional act is a Magical Act." Next, preparing for the ritual—gathering supplies, visualizing, lighting candles, etc.—infuses personal power with the magickal need. During the ritual, using gifts of the Earth—stones, crystals, herbs, and oils—releases vibrational energy which fuses with personal power. Invoking the assistance of the Divine Force and then releasing the energies to work throughout the universe complete the magickal process.

In practicing magick, modern-day Wiccans adhere to a simple moral creed called the Wiccan Rede (from the Old English terms "wicca" ["witch"] and "roedan" ["to guide or direct"]):

Eight words the Wiccan Rede fulfill;
An' it harm none, do what ye will.

The Rede guides Wiccans in the way that the Golden Rule—"As you wish that men would do to you, do so to them"—guides Christians who follow the wisdom of Jesus Christ. However, unlike the Golden Rule, the origin of the Wiccan Rede is uncertain.

Gerald B. Gardner held that the creed was derived from the words of legendary Good King Paulsol: "Do what you like so long as you harm no one." Possibly the Wiccan Rede was created by Gardner as part of his Gardnerian tradition of modern witchcraft. He may have borrowed from Aleister Crowley's Law of Thelema: "Do what thou wilt shall be the whole of the Law."

Despite the murkiness of its genesis, the Wiccan Rede influences spellcasting today. Wiccans respect the free will of living creatures and believe that using magick to harm or to manipulate is an unethical practice. For example, Wiccans believe that a love spell is manipulative if used to take a husband, wife, or significant other away from another or to force someone's affections against his or her free will. Instead, a Wiccan will cast a spell that is aimed at attracting the person who would be best for the Wiccan at that time. Thus, the Wiccan uses magick for good rather than evil purposes and abides by a corollary to the Wiccan Rede: the Threefold Law of Return or the Threefold Law of Karma.

Karma is the cosmic doctrine of cause and effect, stating that every action brings a consequence or a return. Good is returned with good; evil is returned with evil. However, the Threefold Law of Return magnifies the return three times. Therefore, Wiccans who use their powers for good receive three times as much good in return, while Wiccans who use their powers for evil receive three times as much evil in return. In *Witchcraft Ancient and Modern*, Raymond Buckland recognizes that the concept of triple return provides "no inducement for a Witch to do evil." The Threefold Law of Return can be remembered this way:

Be ye young or be ye old,
Whate'er ye do returns three fold.

For some Wiccans, strict interpretation of the Rede prevents them from using magick against criminals. For example, casting a spell to stop a murderer would be perceived as manipulation of the wrongdoer's free will. Other Wiccans interpret the Rede more liberally. They believe that they have a moral responsibility to stop crime using either physical or magickal methods. Just as they would intervene physically to prevent a purse snatching, they would also intervene magickally to stop a rapist. Many Wiccans solve the dilemma through the use of binding spells, a ritual to stop or prevent evil. One of the most remarkable binding spells took place in 1980 in the San Francisco Bay area.

A serial killer known as the Mt. Tam Murderer had been preying on joggers for three years, ambushing and then shooting them. Z. Budapest assembled a group of Wiccans for a public binding ritual during which they called for the murderer to make mistakes during his crimes. Three months later, the trail of errors left by the killer resulted in his arrest and conviction.

In addition to binding rituals, Wiccans perform spells for love, health, money, protection, and other magickal needs. They employ petition magick, color magick, candle magick, cord magick, and element magick. They practice divination through methods such as astrology, charms, palmistry, psychometry, tea-leaf and tarot-card readings, rune casting, and crystal-ball gazing. A veritable library of books is available to introduce the beginner to numerous magickal systems and to lead the beginner through various rituals and spells. However, Scott Cunningham in his book *Wicca: A Guide For The Solitary Practitioner* advises: "If you can't find a ritual to your liking or that fits your needs, create one." That speaks to the individuality as well as the flexibility of Wicca.

Using rituals and spells, Wiccans celebrate the Goddess and the God in the universal rhythms of the seasons. Born at the winter solstice, the Horned God unites with the Goddess in spring, dies at the summer solstice, and is reborn at the winter solstice. Likewise, the energizing rays of the sun grow more abundant at the winter solstice, warming the Earth as the days unfold to spring. In the spring, seeds burst into life, greening the land. The abundance of the land matures through mid-summer. Then at the summer solstice, the vibrant rays of the sun begin their retreat. The abundance of the land is harvested in autumn, then the Earth prepares for her long winter slumber, awaiting the return of the sun.

This cycle is reflected in the Wiccan religious calendar or Wheel of the Year that usually celebrates twenty-one ritual occasions: thirteen appearances of the full moon, called Esbats, and eight festivals marking the changing of the seasons, called Sabbats.

The four major Sabbats are Imbolc, Beltaine, Lammas/Lughnasadh, and Samhain. Wiccans refer to these major Sabbats as days of power, reflecting their genesis as fire festivals in earlier times. The four lesser Sabbats are Winter Solstice, Spring Equinox, Summer Solstice, and Autumn Equinox. Each Sabbat relates a portion of the story about the Goddess and the God:

WINTER SOLSTICE / YULE (around December 21)—The Goddess gives birth to her son, the God. Some Wiccans view the Yule as the time when the Goddess rebirths herself. On the longest night of the year, this Sabbat reminds Wiccans that after death comes rebirth and the return of the light.

IMBOLC (February 2)—Both Mother and Maiden, the Goddess recovers after birthing the God and nurtures her son who is young and growing. This Sabbat is a festival of light, reminding Wiccans that they are purified by the power of the sun following the bleakness of winter. Known as Candlemas, February 2 was the date on which candles for the coming year were made. Imbolc is a traditional time for coven initiations and is an ideal time for Wiccans to plant the seeds of their hopes and dreams for the year. Fertility dances are customary.

SPRING EQUINOX / OSTARA (around March 21)—The Goddess and the God are young and vibrant as they anticipate the exuberant, fertile days of spring. Shoots of new growth in the soil and swelling buds on the trees hold the promise of warmer days to come. Some Wiccans use the week before Ostara to reflect on any injustices they have committed against family and friends. The Wiccan notes the wrongs on a list then strives to rectify the negative acts with positive action. The list is burned during the Spring Equinox celebration.

BELTAINE (April 30)—Having reached maturity, the Goddess and the God fall in love and celebrate that love consensually. Wiccans celebrate Beltaine with laughter, feasting, and fun. Some include the May pole—representing the God—as part of rituals, while others use the cauldron—representing the Goddess—as the focal point of rituals. Beltaine is a traditional time for hivings (i.e., when a coven becomes too large, part of the group leaves to form a new coven), degree ceremonies, new training classes, and other group-related projects.

SUMMER SOLSTICE / SUMMER (around June 21)—The Goddess glows in serenity and fruitfulness while the God is at the peak of his passion and glory. This longest day of the year marks the season between the planting and the harvest. Some Wiccans mark this solstice—a fire festival—by making solar amulets, others harvest herbs and sacred plants, some bring family pets to solstice ceremonies for blessings.

LAMMAS OR LUGHNASADH (August 1)—The Goddess oversees the first harvest while the God loses his strength as the nights grow longer. This Sabbat represents the Wiccan Thanksgiving, when gratitude is shown for the abundance of the earth and for hopes and dreams that have come to fruition. Many Wiccans celebrate with food from the land and the sea; North American Wiccans celebrate Lammas as a grain harvest and include the baking of bread as part of the festivities.

AUTUMN EQUINOX OR MABON (around September 21)—The Goddess as Mother Earth presides over the completion of the harvests. The God prepares to enter the shadow realm. Fields and gardens are ripe with nature's bounty, but a nip in the air holds the promise of the cold months to come. Many Wiccan celebrations focus on eliminating things from one's life—separating the wheat from the chaff—while others focus on honoring the spirits of female ancestors.

SAMHAIN (October 31)—The Goddess is now the Crone, offering wisdom. The God is Lord of the Underworld. Death reigns, but time leads to rebirth once again at Winter. Wiccans reflect on the events of the last year, especially those that have ended or retreated. Believing that on this night a thin veil separates the physical and spiritual worlds, Wiccans remember the spirits of their beloved dead who await reincarnation.

The Wheel of the Year is rotated 180 degrees for Wiccans in the southern hemisphere. For example, Wiccans in Australia celebrate Winter Solstice on June 21. However, not all Australian Wiccans choose to observe this "where-you-are" convention.

In addition to Sabbats, Wiccans celebrate the appearances of the full moon in thirteen Esbats held throughout the year. Esbats represent the time when the Goddess is at her full power, so these are ideal times for spellcasting. Special rituals such as handfastings (i.e., marriages) and Wiccanings/sainings (i.e., christenings) are conducted during Esbats. The consecration of a natural beverage and a cake—the Wiccans' communion—is customary at Esbats.

An important and beautiful Esbat ritual for many Wiccans is Drawing Down the Moon. During this ritual, Wiccans invoke or draw down the spirit of the moon, enabling them to connect with the power of the Goddess and to the power that resides inside them.

WICCAN WORSHIP AND RITUALS

Wiccans worship and conduct rituals either in covens or as solitary practitioners. A coven is a group of Wiccans who work together on a regular basis under the direction of a High Priestess and a High Priest. The High Priestess, who represents the Goddess, and the High Priest, who represents the Horned God, are a spiritual team, training and counseling new Wiccans and guiding ceremonies and rituals.

Wiccans do not solicit converts, so an individual interested in joining a coven must locate a group and ask permission to join. Admission is not automatic. Candidates are screened, trained, and evaluated before admittance to the coven is granted.

Candidates serve an apprenticeship of a year and a day during which they undertake long and intense study of the Craft. At the conclusion of their apprenticeship, if they are deemed worthy for admittance to the Craft, the candidates are initiated in a formal ceremony. Initiation ceremonies vary, depending upon the tradition, but they are rites of passage, marking not only entry into the Craft but the spiritual transformation of the Wiccan. Women are initiated by a High Priest, while men are initiated by a High Priestess. For Hereditary Witches, mothers can initiate their daughters, and fathers can initiate their sons. Contrary to popular misconceptions, initiates do not renounce their faith, Christian or any other; they do not pay homage to Satan, as the Devil is not recognized by Neo-Pagans; and they do not participate in blood sacrifices.

The initiation ceremony is the first of several that new Wiccans experience. Traditions such as Gardnerian and Alexandrian, for example, have systems of advancement, comprised of three degrees or levels. Advancement through each degree requires continued study, and initiation ceremonies mark entry to higher degrees. The highest level—eldership—is attained by Wiccans only after years of study, training, and experience, and the achievement of eldership is an honor for the Wiccan and for the coven.

Traditionally, covens number thirteen individuals: a leader and twelve followers. However, covens can vary in size from three to twenty members. Covens can consist of a mix of women and men, all women, or all men. Some Wiccans consider nine to thirteen members to be the ideal size because this range is large enough to generate effective energy yet small enough to promote group rapport and harmony.

While covens provide comfort and support, some Wiccans feel that they can concentrate more and progress better in their spirituality by pursuing a lone path. Others follow that path because they wish to protect their privacy. These Wiccans are called solitaries. Solitary Wiccans can self-initiate, although some solitaries believe that initiation is merely ceremonial and unnecessary. Estimates indicate that solitaries outnumber those who belong to covens.

Whether working within a coven or as solitaries, Wiccans approach rituals and magick in similar yet individualized ways. While rituals can be traditional or new, rehearsed or spontaneous, wholly spiritual or a combination of spiritual and magickal, Wiccans usually prepare for their ceremonies by purifying themselves, dressing for ritual, and creating a sacred space or magick circle.

The purification rite is a common aspect of many religions. Wiccans view immersion in a tub of cool, salted water as a means of dissolving the day's tensions so that the individual can stand before the Divine Force with a cleansed body and mind. During the bath, some Wiccans burn candles and incense. Others add scented oils or herbal sachets to the water. Of course, some regard ritual bathing as unnecessary and do not include the purification rite as a prelude to their rituals.

The next step is dressing for ritual. Some traditions believe that being skyclad, or naked, is preferable for ritual, since that is the natural state of the human body. However, ritual nudity is not embraced by all Wiccans and thus remains a personal preference.

ᔕ "To Your Health" ᔕ

In her book, *A Victorian Grimoire,* author Patricia Telesco shares directions for making a small, homemade doll called a poppet which can be used in sympathetic magick for healing.

"For example, if you have a friend who has been plagued by colds, sew up a little figurine filed with herbs of healing and revitalization (eucalyptus and lemon are especially good for colds). In all good conscience, you should first ask your friend's permission to help, so that you can personalize the poppet to represent him/her. While you work on the figurine, you should visualize the sickness of your friend being poured into it, even as you stuff the herbs. Next, chant a small verse, something like, "With love you are stitched, with love you are made, all sickness I banish, instead health now inlaid. As a needle to thread, be this poppet to (name), so that (he/she) may rise joyfully out of their bed."

Depending on your viewpoint, you can now do one of two things with the poppet. One is to give it to the intended individual that they might carry their health with them. The second is to bury the poppet, thus burying the sickness. Either method is equally effective; the only difference is which one makes more sense to you."

A simple robe or other comfortable garments made of natural fibers such as cotton, wool, or silk are appropriate for ritual dressing. Wiccans often choose the shade of their robes from a palette that identifies the specific vibration of the color. For example, a blue robe is favored by those conducting healing rituals. Black robes are popular, but the color does not symbolize evil. A color of protection, black represents the universe, which is the source of divine energy.

Jewelry with religious or magickal designs can be part of ritual dressing, too, but is not essential. Pearls, emeralds, and silver honor the Goddess, while diamonds, gold, and brass honor the God. Crescents, ankhs, and pentagrams are the meaningful designs that Wiccans prefer.

The next step involves creating a sacred space or magick circle. Wiccans create places of power indoors or outdoors, and in these sacred spaces the Deities are honored and magickal rituals are practiced. Usually nine feet in diameter, the circle is cast by visualizing energy and walking in a clockwise circular movement called deosil. The primary points are marked with glowing candles, appropriate objects, or ritual tools.

At the North, which represents the Earth, the element of fertility, Wiccans can place herbs, a bowl of salt or soil, crystals, stones, or money. At the East, which represents Air, the element of the intellect, Wiccans can place a feather or an empty bowl. At the South, which represents Fire, the element of change, Wiccans can place a burning candle, incense, or a red ball. At the West, which represents Water, the element of the emotions, Wiccans can place a bowl of water or sea shells. These objects can also be aligned in their proper directions on the altar, which is at the center of the circle, usually facing North, the direction from which energy flows out of darkness into light.

The left side of the altar is the domain of the Goddess, while the right side of the altar is the domain of the God. The middle of the altar is dedicated to both. The ritual tools sacred to the Goddess and the God are positioned in a pleasing arrangement in their respective domains. Wiccan ritual tools include:

ATHAME: A tool of power manipulation sacred to the God, the athame, or magick knife, directs the energy that Wiccans raise during rituals. Traditionally a dull, double-edged knife with a black handle, the athame serves a ritualistic rather than a practical purpose.

BELL: When rung, this ritual tool that is sacred to the Goddess unleashes vibrations that banish evil spirits, create positive energies, or signal the beginning or end of a spell.

BESOM: Sacred to both the Goddess and the God, the besom, or broom, is a purifier used by Wiccans to cleanse an area of negative energy before beginning a ritual. The bristles need not even touch the floor; while brushing, the Wiccan need only visualize the sweeping away of psychic debris. The traditional formula for making a magickal broom incorporates a staff of ash for protection, a brush of birch for purification, and a binding of willow for healing and love.

BOLLINE: The bolline is the Wiccan's working knife. This white-handled knife fulfills the practical purpose of cutting wands, cords, and sacred herbs or inscribing symbols onto candles, wood, and clay.

BOOK OF SHADOWS: This Wiccan workbook, or grimoire, is a personal volume for the recording of beliefs and practices such as laws and ethics, incantations, ritual patterns, spells, herbal recipes, dances, divination methods, and other notes. Books of shadows vary from tradition to tradition, from coven to coven, and from solitary to solitary. By custom, the Book of Shadows is kept by the High Priestess or High Priest. New Wiccan initiates borrow the master copy and create their own volume by hand-copying from the original and adding personal, meaningful material. Ordinarily, a Book of Shadows is kept secret, although over the years some books of shadows have been published and shared with the public.

CAULDRON: Sacred to the Goddess, the cauldron is a container of transformations. Wiccans use cauldrons to burn fires or incense during rituals or to prepare herbal remedies for healing. Traditionally made of iron, cauldrons rest on three legs and have an opening that is smaller than its widest part.

CENSER: The censer is an incense burner that contains the sticks, cones, or blocks of incense that smolder during Wiccan rituals, carrying messages on the smoke to the Divine Forces. Many Wiccans prefer to use granulated incense that is burned on self-igniting charcoal briquettes. The censer can also be used to burn herbs, wood, or other substances to purify the air prior to rituals or to raise the vibration of the magickal need.

CRYSTAL SPHERE: Often made of quartz or leaded glass, the crystal ball is used for contemplative divination. The crystal sphere symbolizes the Goddess and can also be used to receive messages from the Divine Forces.

CUP: This stemmed cauldron represents the Goddess and often contains the beverage consumed during a ritual.

PENTACLE: The pentacle is a flat piece of metal, wood, earthenware, or clay inscribed with Wiccan symbols, most often the pentagram, which is an encircled five-pointed star with one point upright. The points symbolize the five metaphysical elements of the ancients—Earth, Air, Fire, Water, and Spirit—and the circle encompassing the star represents the God-Goddess or Divine Force. By tradition, the topmost point of the pentagram represents Spirit, the upper right-hand point represents Water, the lower right-hand point represents Fire, the lower left-hand point represents Earth, and the upper left-hand point represents Air.

The pentagram is as sacred to Wiccans as the cross and fish are to Christians and as the Star of David is to Jews. As Satanists turn the cross upside down, they reverse the pentagram, so that the elements of Fire and Earth are at the top and Spirit is at the bottom. However, the upright pentagram represents Wicca/Witchcraft and should not be confused with the inverted Satanic symbol. During Wiccan rituals, the pentacle holds amulets, charms, or other objects that will be consecrated during the rite.

WAND: The wand is a tool of invocation that calls spirits to join rituals. Wiccans also use the wand to direct energy, to trace symbols or a circle on the ground, or to stir cauldron concoctions. Willow, elder, oak, apple, peach, hazel, and cherry are the traditional woods favored by Wiccans for their wands. Wiccans do not worry about finding the right wand; they believe that the ideal wand will come to them.

Once the ritual tools are in place and the circle has been cast, Wiccans decide on a goal for the magickal ritual then visualize that desire by focusing on a symbol such as a burning candle. Next, they dance around the circle, chanting, singing, clapping hands, or drumming to form psychic energy called a cone of power. As the tempo of the activity increases, the cone of power gradually rises over the circle. Highly attuned individuals such as the High Priestess or High Priest frequently see the energy as silver or silver-blue light shimmering above the participants. When the energy reaches it peak, the High Priestess or High Priest signal the participants to release the power, which they do in a burst such as rushing toward the burning candle and shouting out their intention.

The cone shape is significant to Wiccans because it represents both the circle and the triangle. The circle symbolizes the sun and the cycle of birth, death, and rebirth. The triangle symbolizes the three faces of the Goddess. In Witchcraft lore, Witches usually wear tall, conical black hats.

Whether they call themselves Witches or Wiccans, practitioners view Wicca as a multifaceted crystal, uniting religion, mind power, magickal systems, respect for nature, wisdom and learning, and love for and faith in the Divine Forces. Dressing in black, joining a coven, and performing spells do not make a person a Witch. Only by undertaking intense and long study of the Craft; believing in and adhering to spiritual laws; and embracing a philosophy of living wisely, with harm to none, and in harmony with nature can an individual lay claim to the desired status of Witch. So mote it be!

ॐ "Prosperity, Come To Me" ॐ

In her book, *Easy Enchantments: All the Spells You'll Ever Need for Any Occasion,* author Lexa Rosean shares the "Prosperity Water Spell," a modern spell she designed by blending a number of ancient customs. The ingredients are:

> 10 pennies, preferably ones found facing
>   heads-up on a road or street
> 1 empty, clear jar
>   spring water
>   green food coloring
> 1 green candle
>   potting soil

"Once you have your ten pennies, place them in an empty clear jar. Fill the jar with spring water and three drops of green food coloring. On the next full moon leave the jar (lid off) under the light of the moon. You may place it on a windowsill where the moon is sure to shine, or in a garden or terrace. If you do not have access to any of these places, go outside with the jar and hold it up to the light of the full moon for at least thirteen minutes. The longer the jar is exposed, the more powerful the potion, but thirteen minutes is the minimum amount of time required to empower the water. You must close the lid on the jar and take it inside before sunrise. On the following evening, seal the lid of the jar by dripping the wax of a green candle round and round the perimeter of the jar, sealing the space between the neck of the jar and the lid. Bury the jar in some rich dark earth. You can do this outside in a garden or indoors with a pot and some potting soil. Once you have buried the jar, trace an invoking pentagram (five-pointed star) on the surface of the soil. To draw an invoking pentagram begin at the top point and move down diagonally to the left. Continue up diagonally to the center right point. Go across horizontally to the center left point. Move down diagonally to the bottom right point and continue up diagonally to meet the original top center point. If you visualize the pentagram as a person standing with arms and legs outstretched this should be easy to imagine. The top center point is the head. The right and left center points are the arms and the right and left bottom points of the star are the legs.

"The pentagram is a symbol of earth and prosperity. By burying your jar in the earth you are fusing it with the power of the earth goddess. The copper of the pennies also represents the earth element. Pentagram, soil, and copper infuse your water with the triple aspect of earth, therefore the water will be thrice blessed. Keep the jar buried until the next new moon. Wait 24 additional hours and then dig up the jar. Break the wax seal and sprinkle this water around home, business, or person anytime you want to bring more prosperity into your life."

NINE

A Witches Who's Who: From Historic to Contemporary Times

HROUGHOUT history, many fascinating individuals have been associated with Wicca and Witchcraft. The following compendium of twenty-five notables presents a Witches Who's Who from historic to contemporary times.

ADLER, MARGOT (1946–) An American Witch who prefers to describe herself as a Pagan, Margot Adler chronicled the rise of Neo-Paganism in the United States in the landmark 1979 book, *Drawing Down the Moon*.

Adler was born in Little Rock, Arkansas, and grew up in New York City. She is the granddaughter of famed psychiatrist Alfred Adler. Raised in a nonreligious home, Adler as a child felt drawn to the ancient Greek deities, particularly Artemis and Athena. While in high school, Adler began an exploration of various religions.

She graduated from the University of California at Berkeley with a bachelor's degree in political science and focused her energies on political action, including the fight for civil rights in Mississippi in 1965 and the political protests at the Democratic convention in Chicago in 1968.

She completed a master's degree in journalism in 1970 at the Graduate School of Journalism at New York's Columbia University and took a job as a broadcast journalist for radio station WBAI. Adler joined the staff of National Public Radio in 1979.

A trip to England to investigate the history of the Druids led to her uncovering the existence of Neo-Pagan groups and to her discovering Witchcraft. After listening to an audiotape of the "Drawing Down the Moon" ritual and the "Charge of the Goddess" address, Adler's girlhood memories of the Greek goddesses Artemis and Athena were rekindled. She felt the empowerment of connecting to the Goddess and determined to explore that path of spiritual development.

She studied initially with a Brooklyn group that was sponsored by the New York Coven of Welsh Traditional Witches. She eventually joined a Gardnerian coven, then was initiated as a first-degree Gardnerian priestess in 1973. She established a Pagan Way grove in Manhattan and began researching the Neo-Paganism movement and interviewing individuals in the Neo-Pagan community. That research culminated in the landmark book *Drawing Down the Moon*, published in 1979 and revised in 1986. In the book, Adler focused on earth-centered spirituality and explored for the first time a wide range of belief systems including Witchcraft and Wicca, Neo- and Classical Paganism, Odinism, Druidism, Shamanism, the Church of All Worlds, and the New Reformed Orthodox Order of the Golden Dawn. The book became a landmark work.

In 1988, she married Dr. John Gliedman. American Wiccan high priestess Selena Fox officiated at their handfasting, or rite of marriage, and the *New York Times* covered the event in its society pages—the first handfasting to be so reported.

AGRIPPA (HEINRICH CORNELIUS AGRIPPA VON NETTESHEIM) (1486–1535) One of the most influential occultists of the sixteenth century, Agrippa was a scholar ahead of his time whose interests in the magickal arts nearly caused his condemnation as a witch.

Agrippa was born in Cologne, Germany. He was a superior student at the University of Cologne, mastering eight languages and delving into magick, alchemy, the Kabbalah, and Hermetica. He received a doctorate of divinity in 1509 from the University of Dole in France.

He recorded his extensive knowledge of magick and the occult in a three-volume work, *De Occulta Philosophia*. Within the work, he argued that magick originated not from the Devil but from natural psychic gifts. He reasoned that an individual's will and imagination could fuel magick and that a human being's highest potential could only be achieved by observing and assimilating nature's harmonies. He believed in astrology, numerology, divination, and the power of gemstones. He called the astral body the "chariot of the soul" and maintained that it could leave the physical body.

His radical views and his sharp temper kept him drifting from job to job across Europe for years. The Church denounced him as a heretic, and infuriated civic authorities often ran him out of town. His most infamous incident occurred in Germany when he successfully defended a woman accused of witchcraft.

At the woman's trial, the principal evidence presented was the fact that her mother had been burned as a witch. Agrippa offered a theological defense, stating that the daughter could be separated from Christ only by her own sin, not by the sin of her mother. The woman's acquittal so outraged the Inquisitor that he threatened to indict Agrippa for aiding a witch. That incident solidified support for the conclusion that Agrippa himself was a witch.

Agrippa's reputation as a black magick practitioner preceded him wherever he went and generated a collection of amazing tales about his life. Reportedly, Agrippa conjured the spirit of Rome's greatest orator, Cicero, to deliver a lecture for him. At the conclusion of the inspiring oration, the audience was moved to tears.

When traveling, Agrippa purportedly paid for his lodging with gold coins that later turned into seashells in the hands of the innkeepers.

Once, when Agrippa was on the road, a young man gained access to his study, discovered a book of spells on a desk, and started reading aloud. The young man was shocked when a demon materialized, demanding to know why the youth had summoned him. Terrified, the young man stood mute. Enraged, the demon attacked the youth, strangling him and leaving him dead on the floor.

Agrippa found the corpse when he returned and was frantic with horror and confusion. Notifying the authorities or trying to dispose of the body could result in his being accused of murder. What could he do? According to the story, Agrippa conjured the demon that had killed the young man and commanded the fiend to restore life to the corpse. When the corpse had been reinvigorated, Agrippa ordered it to walk to the marketplace and then to collapse, simulating a natural death. However, the strangulation marks on the throat of the corpse were telling and led the authorities to Agrippa. He fled the town to avoid prosecution.

A familiar in the form of a large black dog supposedly accompanied Agrippa wherever he went. As Agrippa lay dying, he said "Begone, wretched animal, the entire cause of my destruction." Upon hearing those words, the familiar ran from the house and jumped into a river.

Several of the tales connected to Agrippa inspired German writer Johann Wolfgang von Goethe when he penned *Faust*.

Toward the end of his life, Agrippa's reputation caught up with him. Around 1530, Charles V jailed Agrippa for one year for heresy. When he was released, he returned to Cologne, but he was tossed out of town and banished from Germany. He sought refuge in France but was jailed for having previously made unkind remarks about the queen mother. After his release, he spent his final days in Grenoble, dying in 1535.

ANDERSON, VICTOR (twentieth century) Victor Anderson cofounded the Faery Tradition of Witchcraft.

Anderson was born in the southwest United States in the early 1900s, and during his childhood, his family relocated to Oregon. There, at the age of 9, he encountered an elderly woman sitting skyclad, naked, in the middle of a circle, tending to brass bowls brimming with herbs and teas. When she revealed to him that he was a Witch, Anderson removed his clothing and underwent a sexual initiation. A vision overtook him. He and the elderly woman floated in darkness, clinging to one another until she transformed herself into the Goddess. Then the vision transitioned Anderson to a place of thick tropical vegetation under an expansive sky studded with stars and a glowing green moon. From out of the thicket, the Horned God approached with phallus erect and a blue flame shooting from his head. The vision dissolved. Anderson found himself in the circle with the elderly woman, and she taught him rituals using the ingredients in the brass bowls. Before Anderson dressed to return home, she cleansed him with oil, butter, and salt.

Subsequently, Anderson joined a coven that practiced a kind of Witchcraft focused on living harmoniously with nature, practicing magick, and celebrating with music and dance. They called the Pagan gods they worshipped "The Old Gods" and "The Old Powers."

After reading Gerald B. Gardner's book, *Witchcraft Today,* Anderson was inspired to establish his own coven. Anderson and family friend Gwydion Pendderwen cofounded the Faery Tradition and cowrote the liturgy used in that Tradition.

BLYMIRE, JOHN (1895–?) John Blymire was at the epicenter of a sensational murder trial that rocked the sleepy Pennsylvania Dutch farm country of York, Pennsylvania, in 1929.

York County, Blymire's birthplace, is an area rich in the lore and superstition of the Pennsylvania Dutch. The early German settlers who established farms in this unique area of the state, still known today as the "hex belt," held strong beliefs in folk magick, witchcraft, and witches. Blymire's father and grandfather were "powwowers," witches who cured illnesses through sorcery, placed hexes on individuals, protected people from hexes, and broke hexes placed by other witches. For the Pennsylvania Dutch, a hex or spell can be either positive or negative and is cast by a powwower or professional witch. The services of the powwower are solicited by an individual and paid for with a voluntary contribution.

During his childhood, Blymire acquired the skills of the powwower by working as an apprentice to his father and grandfather. He experienced his first cure at age 7 when he helped to remedy his grandfather's urinary problem. Despite this initial success, Blymire's skills as a powwower were modest. He quit school at age 13, found work in a cigar factory in York, and lived alone in a succession of rooming houses. After word leaked out that his family had powwowing abilities, Blymire's coworkers brought their health problems to him.

One man suffered from a wheal in his right eye and asked Blymire if he could cure the affliction. Blymire agreed to try and asked the coworker to bring an unwashed supper plate to the factory the next day. Pressing the dirty side of the plate against the infected eye, Blymire chanted mysterious words, threw the plate on the ground, and smashed it into pieces with his feet. Blymire then made the sign of the cross three times on the man's eye and promised that the eye would be healed by the following day. It was.

Blymire's curative powers extended to animals, too. In 1912, an apparently rabid collie ran amok through the streets of York, snarling and foaming at the mouth. As the animal charged a group of workers exiting the cigar factory at the end of their shift, Blymire confronted the dog, uttered an incantation, and made the sign of the cross on the collie's head. Suddenly, the dog ceased foaming at the mouth, licked Blymire's hand, and then followed him home, tail happily wagging. That incident cemented in the mind of the community Blymire's reputation as a powwower. However, soon after, Blymire began experiencing strange symptoms.

Fearing that a jealous powwowing competitor had put a hex on him, Blymire consulted his father and grandfather in an effort to reveal the identity of the hexer. The Pennsylvania Dutch believe that a hex cannot be broken until the name of the one who cast the spell is known. Blymire's father and grandfather could neither discover the identity of the hexer nor remove the spell.

Not knowing what else to do, Blymire left his job at the cigar factory in 1913 and traveled across the county, seeking help from other powwowers and working at odd jobs to pay for the voluntary contributions. No one was able to help him, and soon he was nearly penniless.

His luck and his health seemed to improve after he met 17-year-old Lily Halloway, whom he married in 1917. During the first year of their marriage, Blymire put on some pounds, found a full-time job, and increased his powwowing business. Then dark days returned. Their firstborn son died at five weeks of age. Their second child died after living only three days. Blymire's symptoms returned, and he lost his job. His life took another downward spiral; and eventually, Lily divorced him.

Blymire persisted in trying to unmask the person who had hexed him. In June 1928, he met with Nellie Noll, a powerful witch who revealed the identify of the hexer: Nelson Rehmeyer.

Known as "The Witch of Rehmeyer's Hollow," Rehmeyer was a powwower who lived eight miles away from the Blymire family farm. Rehmeyer had treated Blymire when he had been seriously ill as a child. Blymire had even worked for Rehmeyer, digging potatoes on his farm.

Noll convinced Blymire that Rehmeyer was the culprit by having Blymire stare at the face of George Washington on a dollar bill. As he did, he saw Washington's face vanish and Rehmeyer's face appear. Noll explained the two ways that Blymire could break Rehmeyer's curse. Blymire could steal and burn Rehmeyer's grimoire, a handbook of powwowing magick, or snip a lock of Rehmeyer's hair and bury it deep under ground.

Blymire recruited two accomplices to help with the covert action: John Curry, a friend from the cigar factory; and Wilbert Hess, the son of a local farmer. Both Curry and Hess believed that Rehmeyer had cursed them, too, and were desperate to do anything to end their suffering.

The three visited Rehmeyer's home on a November night with the intention of either taking the book or clipping Rehmeyer's hair. Rehmeyer welcomed the trio, and they spent the evening talking. Sensing the presence of a power stronger than his own, Blymire became frightened and aborted his plot. He and his cohorts left but returned on November 27.

After being welcomed in, Blymire immediately demanded that Rehmeyer surrender his book. When Rehmeyer refused, Blymire became enraged, grabbed him, and started beating him. Curry and Hess joined the fray.

Curry tied up Rehmeyer's legs with rope. Blymire twisted another piece of rope around Rehmeyer's neck, choking him. Hess kicked and pummeled the fallen man repeatedly, and Curry hit Rehmeyer over the head three times with a block of wood. The assaults continued until Rehmeyer moaned one final time and then died. "Thank God! The witch is dead!" Blymire shouted. The men tore the house apart, searching unsuccessfully for the book, then took less than $3 in change that they found and left.

A neighbor discovered Rehmeyer's body on November 30 and notified the police. The evidence trail led to Blymire who confessed and exulted that he had killed the witch who had cursed him. He and his accomplices were arrested, and their story—dubbed the "voodoo murder"—exploded in the media. Reporters from all over the world exposed the use of folk magick and the belief in superstitions among the Pennsylvania Dutch and generated enough negative publicity to anger presiding judge Ray P. Sherwood. Sherwood instructed the attorneys for the defendants that he would not admit evidence of or allow references to witchcraft during the proceedings.

The trials began on January 9, 1929. The motive for the murder was established as robbery. Expunged of their references to powwowing and hexes, the confessions were admitted into evidence. Although the jury might have been sympathetic had they known the full story, they delivered guilty verdicts on the counts of murder in the first degree for Blymire and Curry. They found Hess guilty of murder in the second degree.

The men were sentenced on January 14. Blymire and Curry received life imprisonment, and Hess received ten to twenty years. Curry and Hess were released on parole in 1934, while Blymire was released on parole in 1953. All three returned to York County, living out their days peacefully in quiet, rural Pennsylvania Dutch country.

BUCKLAND, RAYMOND (1934–) An Englishman who settled in America in 1962, Raymond Buckland is credited with introducing modern Witchcraft to the United States, founding the tradition of Seax-Wica and serving as one of Witchcraft's primary spokespersons for more than twenty years.

Buckland was born in London and reared spiritually in the Church of England. When Buckland was about 12, an uncle introduced him to Spiritualism and the occult, which sparked further interest in Witchcraft and magick. After graduation from King's College School and service in the Royal Air Force, Buckland immigrated to the United States.

The books *The Witch-Cult in Western Europe* by Margaret A. Murray and *Witchcraft Today* by Gerald B. Gardner influenced Buckland to follow the path of the Craft. He was so impressed with the latter that he wrote to Gardner, and the two forged a relationship through their mail and telephone communications. Eventually, Gardner designated Buckland as his United States spokesperson.

Buckland was initiated by Gardner's high priestess, Lady Olwen (Monique Wilson), in Perth, Scotland, in 1963. Buckland returned to the United States to establish his own coven and to begin a Museum of Witchcraft and Magic similar to the museum that Gardner operated on the Isle of Man.

Buckland solidified his reputation as spokesperson for the Craft with the publications of *A Pocket Guide to the Supernatural, Witchcraft Ancient and Modern,* and *Practical Candleburning Rituals.* By 1973, Buckland's museum collection had outgrown his Long Island basement, so he rented a building to house the artifacts and resigned from his job at British Airways to operate full-time the first Museum of Witchcraft and Magic established in the United States.

Unfortunately, Buckland's personal life went into a tailspin. His marriage ended, he relinquished leadership of his coven to his high priest and high priestess, and he relocated to New Hampshire. There he met his second wife, reestablished the museum, and left the Gardnerian tradition.

Buckland had become disenchanted with Gardnerian Witchcraft and decided to create a new egalitarian tradition based on the Saxon heritage. He called this Seax-Wica. In 1977, Buckland opened a correspondence school, the Seax-Wica Seminary, which educated students worldwide until the operation closed in the 1980s.

When his second marriage ended after nearly ten years, Buckland closed the museum and married Tara Cochran. The couple relocated to San Diego and practiced Witchcraft as solitaries.

Buckland published his eleventh book, *Buckland's Complete Book of Witchcraft*, in 1986 and has written screenplays, novels, and newspaper and magazine articles. He lectures at universities and serves as technical advisor for films and plays concerning the occult.

BUDAPEST, Z. (1940–) Hungarian-born Z. Budapest, born Zsusanna Mokcsay, established the main branch of feminist Dianic Wicca.

According to Budapest, her family history boasts a long lineage of women herbalists and healers, including her grandmother, Ilona, with whom Budapest has a strong spiritual connection. In 1943, when Budapest was 3 years old, the death apparition of her grandmother appeared to bid her farewell; and since then, Ilona has remained a protective spirit for her.

The Hungarian revolt of 1956 drove Budapest from her homeland to Austria. There she continued her education and received a scholarship to attend the University of Chicago.

Budapest settled in the United States, married, and raised two sons. When her marriage ended in 1970, Budapest moved to California. She attended a rally in Los Angeles commemorating the fiftieth anniversary of women's suffrage, and was attracted to the feminist movement.

Budapest took a staff position at a local women's center. She became enlightened about the pain women suffered in a male-dominated society and in a religion that focused on a male supreme deity. Realizing that women could be helped by a female-centered theology, Budapest gathered together a half dozen friends and held sabbats that honored the Goddess.

On the winter solstice in 1971, Budapest established the Susan B. Anthony Coven. By 1976, the core group numbered nearly forty women. Many coven activities drew close to three hundred participants, and sister covens spread to five other states.

Dianic Wicca became a formidable force in the worlds of Witchcraft and feminism under Budapest's guidance. Her self-published work *The Feminist Book of Lights and Shadows* (later published commercially as *The Holy Book of Women's Mysteries*) oriented practitioners to the rituals, spells, and lore of Dianic Wicca. She also ran a successful shop, The Feminist Wicca.

By the early 1980s, environmental pollution in the Los Angeles area convinced Budapest to relocate to Oakland. She established a new coven, the Laughing Goddess, but internal discord led to its eventual dissolution. Believing that the future of the world depends on "Global Goddess Consciousness," Budapest continues her work by lecturing; training students to become priestesses; and organizing festivals, retreats, and national conferences.

BUTTERS, MARY (circa 1800) "The Carmoney Witch," Mary Butters enjoyed a reputation as a skilled herbalist and spellcaster in her Ireland hometown until a magick ritual turned deadly.

In August 1807, Carmoney, Ireland, resident Alexander Montgomery was frustrated with his cow. Although she was a good milk producer, no butter could be churned from her output. When his wife suggested that the cow was bewitched, Montgomery hired Mary Butters, "The Carmoney Witch," to perform an exorcism.

With her sack of magickal ingredients, Butters arrived at the Montgomery farm. She dispatched Montgomery and a young man named Carnaghan to the barn where she directed them to stand by the cow's head with their coats turned inside out. She instructed the pair to remain there until she summoned them.

In the kitchen, Mrs. Montgomery, her son, and an elderly woman named Margaret Lee watched Butters prepare the ritual. Butters sealed the windows, doors, and chimney. Then she placed a large pot on the fire; added milk, needles, pins, and crooked nails; and stirred the mixture slowly.

In the barn, as the hours ticked by, both Montgomery and Carnaghan grew worried. At dawn, the two hurried to the house where they discovered everyone prostrate on the floor. Mrs. Montgomery and her son were dead, and Lee died several minutes later. Butters was barely alive but survived.

An inquest was held on August 19 during which a determination was made that the unfortunates had suffocated as a result of Butter's smoke and "noxious ingredients." In her defense, Butters reported that a black man carrying a large club had appeared during the spell. She claimed that he struck each person with the weapon, killing Mrs. Montgomery and her son and knocking Lee unconscious. Butters stated that she was merely stunned by the blow.

Butters was to have stood trial in Carricfergus in March 1808, but the charges against her were withdrawn. Despite the tragic circumstances, the Butters incident was transformed into a comical ballad that derided the participants. The song became popular in the community.

CABOT, LAURIE (1933–) "The Official Witch of Salem," Laurie Cabot founded the Witchcraft As A Science tradition and the Witches League for Public Awareness, a United States-based organization dedicated to ending prejudice and bigotry toward Witches and Witchcraft.

From the time she was a child, Cabot felt a connection to Witches. Her father was a descendant of the Cabots from the Isle of Jersey, an island off the coast of England well known for Witchcraft, and Cabot believes that her Witchcraft lineage stretches back some five thousand years.

Her skills at extrasensory perception blossomed by age 6. During adolescence, Cabot's interests in comparative religions, science, Witchcraft, the occult, and the paranormal led to her becoming schooled in the Craft. She was initiated at the age of 16.

In the late 1960s, Cabot moved from Boston to Salem, Massachusetts, vowing to live her life as a Witch and to teach the public about Witchcraft as a science. She adopted the daily dress of a long black robe, shining pentacle, and black eye makeup which exposed her to ongoing ridicule from the general public and criticism from other Witches. Undeterred, Cabot taught courses in Witchcraft as a science in high school and college continuing education programs; provided tarot-card and aura readings; worked occasionally with police departments across the country to solve crimes; and ran the successful enterprise, Crow Haven Corner, one of the major tourist attractions of Salem.

In 1973, Cabot organized Salem's first Witches' Ball, a costume party that celebrates Samhain or All Hallow's Eve. The occasion has since become an annual event in Salem, bringing together participants and media representatives from around the world. In 1977, Massachusetts Governor Michael Dukakis bestowed upon Cabot the title of "The Official Witch of Salem."

Eleven years later, Cabot founded the Temple of Isis, a chapter of the National Alliance of Pantheists. She became an ordained minister through the National Alliance of Pantheists, and she founded a school of her own through which she teaches her unique approach to the Craft.

In 1986, Cabot protested the filming of John Updike's *The Witches of Eastwick* because Cabot believed the movie reinforced inaccurate, negative stereotypes about Witches and Devil worship. In response, she established the Witches League for Public Awareness to educate the public and effect an end to prejudice and bigotry toward Witches and Witchcraft.

CROWLEY, ALEISTER (1875–1947) Maligned by some and esteemed by others, occultist Aleister Crowley is considered by many to be the greatest practitioner of magick of the twentieth century. Born in Warwickshire, England, Crowley believed himself to be the reincarnated spirit of great occultists such as Pope Alexander VI and Eliphas Levi. Crowley became interested in the occult as an adolescent and harbored fantasies about meeting a wicked, independent scarlet woman who would degrade him.

Reading Arthur Edward Wait's *The Book of Black Magic and of Pacts* persuaded Crowley to pursue magick as a vocation. In 1898, he joined the Hermetic Order of the Golden Dawn, discovered his natural facility for magick, and advanced swiftly through the hierarchy. Quarrels with the chief of the Order as well as with other members resulted in Crowley's subsequent expulsion.

Crowley continued his studies on his own, traveling widely and absorbing the wisdom of Buddhism, Tantric Yoga, and the *I Ching*. His learning prepared him well for a series of communications he reportedly received from Aiwass, a spirit from the astral plane whom Crowley described as his Holy Guardian Angel. Crowley further identified Aiwass as a solar-phallic energy that was worshipped by the Sumerians and the Egyptians.

For one hour on each of three consecutive days in April 1904, the voice of Aiwass manifested itself to Crowley and dictated the text of Crowley's *The Book of the Law*. The volume contains the Law of Thelema: "Do what thou wilt shall be the whole of the Law," meaning that a person must do what he or she must do and nothing else.

Crowley used enochian magick to communicate with angels and spirits and to travel through various planes of consciousness. He believed that by 1909 he had united his own consciousness with the universal consciousness, and by 1921 he believed that he had attained the very top of the occult hierarchy, Ipissimus, and had been transformed into a god. In 1922, Crowley became head of the magickal order, Ordo Templi Orientis.

On the earth plane, Crowley was married twice but had relationships with a series of scarlet women, including Leah Hirsig. She indulged Crowley's baser instincts with alcohol, drugs, and sexual magick. Crowley spent his later years in poor health, including being addicted to heroin, and in financial decline. At his death in 1947, he left a body of published works, both fiction and nonfiction, as his legacy. Many regard his book *Magick in Theory and Practice* as one of the best books about ceremonial magick.

FOX, SELENA (1949–) Selena Fox is an American Wiccan high priestess who founded Circle Sanctuary, a legally recognized Wiccan church that has a worldwide Pagan ministry, and Wiccan Shamanism, a religion that blends Witchcraft rituals, contemporary psychology, and shamanistic practices.

Fox's fundamentalist Southern Baptist upbringing in Virginia clashed with the psychic visions and out-of-body experiences she had as a child. As a teenager, she devoured books on parapsychology, developed her skills at tarot-card readings, and eventually left the church.

Fox attended the College of William and Mary where, as president of the classics honor society, she led a reenactment of a Pagan rite of spring. This was her first Pagan ritual. After receiving a bachelor of science degree in psychology in 1971, Fox met a Hereditary Witch who introduced her to the Craft. Fox realized that the Wiccan religion was her spiritual path.

During a meditation in October 1974, Fox envisioned the concept, name, and logo for Circle Sanctuary, also called Circle, which began as an informal coven near Madison, Wisconsin. Fox and her then-partner Jim Alan developed the chants and songs used in the group.

Circle expanded into a leadership role in the Neo-Pagan community, offering a networking service, sponsoring gatherings, and providing information on the movement to the media and the public. In 1978, Fox incorporated Circle Sanctuary as a Wiccan church and worked full-time in her ministry. Circle Sanctuary is headquartered on a nature preserve located near Barneveld and Mt. Horeb, Wisconsin.

Fox presents lectures, workshops, and seminars on Paganism throughout North America and offers spiritual healing services such as nature therapy, dream work, and guided visualization. She serves as a media spokesperson for Wicca and Paganism and is a leading activist for Pagan religious freedom. In 1985, Fox led the fight to defeat in the United States Congress the Helms Amendment which would have eliminated tax-exempt status for Wiccan churches.

Fox created Wiccan Shamanism, an ecumenical and multicultural religion that incorporates outdoor rituals at sacred nature locations; drumming, dancing, and using rattles; meditation; group and one-on-one healing sessions; dreamcraft; positive magick; and herbology.

GARDNER, GERALD B. (1884–1964) Christened by the English media as "Britain's Chief Witch," Gerald B. Gardner helped to revive the practice of Witchcraft during the twentieth century and is known as the father of modern Witchcraft.

Born near Liverpool, England, Gardner claimed that his family roots extended to an ancestor, Grissell Gairdner, who was burned as a witch during the 1600s in Newburgh, Scotland. Gardner's grandmother was reportedly a Witch, and several distant relations were said to have been gifted with psychic abilities.

His attraction to spirituality was stimulated during the years he worked on tea and rubber plantations and in civil service to the British government in the Far East. In 1936, he retired from government work and settled with his wife in Hampshire, England. In the New Forest region, Gardner was introduced to members of the Fellowship of Crotona, a Masonic order with interests in the occult. The group established "The First Rosicrucian Theatre in England," which staged plays dealing with occult themes.

Operating within the Fellowship of Crotona was a secret sect whose members believed themselves to be Hereditary Witches descended from those who had practiced the Craft since the Middle Ages. Their high priestess was Old Dorothy Clutterbuck, and she initiated Gardner into the coven in 1939.

After World War II began, fear was rampant that Hitler would invade England. For Lammas (August 1) in 1940 Gardner, the other members of his coven, and Witches from covens in southern England converged in the New Forest for "Operation Cone of Power." Hundreds of skyclad Witches formed a magick circle and raised psychic energy to prevent Hitler's armies from crossing the sea. The energy drain of the ritual was believed to have contributed to the subsequent deaths of five Witches. Gardner maintained that this was the most notable modern-day use of a cone of power.

In 1946, Gardner met Aleister Crowley, who made Gardner an honorary member of the magickal order Ordo Templi Orientis. According to some sources, Gardner obtained from Crowley information about Craft rituals that Gardner later blended into his own.

Following the repeal of the English law against Witchcraft, Gardner became the "resident Witch" at the Museum of Witchcraft and Magic on the Isle of Man. Gardner acquired the museum from its owner, Cecil Williamson, and contributed his extensive collection of Witchcraft artifacts to the museum. He also established his own coven, initiating Doreen Valiente in 1953. The two collaborated on ritual and nonritual material that formed the Book of Shadows for the tradition of modern Witchcraft that would eventually bear Gardner's name.

Gardner wrote two novels about the Craft before the repeal of the law against Witchcraft, and his first nonfiction book, *Witchcraft Today*, debuted in 1954 with an introduction written by Margaret A. Murray. The book generated intense interest in Witchcraft, thrusting Gardner into the media spotlight and causing new covens to sprout up throughout England. He published a follow-up book, *The Meaning of Witchcraft*, in 1959.

In 1963, just prior to leaving for Lebanon for the winter, Gardner met Englishman Raymond Buckland, who carried the Gardnerian tradition to the United States. On Gardner's return trip by boat from Lebanon, he died of heart failure on February 12, 1964. Gardner's influence on modern Witchcraft remains strong today.

GLENDOWER, OWEN (circa 1350 to circa 1416) The Welsh leader known as "King of the Witches," Owen Glendower led a successful albeit short-lived revolt against Henry IV of England in the early 1400s.

Believing himself descended from Prince Llewelyn ap Gruffud, Glendower initiated a guerrilla war against the English with help from his allies, the Percy family and the throne of France. Within a few years, most of the English had fled Wales; and in 1405, Glendower established his own parliament. However, by 1409 the military superiority of the English, led by the future Henry V, had stripped Glendower of his power.

Despite being vanquished by the English, Glendower sustained the devotion of his followers. His followers worshipped the Great Goddess and recognized Glendower's claim that he was her earthly consort. Legends relate that Glendower made human sacrifices to and engaged in ceremonial sexual intercourse with the Great Goddess.

Five centuries later, Alexander Sanders professed himself to be a direct descendant of Glendower and appropriated the title "King of the Witches" as his own.

GOWDIE, ISOBEL (circa 1662) Self-professed witch Isobel Gowdie was tried for witchcraft in Scotland in 1662 after revealing scandalous stories about participating in covens and cavorting with the Devil and his demons.

In the spring of 1662, the austere citizens of Auldearne, Morayshire, in Scotland reeled at the sensational tales they heard from a young, attractive, redheaded neighbor, Isobel Gowdie. In four confessions offered voluntarily during April and May, Gowdie declared that she was a witch, and she shared the lurid details of her fifteen-year relationship with the Devil.

She proclaimed that she had first encountered the Devil in Auldearne in 1647 when he appeared to her in the shape of a man in gray. After recruiting her for his service, the Devil baptized Gowdie as a witch by biting her shoulder and sucking the wound, sprinkling the blood over her head, and renaming her Janet. Gowdie testified that she was initiated into a coven of thirteen members which held regular sabbats that included dancing, feasting, and sexual orgies with the Devil and his demons.

Gowdie's husband, farmer John Gilbert, was among the most shocked by her disclosures. How was she able to be away without his knowledge? Gowdie explained that she had placed a broomstick next to him in their bed, so he never knew when she was gone.

Gowdie stated that the witches cast spells on beanstalks and rushes by chanting "Horse and Hattock, in the Devil's name," enabling them to fly to the sabbats. Once there, Gowdie related, the witches took turns having sexual intercourse with the Devil. Gowdie revealed that the Devil possessed enormous genitals; that his large, scaly penis made penetration excruciating; and that his semen felt icy cold. But she insisted that having intercourse with the Devil gave her more pleasure than she had ever experienced with a mortal man.

Gowdie also detailed the mischief in which she and the other witches engaged while in service to the Devil. They raised terrible storms by striking a stone with a wet rag while intoning "I knock this rag upon this stone / To raise the wind in the Devil's name / It shall not lie, until I please again." They made fertile farmland sterile by turning over the soil using a miniature plow pulled by toads. They shot magick elf arrows made by fairies at people and animals with the intention of maiming or murdering them.

The authorities immediately seized Gowdie and searched her body for a Devil's mark, a brand made by the Devil on the bodies of his initiates. Finding one, they arrested her and ordered a trial. During the proceedings, Gowdie named the other Auldearne witches and testified that the coven was led by a woman named Jean Marten. Gowdie swore that all of the coven members could transform themselves into animal shapes and that each member had her own familiar. Gowdie testified that she had shot and killed a woman with an elf arrow and that members of the coven had killed several children by making and then destroying clay images of them. She shocked the community further by declaring, "I do not deserve to be seated here at ease and unharmed, but rather to be stretched on an iron rack: nor can my crimes be atoned for, were I to be drawn asunder by wild horses."

Gowdie's fate at the conclusion of her trial is uncertain because the official record is incomplete. However, she and the other members of her coven whom she named were most likely executed.

The coherence of her testimony and the remorse she expressed for her actions have contributed to the debate about Gowdie's motivation for divulging her deeds when she was neither under suspicion nor coerced to confess. Some authorities speculate that Gowdie was insane or emotionally disturbed. Others believe that she used a vivid imagination to counteract a dull existence, that the fantasy became reality for her, and that the only way to fuel the fantasy was to make a public confession. Some think that Gowdie's coven chose her as a Satanic sacrifice, while others suggest that a rift in the coven led Gowdie to expose herself and her associates.

JONES, MARGARET (circa 1648) In 1648, Margaret Jones became the first witch executed in Massachusetts Bay Colony.

Jones was among the early settlers in Massachusetts, and she worked as a midwife and lay healer. When the conditions of her patients worsened, Jones was accused of having a "malignant touch." Her medications supposedly had "extraordinary violent effects."

When patients refused her medical advice, Jones reportedly bewitched them so that "their diseases and hurts continued, with relapse against the ordinary course, and beyond the apprehension of all physicians and surgeons." Jones was also accused of possessing psychic powers: "Some things which she foretold came to pass accordingly; other things she could tell of . . . she had no ordinary means to come to the knowledge of."

She was arrested, jailed, and tried; and a parade of witnesses testified against her. She defended herself vigorously, denounced those who condemned her, but was convicted and sentenced to hang. She was executed in Boston on June 15, 1648. Records at the time recorded: "Her behavior at her trial was intemperate, lying notoriously, and railing upon the jury and the witnesses. In like distemper, she died . . . The same day and hour she was executed, there was a very great tempest at Connecticut, which blew down many trees, etc."

KYTELER, LADY ALICE (circa 1324) Wealthy aristocrat Lady Alice Kyteler of Kilkenny, Ireland, bears a dual distinction. She was the first person tried for witchcraft in the Emerald Isle, and she was among the first of those accused of witchcraft in the Middle Ages to be charged with heresy. Thrice-married Lady Alice Kyteler had inherited much of her vast wealth from her succession of husbands, making her one of the richest widows of the region. When she married a fourth time, husband Sir John le Poer subsequently became ill with a mysterious emaciating disease, and a housemaid suggested that le Poer was a victim of witchcraft. He suspected Kyteler. After le Poer allegedly discovered magick powders and potions in a locked chest belonging to his wife, he was convinced. Le Poer and several of Kyteler's children accused her of having used witchcraft to cause the deaths of her prior husbands and of having used her evil concoctions to cause le Poer's present illness.

Le Poer brought his charges to the Bishop of Ossory, who launched an inquisition in 1324. The Bishop may have been motivated by the desire to root out sorcery, or he may have been prompted by the knowledge that he could confiscate Kyteler's fortune if she was found guilty.

During the investigation, various allegations were made against Kyteler: She had denied God; she ritually sacrificed live animals to the Devil; she caused death and disease among the populace by mixing weird ingredients (such as worms; spiders; fingernails from dead men; hair; and brains from dead, unbaptized infants) in the skull of a decapitated thief; she consorted with a demon named Robin who took the shape of a cat or a hairy black dog; she used witchcraft to foretell the future and to compel her husbands to bequeath their estates to her and to her eldest son, William Outlawe. Witnesses charged that Kyteler had been seen sweeping the streets of Kilkenny with a broom, moving the debris toward the home of her favorite son, chanting: "To the house of William, my son / Hie all the wealth of Kilkenny town."

At the conclusion of the investigation, the Bishop declared that Kyteler was the leader of a coven of sorcerers and sought her arrest. Outlawe came to his mother's defense by rallying the support of the family's influential friends, and the Bishop's efforts were thwarted. Then the Bishop excommunicated Kyteler and ordered her to appear before him. She refused and escaped to Dublin.

In response, the Bishop charged Outlawe with heresy. Kyteler used her influence to have the Bishop arrested, and he was jailed for seventeen days. He retaliated by censuring the diocese; but his interdict was lifted under pressure from the Lord Justice, a friend of Kyteler's family.

The Bishop attempted several other times to have Kyteler arrested, forcing her to flee to England. In Kilkenny, she was tried and convicted of witchcraft in absentia, but she did not serve a sentence for her crimes. Instead, she lived in peace and comfort in England for the remainder of her life. Others fared less well.

Her maid Petronilla was arrested, and the Bishop had her flogged until she admitted that all of the charges against Kyteler were true. Petronilla also named eight others as witches who were part of Lady Alice's coven. Following excommunication, Petronilla was condemned and burned alive in the Kilkenny marketplace on November 3, 1324, making her the first person burned to death for heresy in Ireland. Some of the alleged sorcerers named by Petronilla fled the area before they could be arrested. Others suffered a range of punishments, including banishment from the diocese, excommunication, whipping, and execution by burning.

LAVEAU, MARIE (?1794–1881), (1827–?1897) The famed "Voodoo Queen of New Orleans" who led voodoo worshipers in nineteenth-century Louisiana, Marie Laveau was in reality two women, a mother and daughter who sensationalized the ancient practice of the Vodoun religion in North America.

A free woman of color, the first Marie Laveau was a melange of black, white, and Indian ancestry which contributed to her statuesque beauty. She married in 1819, but her husband left her soon after, and his death was reported five years later. Laveau supported herself as a hairstylist, catering to wealthy white and Creole women in New Orleans. Laveau listened as they revealed secrets about their lives, intrigues concerning their families, and gossip surrounding their friends.

Around 1826, Laveau met a quadroon, a person one-quarter black, from Saint Domingue (now Haiti), Louis Christophe Duminy de Glapion. The pair decided to live together in unwedded bliss. Laveau gave up her hairstyling business, and they started a family that eventually numbered fifteen children. While tending to her tiny ones, Laveau, a devout Catholic, saw opportunities in the practice of voodoo (now referred to as Vodoun), a religion that had arrived on American shores with the first groups of slaves from Africa and the West Indies.

Voodoo practitioners serve a pantheon of gods called loas and believe that the father of the loas is the Great Serpent, Danbhalah-Wedo. Secret rituals and ceremonies can include animal sacrifice, chanting, drumming, dancing, and magick to effect either good or evil.

In southern Louisiana in the early 1800s rumors spread about clandestine rites that slaves conducted at Lake Pontchartrain: worshipping snakes, dancing wildly, drinking to drunkenness, engaging in sexual intercourse, and employing magickal powers to overcome enemies and to ensure favorable futures. Fearing that the slaves were plotting against them, white slave owners pressured the New Orleans Municipal Council to pass a resolution prohibiting blacks from congregating. The 1817 ordinance restricted blacks to gathering only on Sundays and only in a specially designated area in New Orleans called Congo Square. For nearly two decades, most of the blacks who assembled at

Congo Square on Sundays were voodoo practitioners, serving the loas through dancing and singing.

In the early 1830s, Laveau recognized that infighting among the numerous voodoo queens reigning in New Orleans loosened the control of the Sunday Congo Square dances and the secret ceremonies held out in the bayous. Laveau wrested power from the queens through various means, including the use of gris-gris, or voodoo charms.

Laveau transformed the secret ceremonies at Lake Pontchartrain into public exhibitions, inviting the press, the police, and anyone interested in taboo pastimes. She charged admission, creating a profitable business for herself. Laveau incorporated many aspects of Catholicism in the voodoo rites, including incense, holy water, prayer, and images of the saints. She organized secret sex orgies, pairing wealthy white men with alluring black and mixed-race women at an establishment called "Maison Blanche" or White House. Laveau became the star of the Sunday Congo Square dances, arriving before the other attendees and dancing with her snake much to the amazement of the fascinated audience that gathered to watch.

Parlaying the personal secrets she had gained as a hairstylist with her extensive knowledge of magick and her flamboyant personality, Laveau transformed herself into a potent force in the community. Blacks crowned her their queen; and whites flocked to her for potions, spells, and readings. Her fame so saturated the area that consulting Marie Laveau became a fashionable amusement for anyone visiting New Orleans.

In 1869, Laveau, then in her 70s, abdicated her throne. Her successor, daughter Marie Laveau Glapion, moved seamlessly into the role of voodoo queen. She assumed the identity of Marie Laveau, and many outside the circle of voodoo could not discern a difference between mother and daughter.

Born on February 2, 1827, Marie Laveau Glapion shared many of her mother's fine physical features, although she had lighter skin than her mother. Laveau Glapion apprenticed for her role of voodoo queen by working as a hairstylist and then operating a Bourbon Street bar and brothel.

She was renowned as a madam, procuring for white men whatever sexual pleasures they desired. Her parties at Maison Blanche featured vintage wine and champagne, delectable food, and provocative music. The police seldom raided her establishment. Not only did they fear Laveau Glapion and the voodoo power she held, but they also feared the wrath of many of her guests—high-ranking politicians and officials.

When mother Marie died on June 6, 1881, newspapers splashed their pages with accounts of her beauty, her life, her piety and good works with little mention of her association with voodoo. However, the public knew that "The Voodoo Queen of New Orleans" was dead. The notorious public persona of Marie Laveau ended with mother Marie's demise, and thus the career of Laveau Glapion, who had assumed her mother's identity so flawlessly, ended as well. Laveau Glapion faded from the glare of media scrutiny and continued her work in obscurity until her own death, reportedly by drowning during an 1897 storm on Lake Pontchartrain.

The charismatic Marie Laveau reportedly haunts the cemeteries where mother and daughter are buried. Vodoun faithful who seek Laveau's assistance conduct a ritual during which they place an offering of food, money, or flowers on the gravesite; turn around three times; state their petition; then use a red brick to scratch a cross on the tombstone. Some individuals claim to have seen Laveau's spirit in Congo Square, around Lake Pontchartrain, and in the French Quarter.

LEEK, SYBIL (1923–1983) English Witch, astrologer, and author, Sybil Leek publicized the revival of Witchcraft in the Western world during the 1960s.

Leek was born in Midlands, England, to a family of Hereditary Witches with strong psychic abilities. At age 9, Leek met British occultist Aleister Crowley, who predicted that Leek would one day continue the work he had begun. Leek was initiated into the Craft in early adulthood, joined a 700-year-old coven near the Burley area of the New Forest, and ultimately became the coven's high priestess. She experienced a mystical epiphany in the 1950s during a spring walk in the New Forest. A vivid blue light descended upon her, blessing her with a feeling of serenity and with the knowledge that her life's mission was to be an emissary for Witchcraft.

The British media responded enthusiastically to Leek, but the resulting publicity brought a crush of tourists and autograph seekers to her small village and overwhelmed Leek's successful antique business. Under increasing local pressure to denounce Witchcraft, Leek gave up her business and moved from the area. She relocated to the United States in the early 1960s and established herself as an astrologer and author. In 1968, she published her first book, *Diary of a Witch*, which detailed her life as a modern-day practitioner of Witchcraft. The tremendous public response made Leek a media magnet.

Wearing her trademark cape and flowing gown and sometimes bearing her jackdaw Mr. Hotfoot Jackson on her shoulder, Leek made the rounds on the media circuit, educating the masses about Witchcraft and debunking myths and stereotypes about Witches. Leek completed her life's mission by writing more than sixty books; publishing an astrology journal; writing an internationally syndicated column; and speaking to groups about subjects such as the holistic philosophy of Witchcraft, the differences between Witchcraft and Satanism, and the concept of reincarnation.

LEVI, ELIPHAS (1810–1875) Eliphas Levi was a French occultist whose investigations and books stimulated interest in magick during the nineteenth century.

Born in Paris as Alphonse Louis Constant, Levi was drawn to magick and the occult as a young boy. After a failed career as a priest, he assumed the name Magus Eliphas Levi and began investigating the magickal arts. His first experiment with necromancy took place in 1854 when he attempted to conjure the spirit of the ancient Greek practitioner of magick, Apollonius of Tyana. Necromancers summon the spirits of the dead for information about the future.

According to Levi, he prepared for the ritual by eating a vegetarian diet for two weeks and fasting for one week. He also meditated on Apollonius and engaged in imaginary conversations with him. On the appointed day, a white-robed Levi positioned a table covered with white lambskin in the center of his magick chamber, a room adorned with wall mirrors. On each end of the table, he placed a metal bowl containing a lighted taper. His incantations began.

Levi reported that he grew colder and colder as the hours passed and the ritual deepened. After twelve hours, Levi sensed the floor shaking and saw a spirit come into view in one of the mirrors. Three times Levi invited the apparition to materialize. The grayish ghost finally appeared, enveloped in a shroud. The feeling of coldness intensified, filling Levi with fear and making him unable to voice the questions he had intended to ask. The apparition telepathically answered the questions with the responses "death" and "dead." Then Levi watched in horror as the spirit reached out and touched the ritual sword that Levi held. Instantly, Levi's arm lost all sensation. The sword clattered to the floor, and Levi collapsed.

Not certain that he had conjured the spirit of Apollonius, Levi performed subsequent rituals. He claimed that he succeeded in summoning forth Apollonius on several occasions.

Levi's first book, *The Dogma and Ritual of High Magic*, was published in

1861. His other books included *A History of Magic, Transcendental Magic,* and *The Key of Great Mysteries.* Levi is widely known for his drawing of "the Baphomet of Mendes," a compilation of elements that Levi claimed represented the ultimate power in the universe.

Among Levi's many admirers was the popular English author, Sir Edward Bulwer-Lytton. Levi and Bulwer-Lytton became members of an occult group that studied magick; astrology; mesmerism; and scrying, a method of divination in which the sorcerer concentrates on a shiny object until a vision appears. The Hermetic Order of the Golden Dawn incorporated Levi's magick in their rituals. Born on the day that Levi died, Aleister Crowley believed that he was Levi's reincarnated spirit.

PENDDERWEN, GWYDION (1946–1982) Gwydion Pendderwen cofounded the Faery Tradition with Victor Anderson; contributed a collection of liturgical materials to the Tradition; established Nemeton, which originated as a Neo-Pagan networking organization; and began Forever Forests, an organization dedicated to planting trees and raising ecological consciousness.

Pendderwen was born and raised in California. As a boy, he met Victor Anderson after Anderson halted a fistfight between his son and Pendderwen. Pendderwen grew to be a family friend; Anderson schooled him in Witchcraft and eventually initiated him. The two went on to found the Faery Tradition and create the ritual material for the Tradition, borrowing inspiration from the Alexandrian Book of Shadows.

His interest in Celtic folklore led to his learning Welsh and becoming involved in Celtic nationalism. He served as Court Bard for the Society for Creative Anachronism's Kingdom of the West. Pendderwen gained fame within the Pagan community with his 1972 recording *Songs of the Old Religion,* a beautiful collection of sabbat and seasonal songs as well as love themes to the Goddess.

In 1970, Pendderwen helped establish a Neo-Pagan networking organization, Nemeton, which is the Welsh word for "sacred grove." Regional affiliates contributed to the spread of Wicca and Neo-Paganism across the United States. Nemeton was assimilated into the Church of All Worlds in 1978.

To pursue his artistic endeavors, Pendderwen left his full-time job and retreated to a rural area in Mendocino County. In a cabin without electricity, he and his cat lived a solitary life for a number of years. He became inspired by a Pagan deity of the woodlands, the Green Man, which led to Pendderwen's planting trees in the area each winter. Forever Forests grew from this effort, because Pendderwen believed that organized, yearly tree plantings could honor Mother Earth and raise ecological consciousness.

Pendderwen traded his solitary existence for a more public life in 1980. He performed at the first Pagan Spirit Gathering, organized tree planting events, and protested against nuclear power plants. An automobile accident in 1982 ended his life.

PICKINGILL, OLD GEORGE (1816–1909) An influential individual in English Witchcraft, Old George Pickingill claimed to be a Hereditary Witch who could trace his ancestry back to the eleventh century.

Born in Hockley, Essex, in East Anglia, Pickingill claimed that his family's Witchcraft roots began with Julia, the "Witch of Brandon," who lived in a village north of Thetford in Norfolk. Family legend held that in 1071 Julia was commissioned to murmur chants for the dual purpose of inspiring Hereward the Wake's soldiers in their battle against the Normans and confusing the enemy so that their attack would fail. Unfortunately, the Normans burned Julia's village, and she was killed in the conflagration.

Julia's descendant, Old George, carried on the family tradition of worshipping the Horned God. Pickingill was a staunch and open anti-Christian, and he influenced the establishment of the Rosicrucian Society of England and the Hermetic Order of the Golden Dawn.

During a sixty-year period, Pickingill formed the Nine Covens, a group of covens located in Hertfordshire, Essex, Hampshire, Sussex, and Norfolk. Leaders were Hereditary Witches; both men and women could be admitted, but only women performed the rituals. Two notable initiates were said to have been Aleister Crowley and Gerald B. Gardner. Reportedly, Pickingill also led an all-female coven, the Seven Witches of Canewdon.

Pickingill worked as a farmer in the Canewdon district. To his neighbors, he was an irascible, enigmatic man who used magick as a blackmail weapon. If his neighbors failed to supply him with beer, Pickingill threatened to cast spells that would halt their farm machinery. Neighbors whispered that Pickingill enjoyed relaxing by his hedge and smoking his pipe while hundreds of imps harvested his fields. Few people dropped in on him unexpectedly, and those that were invited arrived fearful and left relieved. Many were glad to hear of his death in 1909, and several persons who went to his house to make sure that Pickingill was really dead reported seeing imps skulking about his bedroom.

SANDERS, ALEXANDER (1926–1988) The flamboyant founder of the

Alexandrian Tradition, Alexander Sanders led a sensational life as a Witch and psychic, grabbing headlines in the British press during the 1960s for his astounding yet dubious feats of magick.

Much myth surrounds the larger-than-life figure of the man who called himself Alexander Sanders. According to Sanders, he was born in Manchester, England, where at age 7 he was initiated into the Craft by his grandmother, Mary Bibby.

The ceremony occurred serendipitously. Sanders wandered into the kitchen of his family's home and found his grandmother standing naked in the center of a circle traced on the floor. Declaring that she was a Hereditary Witch, she invited him to join her in the circle, commanded him to strip off his clothes, and then used a knife to nick his scrotum while intoning, "You are one of us now." Sanders borrowed and copied his grandmother's Book of Shadows, learning the rituals of magick at her knee and realizing his natural abilities for clairvoyance and healing touch.

As an adult, Sanders focused his life on using magick to create power and wealth. By 1965, he claimed to have established a hundred covens with more than sixteen hundred initiates. He crowned himself "King of the Witches," believing he was a direct descendent of Owen Glendower, the Welsh leader who had originally borne that title.

The British media found the often-salacious Sanders an irresistible subject and covered his exploits in the tabloids, catapulting him into national prominence in 1969. The publicity spawned a colorful biography, a feature film, and numerous talk-show appearances and speaking engagements. A master media manipulator, Sanders beguiled audiences with stories about his fantastic feats.

He bragged about having created during ritual masturbation a spirit baby that he named Michael. Soon after his creation, Michael vanished to the spirit realm but took periodic control of Sanders, causing him to go wild at parties, hurl insults at people, and engage in other objectionable social behaviors. Sanders reported that as Michael matured he evolved into an invaluable spirit familiar who aided Sanders during healing sessions.

Sanders claimed he banished warts by "wishing them" on a person "who's already ugly, with boil marks I can fill up with the warts," cured heroin addiction and cancer with healing energy, and performed magickal abortions by pointing to the woman's uterus and proclaiming the end of her pregnancy.

Witches were displeased with Sanders's braggadocio, believing that his boastings brought ridicule to the Craft. However, the veneer that was Alexander Sanders eventually crumbled. After the media furor waned, reports surfaced that Sanders had plagiarized most of the materials he used in establishing the Alexandrian Tradition. Experts note how similarly the Alexandrian Tradition parallels the Gardnerian tradition. Ironically, the very term Alexandrian could be considered a misnomer. The man from Manchester had adopted the name Alexander Sanders in place of his own.

STARHAWK (1951–   ) Feminist, peace activist, and author, Starhawk is an American Witch who through her teaching and writing has inspired both men and women to recognize their spirituality and to embrace the Craft.

Starhawk learned Witchcraft during her years as a college student, and one of her teachers was Z. Budapest. Subsequently, Starhawk became a teacher, offering a Witchcraft course at the Bay Area Center for Alternative Education in San Francisco. From the men and women students in that class, Starhawk formed her first coven, Compost; held a formal initiation ceremony; and later served as the coven's high priestess. Following her initiation into the Faery Tradition, she organized a second coven, Honeysuckle, whose members were women.

Starhawk founded a community of women and men in San Francisco which she named Reclaiming. With a mission of "working to unify spirit and politics," Reclaiming offers courses, public rituals, and training in the Goddess tradition. The community has a magazine and a Web site (http://www.reclaiming.org) that connect people from throughout the United States and around the world. Reclaiming also offers Witch Camps, residential, week-long summer programs in ritual and magick held in various locations in the United States, Canada, England, and Germany.

Starhawk's published works include *The Spiral Dance: A Rebirth of the Ancient Religion of the Great Goddess,* the twentieth anniversary edition of which was published in 1999; *Dreaming the Dark: Magic, Sex, and Politics;* and *Truth or Dare: Encounters with Power, Authority and Mystery.* Her first novel, *The Fifth Sacred Thing,* won the Lambda award for Best Gay and Lesbian Science Fiction in 1994. Starhawk is a major contributor to *The Pagan Book of Living and Dying;* was a consultant for the films *Goddess Remembered* and *The Burning Times;* and cowrote the commentary for *Full Circle,* films in the Women's Spirituality series produced by the National Film Board of Canada.

One of the major voices of ecofeminism, Starhawk travels extensively in

North America and Europe, presenting workshops and lectures. As a political activist, Starhawk was among more than five hundred people arrested in a nonviolent blockade that shut down the opening meeting of the World Trade Organization in Seattle, Washington, in 1999. The blockade highlighted concerns about the effects of global free trade on human rights and the environment.

VALIENTE, DOREEN (1922–1999) Considered by many to be the "mother of modern paganism," Doreen Valiente during the 1950s reshaped the liturgy used by Witches and became a guiding force in the evolution of modern Witchcraft.

London-born Doreen Dominy was raised in a Christian home and educated in a convent school which she left at the age of 15, vowing never to return. She had psychic experiences throughout adolescence, and by her late teens she was a skilled clairvoyant. In 1944, she married Casimiro Valiente, who did not approve of his wife's use of her paranormal abilities.

After Britain's Witchcraft Act was repealed, Valiente contacted Gerald B. Gardner, who initiated her as a witch in 1953. Subsequently, Valiente became high priestess of Gardner's New Forest Coven. The material in the coven's Book of Shadows purportedly owed its origins to the rituals Gardner had been given after his initiation by high priestess Old Dorothy Clutterbuck in 1939 and to material written by Aleister Crowley. Collaborating with Gardner, Valiente revised the various liturgical components, deleting large portions of Crowley's material and adding her own poetic words, including "The Charge of the Goddess" and "The Witches' Rune."

Valiente left Gardner's coven in 1957; established a new coven; then was initiated into a traditional, hereditary branch of Witchcraft in 1964.

Through the 1970s, Valiente shared her inclusive view of the Craft with others in numerous articles and three books: *Natural Magic, An ABC of Witchcraft Past and Present,* and *Witchcraft for Tomorrow.* The latter work explained Witchcraft and provided a Book of Shadows for those interested in self-initiation and in establishing covens.

In 1980, Valiente turned detective, investigating the origins of Old Dorothy Clutterbuck. For years Clutterbuck's very existence had been questioned because of a paucity of information about her. In fact, some believed that Clutterbuck had been a figment of Gardner's imagination. On the night of Samhain in 1980, according to Valiente, she and three other Witches gathered together in a forest in the south of England to commune with Clutterbuck's spirit. Valiente asked for a sign that Clutterbuck approved of the planned search. Suddenly, the lantern at the south quarter of the magick circle fell over and its glass shattered. Valiente accepted this as a signal to move forward with her investigation. She searched local documents, and two years later Valiente uncovered Clutterbuck's birth certificate from 1880, her last will and testament, and her 1951 death certificate.

Valiente died in 1999, leaving no close relatives. She chose as the principal beneficiary of her estate the Center for Pagan Studies in Surrey, England. According to Phyllis W. Curott, president emeritus of Covenant of the Goddess, the New York-based umbrella organization for witches: "She was a wise and wild woman, who definitely ran with the British equivalent of wolves."

WEIR, MAJOR THOMAS (1600–1670) Eight years after Isobel Gowdie shocked the citizens of Auldearne, Scotland, with her confessions of being a witch, Thomas Weir stunned the citizens of Edinburgh with his confessions of practicing black magick.

Weir was an exemplary citizen. He had a distinguished military record as a Parliamentarian soldier and had served as commander of the Edinburgh city guard. He was a pious Presbyterian, revered by many as "Angelical Thomas." He was a devoted family man who lived quietly with his sister and his stepdaughter, Margaret Bourdon. Thus, people were incredulous when Weir announced that he was a longtime practitioner of black magick.

He confessed to having a carved thornwood staff through which he worked his spells and demonic rituals. Weir also revealed that he had engaged in incest with his sister, beginning when she was a teenager and continuing until she reached age 50. Then he preyed on other young girls, including his stepdaughter and his servant, Bessie Weems. He also fornicated with animals, including sheep, cows, and his horse.

Disbelief among the populace only spurred Weir to repeat his confessions until the Lord Provost of Edinburgh felt compelled to launch an investigation. A physician was dispatched to assess Weir's mental status, and when the major was declared sane, he and his sister were arrested and charged with sexual crimes and sorcery.

Their trial was held on April 9, 1670. Major Weir faced charges of incest, adultery, fornication, and bestiality. The sorcery charge against him was not mentioned, apparently because the authorities were mortified that such an esteemed Presbyterian had dabbled in diabolical deeds. Weir was convicted and condemned to die. Later, from prison, Weir declared, "I know my sentence of damnation is already sealed in Heaven . . . for I find nothing within me but blackness and darkness, brimstone and burning to the bottom of Hell."

Weir's sister testified that the pair had made a pact with the Devil, described traveling to Musselburgh in 1648 for a meeting with the Devil, and confessed to keeping a familiar that spun enormous quantities of wool for her. She, too, was found guilty and condemned.

On April 11, Major Weir's execution was carried out on Edinburgh's Gallowhill. He was strangled, and his body was burned to ashes. His sister faced her execution the following day in Edinburgh's Grassmarket. She was hanged.

Thomas Weir's death did not lay to rest his notoriety as one of Scotland's most infamous witches. Reports of strange happenings at Weir's former house at the Head of the Bow in Edinburgh swirled throughout the area for centuries. In *Traditions of Edinburgh*, author Robert Chambers reported in 1825 that: "His house, though known to be deserted by everything human, was sometimes observed at midnight to be full of lights, and heard to emit strange sounds, as of dancing, howling, and what is strangest of all, spinning. Some people occasionally saw the Major issue from the low close at midnight, mounted on a black horse without a head, and gallop off in a whirlwind of flame."

ZELL, MORNING GLORY (1948–   ) Priestess, animal lover, teacher, and author Morning Glory Zell is a practitioner of Celtic Pagan Shamanism and with her husband Otter Zell leads the Church of All Worlds.

Morning Glory Zell was born Diana Moore in Long Beach, California, to an abusive father and a deeply religious mother. Zell attended the Methodist church until she was 13 then, becoming disenchanted, changed to the Pentecostal church. Zell sought help from her new pastor in coping with her father's abuse. She was told: Women are subordinate to men, must obey the will of the Lord, and must bear their suffering with courage. With her growing feminist sensibilities offended, Zell left the Pentecostal church; investigated other Christian denominations, Buddhism, and Zen Buddhism; but found the same male-centered theological perspective.

The Vedanta Society first introduced her to the concept of the Goddess. Her exploration of the ancient Greek gods and goddesses acquainted her with Paganism and with the goddess of the moon and the hunt, Diana. Zell felt a connection to her namesake, and at night she sang to the moon and tried to draw it down. The Goddess became a central force in Zell's life, and she embraced Paganism.

From her childhood days, Zell had experienced clairvoyant dreams, and those around her teased her by calling her a witch. At 17, after reading Sybil Leek's *Diary of a Witch*, Zell realized that she was a Witch and also believed that she had been one in previous lives. After high school graduation, Zell left for a month-long wilderness vision quest in Big Sur. Three weeks of fasting and one week of living off the land led to a dramatic self-initiation into the Craft: Zell dove from a cliff into a deep pool of water and pronounced herself a Witch as she swam to shore.

As she immersed herself in Witchcraft studies, Zell's birth name—Diana—posed difficulties for her. Zell had discovered that Artemis had been granted eternal chastity by Zeus and that the Goddess required her human followers to lead celibate lives. Zell desired to marry and to raise a family and thought that her birth name might hinder those goals. Thus, at age 19, Zell renamed herself Morning Glory.

With a new name, Zell abandoned life in California for the open road and the opportunity to join a commune in Eugene, Oregon. Along the way, she met a hitchhiker named Gary with whom she fell in love. The pair joined the commune; and when Zell was 21, they joined their lives in an open marriage. The next year their daughter Rainbow was born.

Zell experienced a clairvoyant dream in 1971 during which she saw the detailed image of a man and knew that she would meet him and have her life forever altered. She met him—Tim "Otter" Zell—in 1973 at the Gnosticon Aquarian festival in St. Paul, Minnesota, where he presented the keynote address. She immediately recognized him from her dream and approached him after his talk. They experienced an instant union of their spirits and knew that they would never part from one another.

Morning Glory ended her marriage to Gary and married Otter in 1974. She became a priestess of the Church of All Worlds (CAW) that Otter had helped to establish.

Formally chartered in 1968, the Church of All Worlds was the first federally recognized Neo-Pagan earth religion in the United States. CAW was also the first Neo-Pagan group to use the term "Pagan" in connection with the so-called "Earth Religions" that emerged in the 1960s. Morning Glory Zell was named vice president of CAW in 1988.

In addition to her work with CAW, Morning Glory Zell is active in wildlife animal rescue. She pursues studies in mythology, history, comparative third world religions, zoology, natural history, and the magickal and psychic arts. She has an extensive collection of Goddess figures from around the world and uses them in conjunction with her lectures, workshops, and classes. She is also a writer with published works of fiction, nonfiction, and poetry to her credit.

TEN

Witches and Witchcraft in Popular Culture

❧

N every age, images of witches and witchcraft have colored the tapestry of popular culture. From folklore, music, and film to television and books, witches exert a magickal, captivating presence. They are the spellcasters, and we are all under their spell.

The malevolent image of witches and witchcraft in folklore is often the first image to which most children are exposed. Some twentieth century psychologists such as Sigmund Freud, Carl Jung, and Bruno Bettelheim have attributed elements of fairy tales to manifestations of universal fears. These universal fears, which are expressed in the stereotyping of witches and witchcraft, are reinforced in other forms of entertainment to which children are exposed as they grow and mature.

FOLKLORE

The magick of tales, fables, and legends—what the Germans call "Marchen"—captivates eager audiences of all ages. German folklorists Jacob and Wilhelm Grimm gathered folktales from the oral and literary traditions of Germany, Scandinavia, Spain, the Netherlands, Ireland, Scotland, England, Serbia, and Finland. Fascinated by the many common, recurring motifs evident in the tales, the Brothers Grimm published *Kinder-und Hausmarchen* in 1812. Generally known as *Grimm's Fairy Tales,* this collection of 210 nursery and household tales was meant for both children and adults.

Readers discovered a rich trove of lore. The Grimms included complete tales, story fragments, and hybrids, as well as scholarly footnotes about the tales. For the hybrids, the Grimms blended two or more undeveloped stories, added and subtracted various elements, and created a single, well-rounded tale. Their compendium circulated widely throughout Germany and eventually around the world. Today translations exist in more than 160 languages, including Inupiat in the Arctic and Swahili in Africa.

The witch is one of the common, recurring motifs evident in the tales of the Brothers Grimm. Some of the tales featuring witches include:

RAPUNZEL. A husband steals fresh, green rampion for his ailing wife from the vegetable garden of a powerful witch. When the witch catches him, she extracts a promise that, in return for all the rampion needed to make the wife well, the couple will give to the witch their firstborn child. After the wife gives birth to a beautiful baby girl, the witch claims the child and names her Rapunzel, another word for rampion.

Rapunzel grows into a beautiful, 12-year-old girl with long, luxuriant golden tresses. Fearing the loss of one so lovely, the witch shuts Rapunzel up in a high tower with neither door nor staircase, only a small window. When the witch visits, she stands beneath the window and calls: "Rapunzel! Rapunzel! Let down your golden hair." Obediently, the girl lets her braided hair fall toward the ground, creating a ladder for the witch to climb to the tower.

Life in the tower is lonely for Rapunzel, and she eases her solitude by singing. A prince riding through the forest hears her melodious voice and follows it to the tower. There he witnesses the ritual of the witch calling for Rapunzel to let down her hair and the witch scurrying up the flaxen ladder. When the witch leaves, the prince calls out to Rapunzel to let down her hair, and he makes haste to the tower window.

At first, Rapunzel is alarmed when the handsome prince enters the room. However, he is so charming that they talk happily for hours and soon find that they are in love. The prince asks Rapunzel to be his wife, and she agrees. But how will she escape from the tower? She asks him to bring skeins of silk that she can weave into a long, sturdy ladder that will assist in her departure.

The silken ladder grows longer and stronger and is almost finished. However, by mistake, Rapunzel reveals to the witch that the prince has been a frequent visitor. Enraged that Rapunzel has deceived her, the witch cuts off Rapunzel's hair and banishes her to a remote part of the forest.

That night when the prince returns to the tower, the witch lets down the severed locks of Rapunzel's hair for him to climb. He is shocked when he encounters the witch who tells him that he will never see Rapunzel again. In grief and despair, the prince leaps from the tower window and lands in a thorny thicket that blinds him. Sad and sightless, the prince wanders aimlessly through the forest until he hears the melodious voice of his beloved. He follows the sound, and the prince and Rapunzel are reunited. Her tears of joy fall into his eyes, and his sight is restored. They live happily ever after.

JORINDA AND JORINGEL. A beautiful maiden named Jorinda promises to marry a handsome youth named Joringel, and they spend their courtship days enjoying each other's company during long walks in the nearby forest.

In an old castle in the middle of the forest lives a witch who can turn herself into a cat or an owl. In these shapes, she hunts for birds and wild beasts that she captures for her supper. The witch also guards the castle grounds from trespassers. If a man comes too near the castle, she casts a spell that forces him to stand frozen to the spot until the witch chooses to release him. If a lovely maiden comes too near the castle, the witch casts a spell that changes the girl into a bird then shuts the bird in a cage and takes it into the castle.

One day while walking hand in hand in the forest, Jorinda and Joringel lose their way and soon find themselves outside the witch's castle. Above them, a screech owl with red glowing eyes circles Jorinda and Joringel three times ᵗʰen lands behind a bush. From behind the bush the witch emerges. Suddenly, ⁱᵃ is transformed into a nightingale, while Joringel becomes rooted to the witch places Jorinda in a cage.

ⁱeads with the witch to return his beloved, but the witch tells him that he will never see Jorinda again. The witch hurries to the castle with the caged Jorinda and removes the spell from Joringel, who falls to the ground, weeping piteously. At last, he walks forlornly back to the village.

That night, Joringel dreams of finding a blood-red flower in the center of which is a large, luminescent pearl. In the dream, he plucks the flower and takes it to the castle. Everything he touches with the flower becomes free of the witch's enchantment. The dream also tells him that this is the means by which he can free Jorinda.

The next day, Joringel sets off to search over hill and dale for the mysterious flower. On the ninth day, he discovers a deep-red flower in the center of which is a large dewdrop, much like a pearl. Joringel carries the flower to the witch's castle. He touches the flower to the door of the castle, and it springs open. He follows the sound of chirping to a great hall where he sees cages filled with thousands of birds. When the witch spies Joringel, she casts her spell to freeze him to the spot, but the mysterious flower protects him. He leaps to her side, touches her with the flower, and her magickal powers cease. The witch flees the castle.

Joringel then touches the flower to each of the caged birds, changing them all back into maidens. When at last he finds the nightingale that is Jorinda in disguise, he is joyous. He touches the flower to the bird's soft feathers, and Jorinda stands before him. They hug each other tightly and then lead the maidens back to the village. Jorinda and Joringel live happily ever after.

MRS. GERTRUDE. Mrs. Gertrude is an old woman who lives in a weird little house at the edge of a small village. The villagers gossip about her, whispering that very peculiar things happen at Mrs. Gertrude's house. A curious little girl overhears the stories. She asks her parents if she may go to Mrs. Gertrude's house to see for herself the strange doings that occur there. Her parents forbid her to go, explaining that Mrs. Gertrude is a wicked witch who does evil things. But the inquisitive little girl, who is also both stubborn and willful, ignores the warning of her parents and goes anyway.

After peeking through Mrs. Gertrude's window, the little girl trembles and falls to the ground at the wonders she has seen. Mrs. Gertrude finds the little girl, looking pale and frightened. The little girl tells her that she saw a black man in Mrs. Gertrude's house. Mrs. Gertrude tells the little girl that the black man was a coal miner.

The little girl tells her that she also saw a green man in Mrs. Gertrude's house. Mrs. Gertrude tells the little girl that the green man was a hunter. The little girl tells her that she next saw a red man in Mrs. Gertrude's house. Mrs. Gertrude tells the little girl that the red man was a butcher.

Then the little girl tells her about the most fearful image she saw: the Devil with flames shooting from his head. A troubled look passes over Mrs. Gertrude's face. "Come inside, dearie," Mrs. Gertrude tells her. "You will see that there is nothing to fear, and you will brighten up my poor little house."

When the little girl crosses the threshold, Mrs. Gertrude quickly bolts the door. "You have seen the witch in her true form," Mrs. Gertrude announces. In an instant, she changes the little girl into a log and tosses it onto the fire. As the flames grow higher, Mrs. Gertrude settles down next to the hearth. "How lovely," Mrs. Gertrude says. "The house is brighter already."

Tales from the Brothers Grimm introduced magick and mystery to readers, beginning in 1812. Five years later in the United States, magick and mystery visited the Bell family of Tennessee with the arrival of an entity that became known in folklore as the Bell Witch.

THE BELL WITCH

In 1817, the prosperous Bell family owned a thousand-acre farm near Adams, a small town in Robertson County, Tennessee about forty miles north of Nashville. The family patriarch John Bell could boast of having a loving wife, Lucy Williams Bell, and a brood of eight God-fearing children. A devout Baptist, John Bell enjoyed a reputation for being an honest and influential man in the community.

The Bell family's troubles began the day that John Bell strolled through his cornfield inspecting the crop and stumbled upon an unusual creature sitting between the corn rows. The beast resembled a dog, but John had never seen a dog like that before. The farmer shivered as he felt the creature's dark eyes bore into him. Aiming his gun, John pulled the trigger, but the beast disappeared.

John did not give the encounter another thought until several days later when he came across a huge fowl perched on a fence. Thinking the bird was a wild turkey, John took aim with his rifle. The creature flapped enormous wings and flew away. The beast resembled a bird, but John had never seen a bird quite like that before. The fowl's face seemed to have human features.

Soon after these eerie occurrences, mysterious happenings began at the

Bell house. The family heard someone pounding on their back door late at night. Each time a sleepy John Bell stumbled downstairs to see what was the matter, no one was there. The noise then moved inside the house. The family heard rapping sounds in various rooms but upon investigation the sounds ceased. They also heard the sounds of a dog scratching on the floors and an invisible rat gnawing on bedposts. The sounds grew louder as the months went by; and after a year, the volume of the noise was so great that it caused the house to shake.

Family members were shaken at night when next the unseen power yanked the covers off their beds. Reporting on the occurrence years later, youngest son Richard Williams Bell wrote that the power then started "slapping people on the face, especially those who resisted the action of pulling the cover from the bed, and those who came as detectives to expose the trick. The blows were heard distinctly, like the open palm of a heavy hand, while the sting was keenly felt, and it did not neglect to pull my hair."

The entity spared no one in the family, not even 12-year-old Betsy. Richard Williams Bell wrote that the power "chose her as a shining mark for an exhibition of its wicked stratagem and devilish tortures. And never did it cease to practice upon her fears, insult her modesty, stick pins in her body, pinching and bruising her flesh, slapping her cheeks, disheveling and tangling her hair, tormenting her in many ways."

Believing that a person bent on mischief was causing the household commotion, John Bell cautioned every family member to keep secret the turmoil under which the family had been living. However, when living in the house became intolerable, John Bell confided in his nearest neighbor and dearest friend, James Johnson.

Johnson suggested that someone within the family might be the prankster and advised John Bell to call in a group of friends to help unmask the culprit. Each of the friends who came to assist was charged with watching one member of the family. However, according to Richard Williams Bell, "All of their wits were stifled, the demonstrations all the while increasing in force, and sister was so severely punished that Father and Mother became alarmed for her safety when alone, and the neighboring girls came almost every night to keep her company."

To protect Betsy, her parents dispatched her to one of the neighbor's homes, "but it made no difference, the trouble followed her with the same severity, disturbing the family where she went as it did at home." The "trouble" continued at the same time at the Bell home, which had by this time become the gathering place for people of the community, desiring to communicate with the unseen power. According to Richard Williams Bell, "It commenced whistling when spoken to, in a low, broken sound, as if trying to speak in a whistling voice, and in this way it progressed, developing until the whistling sound was changed to a weak, faltering whisper, uttering indistinct words. The voice, however, gradually gained strength in articulating, and soon the utterances became distinct in a low whisper, so as to be understood in the absence of any other noise."

The entity was asked repeatedly to identify itself and replied with a different answer each time. At first the entity declared, "I am a Spirit from everywhere, Heaven, Hell, the Earth. I'm in the air, in houses, any place at any time." Another time it responded, "I am nothing more or less than old Kate Batts' witch, and I'm determined to haunt and torment Old Jack Bell as long as he lives."

Kate Batts was a well-known Christian woman in the community. The wife of Frederick Batts, Kate had assumed control of the family business when her husband became disabled. She ran the business successfully but had a reputation for being stubborn, having a mean temper, and unleashing a sharp tongue when provoked. Once, after Kate had had an unsatisfactory business deal with John Bell, she made a public threat to "get" him. Thus, many of Kate's superstitious neighbors called her a "witch" behind her back.

After the entity identified itself with both John Bell and Kate Batts, the community seized upon the commonality and referred to the entity formally as "The Bell Witch" and informally as "Kate."

The Bell Witch was as good as her word, tormenting John Bell and his family for the next three years. John Bell experienced frightening spells during which his face jerked and twisted violently and his tongue swelled enormously. The spells lasted one or two days, after which the witch's anger at John Bell would subside along with his symptoms. Even after he recovered, she continued attacking him.

Richard Williams Bell witnessed a particularly terrifying incident involving his father: "He complained of a blow on his face, which felt like an open hand that almost stunned him. Then his face commenced jerking with fearful contortions. Soon his whole body; and then his shoes would fly off as fast as I could put them on. The situation was trying and made me shudder. I was terrified by the spectacle of the contortions that seized Father, as if to convert him into a very demon to swallow me up. Having finished tying Father's shoes, I raised myself up to hear the reviling sound of derisive songs piercing the air with terrorizing force. As the demoniac shrieks died away in triumphant rejoicing, the spell passed off and I saw tears chasing down Father's yet quivering cheeks."

"Kate" proved to be enigmatic, attacking individuals one moment, playing pranks the next, and even assisting people in trouble. For example, she was a phantasmagorical busybody, prying into the domestic affairs of just about everyone in the community. According to Richard Williams Bell, she "was a great blabbermouth, getting neighbors by the ears, taunting people with their sins and shortcomings." Thus, people in the community began to follow the straight and narrow more straightly and more narrowly lest the witch detect their transgressions and tattle to their neighbors about them.

Kate also assisted people who needed help. One of Betsy Bell's boyfriends decided to explore a local cave—now called "The Bell Witch Cave"—famous for its stalactites. He crawled through the cave on his knees but became stuck in a patch of quicksand. With his candle lost and with no one to hear his cries, the boy thought he would certainly die alone in the dark cave. Suddenly the entire cave was illuminated as if a large lamp had been ignited. Then the boy heard a voice say, "I'll get you out." He had the sensation of strong hands grabbing his legs; and he was pulled out of the quicksand, muddied and nearly suffocated but safe.

Kate also excelled at the art of prophecy. She predicted the coming of the Civil War, the emancipation of slaves, the ascent of the United States as a world power, and the two World Wars. She also predicted the complete destruction of civilization through a fiery cataclysm. Her clairvoyance extended to people in the community, and Kate became adept at giving advice about the more immediate future. For example, Kate warned Betsy Bell repeatedly that if she married her then-beau, Joshua Gardner, the marriage would be a disaster.

The Bell Witch's reputation spread far and wide, bringing people from all parts of the country to John Bell's home. John Bell never failed to provide a meal and a bed at no cost to anyone who came to visit Kate.

One of those who visited Kate was General Andrew Jackson, but Old Hickory did not wish to impose on the hospitality of the Bell family. Jackson and his entourage traveled to the Bell farm on horseback with a wagon loaded with tents and provisions. As they neared the farm, one of the party joked about the correct procedure for eliminating a witch. Suddenly, the wagon halted as if mired in mud. The horses refused to budge and even the strongest men putting their shoulders to the wheel failed to move the wagon. General Jackson reportedly exclaimed, "By the Eternal, it's the witch!" From the bushes near the side of the road, a voice called out, "All right, General, let the wagon move on. I'll see you again tonight." The horses lurched forward, and the wagon moved smoothly along the path to the door of the Bell home.

That evening, Kate made her presence known by the sound of footsteps on the bare floor and by the voice that Jackson had heard in the bushes that afternoon. "All right, General, I'm on hand ready for business." Kate goaded the man who had joked about the best way to destroy a witch: to take a shot at her. He aimed and pulled the trigger, but the gun refused to fire. Then Kate announced that she would teach him a lesson.

Those in the room heard a sound like a punch, and the man fell off his chair. Momentarily dazed, he jumped up screaming that the witch had broken his nose. The front door opened suddenly, and the man dashed out into the night, yelling and running for his life. Later, when Andrew Jackson retold the tale, he was quoted as saying, "I'd rather fight the British at New Orleans than have to fight the Bell Witch."

The Bell Witch soon proved to be too powerful for John Bell. On the morning of December 19, 1820, his family found him in a deep stupor from which he could not be roused. The family members heard Kate bragging, "It's useless for you to try to revive Old Jack. I've got him this time. He'll never get up from that bed again!"

The oldest son, John Jr., rushed to the medicine cupboard to retrieve one of his father's prescriptions. In its place, he found "a smoky looking vial, which was about one-third full of dark colored liquid." When asked about the mysterious vial, Kate replied, "I put it there and gave Old Jack a big dose out of it last night while he was fast asleep, which fixed him." The family tested the medicine on a cat, which whirled around quickly and then died. The vial was tossed into the fire, and a blue flash erupted and shot up the chimney. The next day, John Bell was dead.

His daughter, Betsy, was bereft at his death. The only positive effect seemed to be that Kate was less violent in her attacks on the family. Fifteen-year-old Betsy began to hope that she could find happiness in marriage to Joshua Gardner. But no sooner had Betsy accepted Joshua's proposal of marriage then Kate repeated her oft-said warning, "Don't marry Josh Gardner."

Kate even disrupted Betsy's engagement celebration with tricks and mischief. "Please, Betsy Bell, don't marry Josh Gardner." That was all that the bride-to-be could take. Resigned to the fact that opposing the Bell Witch would be useless, Betsy ended her engagement. Joshua accepted graciously the return of his ring and acknowledged that under the circumstances Betsy had had little choice.

Shortly after the engagement was broken, Betsy's former schoolteacher, Richard Powell, began courting her. They married in 1824.

Apparently, the Bell Witch approved of the match because the entity's effect on the family gradually decreased. The last phenomenon occurred one evening in 1821 when the family sat relaxing by the fire. According to Richard Williams Bell, "Something like a cannonball rolled down the chimney and out into the room, bursting like a smoke ball. A voice clearly called out, 'I am going, and will be gone for seven years. Goodbye to all.'"

In 1828, the promised return of the Bell Witch came to pass. Richard Williams Bell reported that the family heard scratching sounds and had the covers pulled off their beds. He wrote: "We decided not to speak to it and to keep the matter a profound secret. It kept up its disturbances about two weeks and then left forever." Kate also visited the home of John Jr. and promised to return again in 107 years.

In the interim, the marriage of Betsy and Richard Powell endured for seventeen years until his death in 1841. She remained a widow until her death in 1891 at the age of 86. During her life, she never uttered a word about what had happened to her family, despite talk that Betsy had faked the entire episode.

The Bell house was eventually torn down, and over the years various people claimed that the land on which the house had stood was haunted. Others claimed to have experienced strange manifestations in The Bell Witch Cave. The promised return of Kate in 1935 went unfulfilled.

Richard Williams Bell wrote: "People followed every clue, exercised all of their wit, applied all manner of tests, placed unsuspected detectives in and around the house, acted upon all suggestions regarding the suspicion that had been lodged against certain members of the family, and with all their investigations ended in confusion, leaving the affair shrouded in still deeper mystery, which no one to this day has ever been able to account for or explain in any intelligent or satisfactory way."

MUSIC

Music sometimes carries the theme of universal fear established in childhood, that witches are evil and their deeds malevolent. Other times, music centers on the otherworldly quality of witches.

Witches are most often portrayed stereotypically in popular songs ranging from the seductive such as "Witchcraft" to the silly such as "Witch Doctor." Anyone taking a dose of "Love Potion #9" could become "Bewitched, Bothered and Bewildered" by "That Old Black Magic" when listening to the Witches and Witchcraft Top Twenty:

"Abracadabra" by the Steve Miller Band
"Bewitched, Bothered and Bewildered" from *Pal Joey*
"Black Magic Woman" by Santana
"Could It Be Magic" by Barry Manilow
"Ding Dong! The Witch Is Dead" by Fifth Estate, originally from *The Wizard of Oz*
"Do You Believe In Magic" by the Lovin' Spoonful
"Hocus Pocus" by Focus
"Love Potion #9" by the Clovers
"Magic Carpet Ride" by Steppenwolf
"Magic Man" by Heart
"Magic Wand" by Don & Juan
"My Baby Must Be A Magician" by the Marvelettes
"Rhiannon" by Fleetwood Mac
"Season of the Witch" by Donovan Leitch
"That Old Black Magic" by Louis Prima
"We're Off To See the Wizard" from *The Wizard of Oz*
"Witchcraft" by Frank Sinatra
"Witch Doctor" by David Seville
"The Witch Queen of New Orleans" by Redbone
"Witchy Woman" by the Eagles

The Story of "Rhiannon"

Stevie Nicks was inspired to write the song "Rhiannon" after encountering the name in the novel *Triad* by Mary Leader around Halloween in 1974. The ethereal name resonated with Nicks, compelling her to sit down and compose the song in about ten minutes. According to Nicks, she envisioned the song character as a Welsh witch, "a very mystical woman that finds it very, very hard to be tied down in any kind of way, and she's uplifting all through the song." Imagery in "Rhiannon" includes birds, wind, a starless sky, darkness, and heaven. Only later did Nicks discover the genesis of Rhiannon as a Celtic goddess.

In the Celtic religion, Rhiannon is the mare goddess, called Epona in Gaul and Macha in Ireland. She appears in a collection of medieval Welsh tales called *The Mabinogion*.

In the first book of the collection, Pwyll, King of Dyfed, first sees the beautiful Rhiannon astride a white horse, ambling slowly through the Arberth countryside. He falls in love with her. Although Pwyll is on his fastest steed, he cannot overtake the maiden. Rhiannon consents to stop and falls in love with him even though she is betrothed against her will to Gwawl, one of Pwyll's rivals. Pwyll wins Rhiannon from Gwawl; and the couple welcome a son, Pryderi.

Gwawl abducts the child. Rhiannon's maids smear her face with the blood of puppies and falsely accuse her of killing her son. As a punishment, Rhiannon is compelled to serve the royal court as a horse, carrying visitors back and forth. Later, Pryderi is restored to his parents and succeeds his father as ruler of both Dyfed, the beautiful land containing a magick cauldron of plenty, and Annwn, the Otherworld.

In addition to being the mare goddess, Rhiannon is also a muse goddess. The sirens in the ancient Welsh *Triads* as well as in *Romance of Branwen* are called "The Birds of Rhiannon" because of the sweetness of their singing. Birds always accompany Rhiannon as she welcomes the seasons. According to the Rhiannon legend, three of the birds are magickal because their songs have the power to remove pain and suffering. However, the birds—one emerald, one golden, and one snow white—appear only during times of great need, offering solace and healing.

Rhiannon remains an inspiration to superstar Stevie Nicks as evidenced by the evolution of "Rhiannon" since Nicks first composed the song in 1974. In its original incarnation, "Rhiannon" was sung as a slow ballad. In 1975, when Fleetwood Mac recorded the song, "Rhiannon" evolved into its up-tempo version. In 1981, when Nicks launched her first solo tour, she offered her audiences both versions, first as a ballad with just a piano to carry the melody then a rock 'n' roll version with Nicks belting out the song a second time.

She continues concert performances of "Rhiannon" in this way. Additionally, Nicks varies the lyrics to the song as the spirit moves her. For her 1998 boxed set, *Enchanted,* Nicks recorded a simple version of "Rhiannon," offering her strong, clear voice; her talents on the piano; and singer Sharon Celani providing airy, graceful background vocals.

Just as "Rhiannon" is a mutable offering in Nicks's musical catalog, so too is the artist's mystical onstage presence. Nicks enveloped herself in flowing black chiffon in the late 1970s and flowing white chiffon in the early 1980s. She enrobed herself in a hooded velvet cape occasionally. By 1994, Nicks adopted a vintage fringed shawl worn over white chiffon. For the 1998 *Enchanted* tour, Nicks garbed herself in a sparkling gray shawl.

Rhiannon has also inspired Nicks as a visual artist. In 1982, Nicks's best friend, Robin Anderson, was diagnosed with terminal leukemia. Although Nicks had never drawn before, she wanted to create something that Anderson could keep at the end of her bed to remind her of Nicks when they couldn't be together. Nicks painted a portrait of Rhiannon.

That prompted Nicks to create a limited-edition poster of her artwork that was sold at a special benefit concert in Phoenix in 1983. Profits from sales of the poster benefited City of Hope, a cancer research facility. Nicks also allowed the Hard Rock Café to use her Rhiannon painting for a limited-edition series of tee shirts, the sales of which benefited the Special Olympics.

The myth and magick of Rhiannon are infused in superstar Stevie Nicks. As she stated in a 1998 interview on VH1: "I totally believe in magick. Because my life, I think, has been very magick, and magickal things have come true for me time after time after time."

FILM

Through the films in which they are portrayed, images of witches and witchcraft are seared into the minds of moviegoers, sitting in darkened theaters with their gazes drawn to the flickering screen. Here is a retrospective sampling of films that reveal Hollywood's take on witches and witchcraft:

The Wizard of Oz (1939)

The 1939 film was based on the 1900 children's novel, *The Wonderful Wizard of Oz,* by L. Frank Baum. In the film, a tornado whisks Dorothy Gale

(Judy Garland), her house, and her little dog Toto from their Kansas farm to Munchkinland.

The house lands on and kills the Wicked Witch of the East. Her sister, the Wicked Witch of the West (Margaret Hamilton), blames Dorothy for the death and threatens revenge. The Good Witch of the North, Glinda (Billie Burke), bestows upon Dorothy a pair of magickal ruby slippers that belonged to the now-dead Witch. The Wicked Witch of the West desires the slippers for her own.

Wishing to return home, Dorothy travels on the Yellow Brick Road toward the Emerald City in the land of Oz where she hopes to meet the great and powerful Wizard (Frank Morgan) who resides there. Along the way, she encounters a Scarecrow (Ray Bolger) who desires a brain, a Tin Woodman (Jack Haley) who wants a heart, and a Cowardly Lion (Bert Lahr) who needs courage. They all hope that the Wizard of Oz will grant their wishes. When they arrive in the Emerald City, the Wizard grants them an audience and demands, in return for the favors they have asked, that they bring him the broom of the Wicked Witch of the West.

The Winged Monkeys capture Dorothy and Toto and bring them to the castle of the Wicked Witch. The Wicked Witch threatens to kill Dorothy unless she relinquishes the ruby slippers. The Scarecrow, the Tin Woodman, and the Cowardly Lion disguise themselves as the Wicked Witch's guards, enter the castle, and attempt to rescue Dorothy. They are discovered by the Wicked Witch who sets fire to the Scarecrow as a punishment. Dorothy heaves a bucket of water at the Scarecrow to extinguish the flames, and the water splashes on the Wicked Witch. She melts into a steamy puddle on the floor. Dorothy takes her broom, and the friends hurry off to see the Wizard.

After presenting the broom of the "liquidated" Wicked Witch to the Wizard, the friends realize that the Wizard is a fraud. However, the Wizard helps the Scarecrow to understand that he has a wonderful mind, helps the Tin Woodman to feel that he has a tender heart, and helps the Cowardly Lion to believe that he is courageous. The Wizard plans to return to Kansas in a hot-air balloon with Dorothy, but he soars into the ether without her. The Good Witch of the North reappears to reveal to Dorothy that she has always had the power to return home. Dorothy needs only to click the heels of the ruby slippers together three times and to repeat: "There's no place like home."

Dorothy is whisked back to Kansas, to her house, and to her own bedroom where she is reunited with her Uncle Henry (Charley Grapewin) and Auntie

Em (Clara Blandick); the farmhands Hunk (Ray Bolger), Hickory (Jack Haley), and Zeke (Bert Lahr); and Toto, too.

The Wizard of Oz provides a lovely message to viewers that the magick to make one's wishes come true resides inside each person. However, as a counterpoint, the film offers frightening images of witches and witchcraft that were reinforced when, in the days of television, the film became a perennial holiday favorite.

I Married a Witch (1942)

In this saucy fantasy-comedy, a witch (Veronica Lake) executed at Salem, Massachusetts, centuries ago returns to haunt the descendant (Fredric March) of the Puritan who sentenced her to death.

Macbeth (1948)

Shakespeare's play concerning intrigue and murder in Scotland's royal court has been filmed and refilmed since the early years of the twentieth century. However, the production by Orson Welles is a classic. *Macbeth* is one of the major works of literature that strongly influenced the stereotype of witches as evil, old hags.

Commenting on *Macbeth* in *The History of Witchcraft and Demonology* (1926), Montague Summers wrote: "There are few scenes which have so caught the world's fancy as the wild overture to *Macbeth*. In storm and wilderness we are suddenly brought face to face with three mysterious phantasms that ride on the wind and mingle with the mist in thunder, lightning, and in rain. They are not agents of evil, they are evil; nameless, spectral, wholly horrible."

The "three mysterious phantasms" are three unnamed witches gathered on a barren heath as the story unfolds. The ambitious Macbeth seeks their prophecies, and their words induce him to kill Duncan, the king, with disastrous results for Macbeth. As he dies, Macbeth curses the day he first encountered the witches.

The most famous scene occurs in Act IV, Scene 1 which opens with the witches stirring a cauldron containing "eye of newt and toe of frog / wool of bat and tongue of dog / adder's fork and blind-worm's sting / lizard's leg and howlet's wing." They conjure the Greek goddess of witchcraft, Hecate, and other spirits with one of the Bard's most famous couplets: "Double, double toil and trouble; / fire burn and cauldron bubble."

Bell, Book and Candle (1958)

Modern-day witch Gillian Holroyd (Kim Novak) lives happily in a New York City apartment with her Siamese cat familiar, Pyewacket, until the day that handsome publisher Shep Henderson (James Stewart) visits her building. Gillian decides that she must win him, especially when she discovers that he is engaged to an old college rival. Gillian casts a spell over Shep, not realizing that love has put her powers in danger.

Burn, Witch, Burn or *Night of the Eagle (1962)*

Professor Norman Taylor (Peter Wyngarde) derides belief in the supernatural during his college classes then discovers at home that his wife Tansy (Janet Blair) is a practitioner of magick. Despite her protestations that the charms protect their lives and his career, he forces her to destroy the stash of magickal materials. The couple is soon besieged by the curses and spells of faculty wives: witches determined to destroy the Taylors. Posters for the film bearing the teaser "Do the undead demons of Hell still arise to terrorize the world?" capture the essence of how witches and witchcraft are portrayed in the film.

The Conqueror Worm or *Witchfinder General (1968)*

Seventeenth-century witch hunter Matthew Hopkins (Vincent Price) and his sadistic henchman John Stearne (Robert Russell) travel through England, torturing "witches" in order to gain money, power, and sex. After a young soldier (Ian Ogilvy) and his fiancee (Hilary Dwyer) find their world destroyed by the pair, the soldier relentlessly pursues Hopkins and Stearne to exact revenge. This film offered a counterpoint to the usual portrayal of witches as perpetrators of evil and stood in stark contrast to a film from the same year, *Rosemary's Baby.*

Rosemary's Baby (1968)

The publication of Ira Levin's novel *Rosemary's Baby* in 1967 coincided with a resurgence of interest in the occult and with the rise of Neo-Pagan Witchcraft. However, Levin's tale sustained various sensational stereotypes about witches and witchcraft. In the novel, Levin's Devil-worshipping characters refer to themselves as witches. They obey orders from the Devil, and they deliver to him for a satanic rape the woman he has chosen to conceive and bear the Antichrist.

The film version of the novel was directed by Roman Polanski. To assure realism for the rituals and chants, Polanski hired Anton LaVey, founder of the Church of Satan, to serve as an advisor on the film. Not only did LaVey assist in the ritual scenes, he was cast to play Satan in the rape sequence.

In the film, young newlyweds Rosemary (Mia Farrow) and Guy Woodhouse (John Cassavetes) rent an apartment in the sinister-looking Branford building in New York City. From a writer friend, Edward "Hutch" Hutchins (Maurice Evans), they learn about the building's dark past. The building was once home to Adrian Marcato, a witch who claimed to have the power to conjure up the Devil. Cannibal sisters also had resided in the building, and the body of a dead baby was once discovered in the basement.

Rosemary and Guy meet their friendly but odd neighbors, Minnie (Ruth Gordon) and Roman Castevet (Sidney Blackmer). A girl living with the Castevets recently committed suicide. Guy, who is a struggling actor, begins spending time with the couple and learns that they are witches. They promise him professional success if he will allow Rosemary to be raped by Satan, and Guy agrees.

A drugged Rosemary is partially conscious for the ordeal and experiences being surrounded by naked, chanting witches and being raped by a leathery-skinned monster with an enormous penis. However, the next morning Rosemary decides that incident was merely a nightmare.

When Rosemary discovers that she is pregnant, the Castevets persuade her to see Dr. Abraham Saperstein (Ralph Bellamy), who prescribes a daily tonic. Minnie prepares the "vitamin" tonic that contains not fresh herbs but a mysterious substance called "tanis root." The substance, a fungus, is also contained in a silver amulet that the Castevets convince Rosemary to wear. The necklace belonged formerly to the girl who had committed suicide.

Rosemary has a troubled pregnancy which alarms her friend Hutch when he visits and learns about the tanis root. He researches the substance but dies mysteriously before he can bring his findings to Rosemary. At his funeral, Rosemary receives a book, *All of Them Witches,* that Hutch had intended to give her along with a message: "the name is an anagram."

From the book, Rosemary learns about a fungus called "Devil's pepper" that is used in rituals. She reads about the infamous Adrian Marcato and notices that his son's name, Steven, is underlined in the book. She rearranges the letters in the name "Steven Marcato" and deciphers the name "Roman Castevet." Rosemary reads other books on witchcraft and discovers the malevolence of witches. They cast spells that harm or kill people; they use blood and flesh, particularly from babies, in their rituals.

Realizing that she and her baby are in danger, Rosemary turns to both Guy and Dr. Saperstein for help, only to discover that they are part of the conspiracy. Trapped in her apartment by the witches, Rosemary has her baby but is told that it was stillborn. Rosemary discovers later that the baby is alive and being cared for by the Castevets.

Armed with a knife, Rosemary bursts into the Castevets' apartment and finds that the coven has gathered to welcome the Antichrist that they have named Adrian Steven. Rosemary is horrified when she first sees the baby swaddled in black. He has glowing animal eyes, orange hair, and budding horns on his head. The witches soothe her by mentioning that Satan had selected her to be the mother of his child. Rosemary notices the stub of the infant's tail and sees black mittens covering the small, pearly claws on his hands. Fascinated by the creature, she abandons her original plan to kill the baby and herself. Instead, encouraged by the coven members, she mothers the infant, all the while believing that she will be able to divert her child from the path of evil.

Rosemary's Baby had a chilling effect. Viewers were convinced that witches were in league with the Devil, and Wiccans were faced with the task of educating the public about the differences between Neo-Pagan Witchcraft and Satanism. Wiccans faced the same challenge nearly twenty years later when another film about witches and the Devil debuted.

The Witches of Eastwick (1987)

In Updike's 1984 novel, *The Witches of Eastwick,* the three female characters are witches from a sleepy Rhode Island town, and the book perpetuates stereotypes about witches and witchcraft. To relieve the tedium of being single parents and of moving from one lover to another, the women play at the black arts by raising storms, gathering herbs while skyclad, and flying late at night. Each character finds a witch's mark on her body, and all three own large dog familiars.

When Darryl Van Horne relocates to Eastwick, he seduces the women and engages in sexual liaisons with them. His cold bodily fluids and his requests that the women administer the "kiss of shame" are myths associated with the Devil. The women invite Van Horne to join their coven, they indulge in wild parties (sabbats), and the women perform malefic witchcraft.

Not surprisingly, protests erupted when plans to film a screen version of the novel were announced. The producers had originally planned to shoot exterior scenes in Rhode Island. However, in 1986, Laurie Cabot formed the Witches League for Public Awareness (WLPA) to protest the filming. As a result of local protests, the production company moved the location shooting to Cohasset, Massachusetts.

In the film version, the three women characters are only three bored New England women until Darryl Van Horne (Jack Nicholson) appears in Eastwick and brings excitement to their lives. Rich and mysterious, Van Horne moves into a large estate and draws Alexandra (Cher), Jane (Susan Sarandon), and Sukie (Michelle Pfeiffer) into his enchanted world.

They dabble in magick and orgies which are pleasurable forays for a time. Then their spells turn dark. While at a party, Van Horne and the women savor luscious cherries and spit the pits out of their mouths. A rival of the women, Felicia, vomits vast quantities of cherry pits. As Van Horne and the women consume more and more cherries, Felicia continues to vomit and then finally dies.

Alexandra, Jane, and Sukie discover that they are all pregnant by Van Horne. Wishing him to be out of their lives before their babies are born, they construct a likeness of Van Horne in wax and use the figurine to cast out the Devil from their lives. Van Horne leaves amidst amazing special effects which garnered *The Witches of Eastwick* the British equivalent of an Academy Award (BAFTA Film Award) in 1988 for Best Special Effects.

The Witches (1990)

Inspired by the Roald Dahl novel, *The Witches* highlights the attempts of 9-year-old Luke (Jasen Fisher) and his grandmother (Mai Zetterling) to stop the Grand High Witch of the World (Angelica Huston) from turning every child in England into a mouse. Child viewers loved the fantastic critters fashioned for the film by producer Jim Henson's Creature Shop but were also exposed to exaggerated, negative images of witches, including their haglike appearances, their hatred of children, and their poisonous concoctions and diabolical spells.

The Crucible (1996)

Playwright Arthur Miller used the story of the witchcraft hysteria in Salem, Massachusetts, as an allegory about the anti-Communist witch hunting of the early 1950s for his 1953 Broadway play, "The Crucible." Miller penned the screenplay for the 1996 film adaptation.

In the fictional film account, Abigail Williams (Winona Ryder) sneaks out of her house one night to join other young girls in the woods of Salem, Massachusetts, in 1692 for a weird dancing ritual under the full moon. With her dark hair flowing, Abigail drinks rooster blood in a witchcraft charm designed to destroy Elizabeth Proctor (Joan Allen), the wife of the man Abigail loves.

While working as his servant girl, Abigail had an adulterous encounter with John Proctor (Daniel Day-Lewis). He is repentant, and the affair ends when his wife dismisses Abigail. However, Abigail remains in love with him and becomes a young woman scorned.

Abigail's uncle, the Reverend Parris (Bruce Davison) stumbles upon the late night gathering of the girls and accuses them of unholy behavior. Abigail counters his charges with witchcraft accusations against several girls in the village and Elizabeth Proctor. The contagion of false accusations sweeps through the village.

When Judge Danforth (Paul Scofield) is brought to Salem to oversee the trials, he draws a hard line against witchcraft. Then, when evidence against the accused evaporates, he finds retreat impossible. The accused are compelled to confess their guilt or be hanged with tragic results.

Practical Magic (1998)

Based on Alice Hoffman's 1995 novel, *Practical Magic* offers a more enlightened approach to witches and witchcraft compared to other films. However, the film contains some sensational elements that fall within the realm of stereotypes.

The film opens with a flashback sequence. Maria Owens (Caprice Benedetti) is hanged as a witch in Puritan New England; and Maria's young descendants, Sally (Camilla Belle) and Gillian (Lora Anne Criswell) Owens, are orphaned as children. Sent to live with their Aunt Frances (Stockard Channing) and Aunt Jet (Dianne Wiest), the girls are raised unconventionally in a large Victorian house by the sea where their aunts teach them the ancient arts of witchcraft.

The girls learn about the family curse that is their legacy: Any man who falls in love with an Owens woman will face an untimely death. While Gillian is eager to fall in love, Sally hopes that she will not. To ensure that, Sally performs a spell. She writes down the qualities of the man she will love forever—

he has one blue eye and one green eye, he can flip pancakes in the air, and his favorite shape is a star. Convinced that no such man will ever exist, Sally believes she will be safe from the family curse.

The film flashes forward to an adult Gillian (Nicole Kidman) who has moved west and found adventure with the dark, dangerous Jimmy Angelov (Goran Visnjic) and to grown-up Sally (Sandra Bullock) who is married to Michael (Mark Feuerstein) and is the mother of two daughters. When Michael is killed in an accident, a bereft Sally and her children again move in with the aunts. The aunts reveal that they used magick to bring Michael into Sally's life, and Sally vows that her children will never do magick.

Sally receives a frantic telephone call from Gillian, begging Sally to come to Arizona. When Sally arrives, she discovers that Jimmy has beaten Gillian. Jimmy threatens the sisters with a gun. They spike his bottle of tequila with belladonna to knock him out, but he consumes too much and dies. Fearing that they will be jailed for murder, Sally and Gillian bring his corpse back to their aunts' house and perform a spell to raise him from the dead. The spell works, but death has changed him. He tries to strangle Gillian, and Sally hits him with a cast iron skillet, "killing" him a second time. The sisters bury him in the yard, but he haunts them.

Soon, a police officer, Gary Hallett (Aidan Quinn), who is investigating Jimmy's disappearance, arrives to question Gillian and Sally. Gillian tries to distract Hallett by dressing provocatively. Doubting their stories, Hallett questions people in town and obtains intriguing information about the aunts, their nieces, and their witchcraft. He returns to the Owens's house the next morning, helps with breakfast by flipping pancakes in the air, and discovers a distinctive ring that he knows belonged to Jimmy. Gillian prepares a banishing potion that she adds to Hallett's pancake syrup.

Subsequently, Sally confesses that she and Gillian killed Jimmy, but Sally and Gary realize that they are in love. Sally notices that he has one green eye and one blue eye and that he carries a badge in the shape of a star. They are confused about what to do about their mutual attraction and part.

Jimmy's ghost possesses Gillian's body. The aunts intervene by gathering a coven of neighborhood women and performing a rite of exorcism that releases Jimmy's spirit. Jimmy's death is officially recorded as accidental. Hallett returns to begin a relationship with Sally, and on Halloween night the curse of the Owens women is finally broken for good.

While *Practical Magic* is a clever, funny, and romantic film that presents an enlightened view of witches and witchcraft, certain plot elements provide a sensationalized view.

Contributing to the enlightened view are the following elements: showing the aunts encouraging the magickal skills of their young nieces, showing the spell that Sally hopes will help her avoid the Owens curse, having Sally question Gillian's use of belladonna to control Jimmy, having an employee at Sally's herbal shop explain to customers about the differences between Wicca and Devil worship, allowing Sally's children to attend a Solstice celebration, having Hallett question Sally about her Wiccan beliefs and the craft of magick, showing the star as a talisman with power and reflecting that the aunts are witches with integrity.

Contributing to the sensationalized view are the following elements: depicting the aunts performing a love spell in which they prick a dove's heart with a needle and then accept money in payment for the ritual; using the poison belladonna to control Jimmy; showing witches bringing the dead back to life; showing Gillian as the seductive witch temptress; spiking the pancake syrup with a banishing potion; calling upon strangers to assist with an exorcism; performing the exorcism; and having the Owens women "fly" to the ground while clutching black umbrellas.

The Blair Witch Project (1999)

In 1994, three student filmmakers tote cameras and equipment into Maryland's Black Hills to shoot a documentary about a local legend, The Blair Witch. They interview local people about the witch then hike into the woods to find the house where children were ritualistically murdered in the 1940s, allegedly by an agent of the witch.

That's when they become lost. They stumble upon ominous cairns and strange, runelike stick figures. They hear strange noises. They disappear one by one and are never seen again. One year later, their raw footage—videotape and 16mm black-and-white film—is discovered and pieced together for *The Blair Witch Project,* a purported documentary of the students' last days.

Fabricated for the film, The Blair Witch legend began allegedly in 1785 when a local woman, Elly Kedward, was accused of witchcraft and banished to the woods near Blair where she subsequently died. By midwinter 1786, those who had accused Kedward of witchcraft and half of Blair's children had vanished. Terrified, the townspeople abandon Blair.

In 1824, the town of Burkittsville is founded on the former Blair site. One year later, a swimmer on Tappy East Creek, 10-year-old Eileen Treacle, is pulled under the water by a mysterious woman's hand. The girl's body is never found.

In 1886, search parties are sent into the Burkittsville woods to look for missing 8-year-old Robin Weaver. Later, the child stumbles out of the woods unharmed, but one of the search parties vanishes. Several weeks later, the bodies of the search party members are discovered at Coffin Rock. Their arms and legs are tied together, and they have been disemboweled.

From 1940 to 1941, seven children are kidnapped from the Burkittsville area. In May 1941, police find the bodies of the missing children in the basement of a house deep in the woods near Burkittsville. The house belongs to Rustin Parr, a recluse who confesses to murdering the children. He claims he killed them for the ghost of an old woman who haunts the area around his house. He is tried, convicted, and hanged.

Then in 1994, the three student filmmakers disappear from the woods near Burkittsville.

Although *The Blair Witch Project* is pure fiction packaged in a documentary style, countless viewers of the popular film believed that the student filmmakers (Heather Donahue, Joshua Leonard, and Michael Williams) were real and that the Blair Witch was a genuine phenomenon. Thus, many people also believed the stereotype of the evil, murderous witch that was perpetuated in *The Blair Witch Project.* Another element that rankled Wiccans was the use of Wiccan symbols as catalysts for the horror. *The Blair Witch Project* was a blockbuster hit in the summer of 1999, but in the process, Witchcraft took a sizable hit as well.

Artisan Entertainment and Haxan Films promise a sequel to the film that will hit theaters in fall 2000 and a prequel that will debut in fall 2001. Other offerings include television specials on Showtime and on the Sci Fi Network; Blair Witch, a series of adult novels from Pocket Books; The Blair Witch Files, a series of young adult books from Bantam Books for Young Readers; *Blair Witch Volume 1: Rustin Parr, Blair Witch Volume 2: The Legend of Coffin Rock, Blair Witch Volume 3: The Elly Kedward Tale*, personal computer games from Gathering of Developers; and more than 150 licensed products, including posters, models of props, action figures, and Halloween costumes.

TELEVISION

In contrast to the malevolent portrayal of witches and witchcraft in film, witches on television are benevolent, using their powers for good. Whether appearing in a situation comedy, an action series, or a drama, the witches of television often serve as role models for their fans. Television witches show the power inherent in women and the conflicts modern women face in trying to balance various facets of their lives.

"Bewitched"

"So my wife's a witch. Every married man has to make some adjustments." That was the conclusion drawn by Darrin Stephens (Dick York) in the series premiere of "Bewitched," a fantasy situation comedy that aired on the ABC television network from 1964 to 1972. By extension, television viewers had "to make some adjustments" too, because this series banished the stereotype of the ugly, old witch using her powers for evil. Instead, "Bewitched" showcased a beautiful, young witch using her powers for good, always with hilarious results.

The series focused on the domestic difficulties in the home of witch Samantha Stephens (Elizabeth Montgomery), a suburban housewife, and her mortal husband, Darrin, an advertising executive at the McMann & Tate agency. (Dick York was replaced by Dick Sargent in the role after the fifth season.) Central to the difficulties were Darrin's insistence that Samantha not use her witchcraft under any circumstance and the disruptions created by the couple's family and neighbors and by Darrin's employer.

Samantha's mother, Endora (Agnes Moorehead), delighted in using sorcery to meddle in her daughter's marriage and to prove that her mortal son-in-law was an unsuitable match for her lovely daughter. Samantha's father, Maurice (Maurice Evans), resided in London but popped in occasionally to visit his daughter and to bedevil his put-upon son-in-law.

Samantha's cousin, Serena (also played by Elizabeth Montgomery), was a free-spirited playgirl who dallied with Don Juan, Adonis, and Henry VIII and livened up Samantha's domestic life with manipulative witchcraft. Samantha's Uncle Arthur (Paul Lynde) was a witch who loved playing practical jokes. Samantha's Aunt Clara (Marion Lorne) was a lovable witch who had trouble remembering spells and who became easily flustered when the spells went awry as they always did. Samantha's extended family included Dr. Bombay (Bernard

Fox), the family physician, who was always on call to remove unusual spells or to cure witch-specific ailments.

In contrast to Samantha's eccentric family were Darrin's normal, mortal parents. Phyllis and Frank Stephens (Mabel Albertson and Robert F. Simon) adored their daughter-in-law but often required a long rest after visiting Samantha and their son.

Other confused mortals included nosy neighbor Gladys Kravitz (Alice Pearce, later replaced by Sandra Gould) who peeped through keyholes, spied from behind curtains, and peeked through bushes in order to see the odd occurrences at the Stephens house. When she complained to her long-suffering husband, Abner (George Tobias), he frequently told her that she was crazy.

Darrin's neurotic boss, Larry Tate (David White), and his quarrelsome wife, Louise (Kasey Rogers), socialized with Samantha and Darrin during business and personal occasions and remained perplexed by their peculiar lifestyle. Interference by Samantha's family often affected Darrin's work life, resulting in Larry firing Darrin at least twice a month.

The domestic difficulties that drove the weekly episodes were usually resolved by witchcraft, despite Samantha's vow to Darrin not to use her powers. Samantha exercised her powers by casting spells verbally or by twitching her nose. This so-called "witch twitch" made people or objects appear or disappear, bestowed unusual powers to others, or transformed individuals into an array of animals.

When the domestic difficulties spilled over into Darrin's business life, Samantha extricated her husband from jams by using witchcraft to prove a point or to stall for time. At other times she saved her husband's job and impressed clients by foisting off witchcraft-gone-wrong predicaments as advertising-campaign ideas conceptualized by Darrin. In either instance, Samantha managed to convey a sense to Darrin that he rather than she had saved the day.

Samantha and Darrin welcomed a daughter, Tabitha, in 1966 and a son, Adam, in 1971, both of whom inherited their mother's powers of witchcraft. As the series approached the end of its run, episodes found Samantha travelling to distant places and far-off eras and encountering historical persons, disrupting the focus on domestic life in a middle-class, suburban household.

When "Bewitched" ended in July 1972, the cast and crew could reflect on the success of 306 episodes over an eight-year run. During the initial season, "Bewitched" achieved the highest rating of all the new series. For the first five seasons, "Bewitched" enjoyed a consistent position in Neilsen's Top Twelve.

The series was recognized by the television industry and garnered twenty-three Emmy nominations. In 1966, Alice Pearce won Outstanding Performance by an Actress in a Supporting Role in a Comedy for her role of Gladys Kravitz. That same year, Elizabeth Montgomery's real-life husband, William Asher, won for Outstanding Directorial Achievement in a Comedy. In 1968, Marion Lorne won Outstanding Performance by an Actress in a Supporting Role in a Comedy for her role of Aunt Clara. In 1971, Episode 213, "Sisters at Heart," picked up the Governor's Award.

In 1977, a spin-off series, "Tabitha," was launched by ABC, starring Lisa Hartman as the grown-up witch working as an assistant producer for a California television program. The series was cancelled after only twelve episodes. Television viewers would have to wait until 1996 for another series about a young, lovely witch who uses her powers for good.

"Sabrina, the Teenage Witch"

In 1996, Sabrina stepped directly from the pages of the Archie Comics into her new home on the ABC network television series, "Sabrina, the Teenage Witch." In this coming-of-age comedy, Sabrina Spellman (Melissa Joan Hart) lives with two eccentric aunts who are witches, Zelda (Beth Broderick) and Hilda (Caroline Rhea). Completing the household is a sarcastic, talking black cat, Salem (the voice of Nick Bakay) who was a warlock turned into a feline as punishment for his subversive political activities. Sabrina and her loyal boyfriend, Harvey (Nate Richert), attend Westbridge High School.

At the age of sweet 16, Sabrina experiences her first levitation, and her aunts realize that the time has come to tell Sabrina that she is a witch. This rite of passage entails welcoming Sabrina into the coven and offering her a cauldron of her own. "A black pot?" Sabrina asks. "Doesn't anyone shop at The Gap anymore?"

During the series, Sabrina has had hilarious encounters with the mean yet popular Libby (Jenna Leigh Green); the mean and unpopular assistant principal, Mr. Kraft (Martin Mull); the half-witch, half-human hunk, Dash (Donald Faison); the precocious witch from the Other Realm, Dreama (China Jesusita Shavers), who is Sabrina's magickal protege; and Harvey's best friend, Brad (Jon Heurtas), who is suspicious about Sabrina's true identity as a witch. Adding to the witch's brew are Sabrina's part-time job at a college bookstore and romantic entanglements.

Plots focus on the humorous difficulties of good-natured witchcraft. Sabrina has turned Libby into a pineapple and a geek. Sabrina and Harvey's first kiss changed him into a frog. Sabrina has rearranged the fish sticks on her plate in the school cafeteria, exclaiming: "Fishhenge! A deep-fried tribute to the Druids." After disobeying her aunts, Sabrina's guilt reduced her to miniature size. In a more serious vein, during a trip to Salem, Massachusetts, Sabrina and her classmates reenacted the witch trials.

The Halloween 1998 episode, "Good Will Haunting," offered a mixed bag of tricks and treats. Sabrina, Aunt Zelda, and Aunt Hilda reluctantly accepted an invitation from another Spellman family aunt, played by Jo Anne Worley, formerly of "Rowan and Martin's Laugh-In," to attend a boring party. After they arrived, they realized the trick: they were trapped in a lunatic asylum. The treats included the other inmates: Ruth Buzzi, Alan Sues, and Gary Owens, all former "Laugh-In" cast members.

Other incarnations for Sabrina included "Sabrina Goes to Rome" (1998) and "Sabrina, Down Under" (1999) broadcast on ABC's "Wonderful World of Disney" and "Sabrina, the Animated Series," a cartoon that debuted in 1999 on UPN and ABC.

"Buffy, the Vampire Slayer"

In the 1992 film *Buffy, the Vampire Slayer,* air-headed high school cheerleader Buffy (Kristy Swanson) learns that she is "the chosen one" of her generation, the latest in a long line of women vampire hunters stretching back to the Middle Ages. Her slayer trainer Merrick (Donald Sutherland) prepares her for her ultimate showdown with the vampire leader, Lothos (Rutger Hauer), even though Buffy would rather be at the mall shopping with her girlfriends.

The film's premise was translated to television in the series of the same name that debuted on the WB network in 1997. Buffy Summers (Sarah Michelle Geller), her friends, and her Watcher battle vampires, demons, and the forces of darkness while exploring ethical quandaries (such as: Is it okay to kill creatures who are friends? Does Buffy put the Scooby Gang at unacceptable risk? Should Buffy and her vampire boyfriend Angel stay together even if doing so might hurt them both in the long run?).

One of Buffy's friends, Willow Rosenberg (Alyson Hannigan), is the only Jewish member of the Scooby Gang. She is intelligent, a computer whiz, and a dabbler in the occult. Willow has ambitions of becoming a "bad-ass Wicca" as long as her mother doesn't try to burn her at the stake again. Willow has tried her hand at casting spells and continues to explore witchcraft while attending UC Sunnydale.

A spin-off from "Buffy, the Vampire Slayer" is "Angel," a series that premiered on the WB network in 1999, featuring vampire Angel (David Boreanaz) who leaves Sunnydale and Buffy for Los Angeles and the evil people he meets there. Both series depict a world in which the forces of good are constantly at war with the forces of evil with magick serving both sides.

"Charmed"

In October 1998, a new drama series premiered on the WB network, featuring three young, lovely sisters who are also witches. In "Charmed," the three Halliwell sisters—Prue (Shannen Doherty), Piper (Holly Marie Combs), and Phoebe (Alyssa Milano)—are reunited at Warren Manor, the Victorian home in San Francisco, California, where they spent their childhoods. Their old spirit board leads them to the attic and to the discovery of the Book of Shadows, an ancient text that prophesizes the arrival of "The Charmed Ones," three who will become the most powerful in a long lineage of good witches.

Each of the three will inherit one of three ancient family powers: the power to manipulate objects, the power to freeze time, and the power to look into the future. The Book of Shadows predicts that The Charmed Ones will claim their powers on the night of a full moon and that their powers will become stronger as they grow as witches. The sisters realize that they are The Charmed Ones.

Under the glow of the full moon, the youngest sister Phoebe invokes their powers by reciting an incantation. The eldest sister, Prue, receives the power to manipulate objects. The middle sister, Piper, receives the power to freeze time. Phoebe receives the power to look into the future. The sisters also learn that, according to ancient legend, The Charmed Ones are protectors of the innocent and enemies of demons. The dark forces will appear in the guise of normal people, and they will be relentless in their quest to destroy The Charmed Ones and to seize their powers.

The sisters accept their destiny, settling into a daily life together that is fraught with the inevitable conflicts resulting from three dissimilar personalities. Driven by a desire to be successful, Prue scorns Phoebe's free-spirited eccentricities. An earthy and creative soul, Piper often ends up mediating the squabbles between her older and younger sisters. However, all three realize that they must resolve their differences and learn to use their powers wisely in order to fulfill the ancient witchcraft prophecy of The Charmed Ones.

"Charmed" shares with "Buffy" and "Angel" the worldview of the unrelenting struggle between good and evil. Magick is the powerful means to achieve respective goals, and failure to triumph is punished with death and destruction.

BOOKS

Witches on television are restrained in displaying their powers by the limits of special effects. Witches in books are restrained only by the limits of their authors'—and their readers'—imaginations. A young reader can hop aboard Harry Potter's speedy broom, model Nimbus Two Thousand, and battle the opposing team in a Quidditch match (*Harry Potter and the Sorcerer's Stone* by J. K. Rowling). An adult reader can indulge in Rowan Mayfair's attraction to Michael Curry (*The Witching Hour* by Anne Rice) or investigate the murder of an aspiring Witch along with Karen Hightower whose Craft name is Bast (*Speak Daggers to Her* by Rosemary Edghill). Let the imagining begin.

Harry Potter Casts a Spell upon the World

In June 1997, when *Harry Potter and the Sorcerer's Stone* by J. K. Rowling was published in Britain, the juvenile novel zoomed to the top of the adult best-seller lists faster than a Nimbus Two Thousand. Curiously, the same occurred when the book was published in the United States in September 1998.

Harry Potter and the Sorcerer's Stone relates the tale of an 11-year-old orphan, Harry Potter, who has lived ten long, miserable years with his horrible aunt and uncle, Petunia and Vernon Dursley, and their hateful son, Dudley. Harry's life changes when he is granted admission to The Hogwarts School for Witchcraft and Wizardry. Hogwarts is an elite boarding school where potential sorcerers spend seven rigorous years learning about charms, spells, and potions.

During his first year at Hogwarts, Harry not only makes friends—and a few enemies—he helps hatch a dragon and becomes the star of a Quidditch team, scoring points while riding a broom far above the ground. Finding magick in everything from classes to meals, Harry also learns that he has a destiny to fulfill—one that may imperil his life.

The destiny of Harry's creator, J(oanne) K. Rowling, a graduate of Exeter

University and a former teacher, seemed dismal in 1993. Then, Rowling was an unemployed, divorced mother, living on public assistance in a tiny, unheated Edinburgh, Scotland, flat with her infant daughter. "I was very low," Rowling recalls, "and I had to achieve something. Without the challenge, I would have gone stark raving mad."

A scribbler of stories since she was 6, Rowling had received the inspiration for Harry Potter in 1990 while on a train, traveling from Manchester to London. "I was staring out the window," Rowling recalls, "and the idea for Harry just came. He appeared in my mind's eye, very fully formed. The basic idea was for a boy who didn't know what he was."

Rowling accepted the challenge of bringing Harry to life on paper during the low period in her life. She sat at tables in nearby cafes, jotting ideas and scenes for *Harry Potter and the Sorcerer's Stone* on scraps of paper while her daughter napped in her pram. The Scottish Arts Council awarded her a grant to complete the book.

Rowling could not afford to photocopy her manuscript so that the book could make the publishing rounds. Instead, Rowling typed the manuscript twice on a battered old typewriter. The manuscript sold to Bloomsbury (UK) and Scholastic Books (USA). After that, the accolades streamed in.

Harry Potter and the Sorcerer's Stone won the British Book Awards Children's Book of the Year, the British National Book Award, the prestigious Smarties Prize, and the ABBY by American Booksellers. The book was named an American Library Association Notable Book and won rave reviews on both sides of the Atlantic. The *Guardian* (London) proclaimed: "He [Harry] could assume the same near legendary status as Roald Dahl's Charlie, of chocolate factory fame."

The sequel to the first Harry Potter book was *Harry Potter and the Chamber of Secrets*, released in the United Kingdom in July 1998. United States readers, who couldn't wait to see what Harry was up to next, bought copies of the British edition through Internet bookstores. When the U.S. edition was published in June 1999, bookstores across the country were swamped with orders.

In *Harry Potter and the Chamber of Secrets*, Harry finds trouble when he returns to Hogwarts for his second year of school. He misses the express train to school, hijacks a magick car which almost gets him expelled from Hogwarts, then is barred from school property by a crazy elf named Dobby. Things only get worse: Harry breaks an arm playing Quidditch, discovers that he is a parselmouth (one who can talk to snakes—not a good thing for a wizard), and realizes that someone or something is turning Hogwarts students to stone.

The sequel proved as successful as its predecessor. Both novels have sold millions of copies in more than two hundred countries and have been translated into more than thirty-five languages, including Icelandic and Serbo–Croatian.

The third book in the series, *Harry Potter and the Prisoner of Azkaban*, was also eagerly gobbled up by readers. In this book, Harry's life at school is menaced when an infamous murderer, Sirius Black, escapes from the prison fortress of Azkaban with plans to kill Harry. Black is the heir apparent to Harry's archenemy, Lord Voldemort. Even within the walls of Hogwarts, Harry's life is in jeopardy, because a traitor may be among the residents.

When *Harry Potter and the Prisoner of Azkaban* was published in the United States in September 1999, nearly a half million copies sold in the first two weeks.

Children in the U.S. and around the world are completely captivated by this bespectacled sorcerer's apprentice. They read and reread Harry's adventures until the books are well-thumbed and dog-eared. They make up games, stage puppet shows, and put on plays based on the characters and the plots. They emulate the lightning-bolt scar on Harry's forehead with stickers and temporary tatoos, and they besiege book signings wherever author Rowling appears.

"I met a boy at a school in England who recited the first page of the first book to me from memory," Rowling recalls. "When he stopped, he said, 'I can go on.' He continued reciting the first five pages of the book. That was unbelievable."

Rowling envisions the whole series spanning seven novels, one for each year that Harry spends at Hogwarts. The fourth novel, *Harry Potter and the Goblet of Fire*, released on July 8, 2000, was heralded with great fanfare, including sweepstakes sponsored by Scholastic and Barnes & Noble and contests sponsored by Bloomsbury and Amazon.co.uk.

Faithful readers of the series anticipate the November 2001 release of the Warner Bros. feature film based on *Harry Potter and the Sorcerer's Stone*, as well as the first licensed merchandise, which will materialize in late 2000. Mattel plans a line of toys based on characters from the books and the film, while Hasbro plans to produce Harry Potter electronic toys, collector's cards, and candy.

The success of the series has sweetened life for author Rowling. In 2000, she was named author of the year at the British Book Awards; she was made an OBE, or Officer of the Order of the British Empire, for services to children's literature; and she received an honorary doctorate from the University of St. Andrews, Scotland's oldest university, for helping millions of children rediscover "the pure joy of reading."

Because of the magickal elements that are such integral aspects of the Harry Potter books, the series has come under fire in the United States for promoting Witchcraft. In fact, Rowling's series tops the American Library Association's list of "The Most Frequently Challenged Books of 1999."

In response to efforts to ban the Harry Potter books from schools and libraries, the American Library Association passed a resolution in early 2000 praising Rowling's works as having "brought the pleasure of reading to millions of children and adults."

The millions of readers whom Harry Potter has put under his spell all over the world are powerful portents that this sorcerer-in-training will be a mighty wizard, indeed.

Wiccan Fiction for Adults

1. *The Diary of Dorcas Good, Child Witch of Salem* by Rose Earhart
2. *Fantasy With Witches* by Alistair Te Ariki Campbell
3. *The Godmother* by Elizabeth Ann Scarborough
4. *How To Spin Gold: A Woman's Tale* by Elizabeth Cunningham
5. *Lammas Night* by Katherine Kurtz
6. *The Mists of Avalon* by Marion Zimmer Bradley
7. *The Oracle Glass* by Judith Merkle Riley
8. *Speak Daggers to Her* by Rosemary Edghill
9. *The Sub (A Study in Witchcraft)* by Thomas M. Disch
10. *Wicked: The Life and Times of the Wicked Witch of the West* by Gregory Maguire
11. *The Witches' Hammer* by Jane Stanton Hitchcock
12. *Witches Were For Hanging* by Patricia Crowther
13. *The Witching Hour* by Anne Rice

Wiccan Fiction for Children

1. *Beyond the Burning Time* by Kathryn Lasky
2. *Burning Issy* by Melvin Burgess
3. *Enter Three Witches* by Kate Gilmore

4. *Gallows Hill* by Lois Duncan
5. *Jennifer, Hecate, William McKinley, and Me, Elizabeth* by E. L. Konigsburg
6. *Mountain Miracle* by Thomas L. Tedrow
7. *The Other Ones* by Jean Thesman
8. *The Over-The-Hill Witch* by Ruth Calif
9. *The Secret* by R. L. Stine
10. *The Time of the Witch* by Mary Downing Hahn
11. *Wise Child* by Monica Furlong
12. *A Witch Across Time* by Gilbert B. Cross
13. *Witch Week* by Diana Wynne Jones

Bibliography

⟡

Adler, Margot. *Drawing Down the Moon: Witches, Druids, Goddess-Worshippers, and Other Pagans in America*, rev. ed. New York: Viking, 1986.

Ashley, Leonard R. N. *The Wonderful World of Magic and Witchcraft*. New York: Dembner Books, 1986.

Barstow, Anne Llewellyn. *Witchcraze: A New History of the European Witch Hunts*. San Francisco: Harper San Francisco, 1995.

Bell, Charles Bailey. *A Mysterious Spirit: The Bell Witch of Tennessee*. Nashville, TN: Charles Elder Publisher, 1972 (first published in 1934).

Bell, Richard Williams, and M. V. Ingram, eds. *Authenticated History of the Famous Bell Witch. The Wonder of the 19th Century, and Unexplained Phenomenon of the Christian Era. The Mysterious Talking Goblin that Terrorized the West End of Robertson County, Tennessee, Tormenting John Bell to His Death. The Story of Betsy Bell, Her Lover and the Haunting Sphynx*. Clarkson, TN: private printing, 1894.

Bonewits, P. E. I. *Real Magic*. New York: Coward, McCann & Geoghegan, 1971.

Bourne, Lois. *Witch Amongst Us.* New York: St. Martin's Press, 1985.

Bowes, Susan. *Notions and Potions: A Safe, Practical Guide to Creating Magic & Miracles.* New York: Sterling Publishing Co., Inc., 1998.

Boyer, Paul, and Stephen Nissenbaum. *Salem Possessed: The Social Origins of Witchcraft.* Cambridge, MA: Harvard University Press, 1974.

Bracelin, J. L. *Gerald Gardner: Witch.* London: Octagon Press, 1960.

Briggs, Robin. *Witches & Neighbors: The Social and Cultural Context of European Witchcraft.* New York: Penguin Books, 1996.

Buckland, Raymond. *Buckland's Complete Book of Witchcraft.* St. Paul: Llewellyn Publications, 1986.

Budapest, Zsusanna. *The Holy Book of Women's Mysteries,* vol. I rev. Oakland, CA: 1986.

———. *The Holy Book of Women's Mysteries,* vol. II. Oakland, CA: 1980.

Burbank, James. "Yenaldlooshi: The Shape-Shifter Beliefs of the Navajos." *The World & I* (November 1993): 264–272.

Burr, George Lincoln. *Narratives of the Witchcraft Cases, 1648–1706.* New York: Charles Scribner's Sons, 1914.

Cabot, Laurie, with Tom Cowan. *Power of the Witch.* New York: Del Publishing, 1989.

Caporael, Linnda R. "Ergotism: The Satan Loosed in Salem?" *Science,* vol. 192 (April 2, 1976): 21–26.

Carlson, Laurie Winn. *A Fever in Salem: A New Interpretation of the New England Witch Trials.* Chicago: Ivan R. Dee, 1999.

Crowley, Aleister. *Magick in Theory and Practice.* New York: Dover Publications, 1976 (first published in 1929).

Crowther, Patricia. *Lid Off the Cauldron: A Wicca Handbook.* York Beach, ME: Samuel Weiser, 1989 (first published in 1981).

Cunningham, Scott. *Magical Herbalism.* St. Paul, MN: Llewellyn Publications, 1982.

———. *Wicca: A Guide for the Solitary Practitioner.* St. Paul, MN: Llewellyn Publications, 1988.

Curott, Phyllis. *Book of Shadows.* New York: Broadway Books, 1998.

Demos, John Putnam. *Entertaining Satan: Witchcraft and the Culture of Early New England.* New York: Oxford University Press, 1982.

Eliade, Mircea. *Occultism, Witchcraft and Cultural Fashions.* Chicago: University of Chicago Press, 1976.

Evans-Pritchard, E. E. *Witchcraft, Oracles and Magic Among the Azande* abr. ed. Oxford: Clarendon Press, 1983.

Farrar, Janet, and Stewart Farrar. *A Witches Bible Compleat.* New York: Magickal Childe, 1984.

Farrington, Karen. *Dark Justice: A History of Punishment and Torture.* New York: Smithmark, 1996.

Fox, Robin Lane. *Pagans and Christians.* New York: Alfred A. Knopf, Inc., 1986.

Frazer, Sir James G. *The Golden Bough.* New York: Avenel Books, 1981 (first published in 1890).

Frost, Gavin, and Yvonne Frost. *The Magic Power of Witchcraft.* West Nyack, NY: Parker Publishing, 1976.

Gardner, Gerald B. *Witchcraft Today.* New York: Citadel Press, 1954.

———. *The Meaning of Witchcraft.* New York: Magickal Childe, 1982 (first published in 1959).

Ginzburg, Carlo. *Night Battles: Witchcraft & Agrarian Cults in the Sixteenth and Seventeenth Centuries.* New York: Penguin Books, 1985 (first published in 1966).

Glass, Justine. *Witchcraft, the Sixth Sense.* North Hollywood, CA: Wilshire Book Company, 1970.

Goldenberg, Naomi. *Changing of the Gods: Feminism and the End of Traditional Religions.* Boston: Beacon Press, 1979.

Gonzalez-Wippler, Migene. *The Complete Book of Spells, Ceremonies & Magic.* St. Paul, MN: Llewellyn Publications, 1988.

Graves, Robert. *The White Goddess.* New York: Farrar, Straus & Giroux, 1966 (first published in 1948).

Gregor, Arthur S. *Witchcraft & Magic: The Supernatural World of Primitive Man.* New York: Charles Scribner's Sons, 1973.

Grimassi, Raven. *Hereditary Witchcraft: Secrets of the Old Religion.* St. Paul, MN: Llewellyn Publications, 1999.

———. *Italian Witchcraft: The Old Religion of Southern Europe.* St. Paul, MN: Llewellyn Publications, 1999.

———. *The Wiccan Mysteries: Ancient Origins and Teachings.* St. Paul, MN: Llewellyn Publications, 1997.

Grimm, Jacob Ludwig. *Grimm's Fairy Tales: Twenty Stories.* New York: Viking Press, 1974.

———. *Tales from Grimm.* New York: Coward-McCann, Inc., 1936.

Guiley, Rosemary Ellen. *The Encyclopedia of Witches and Witchcraft.* New York: Facts On File, Inc., 1989.

Hansen, Chadwick. *Witchcraft at Salem.* New York: New American Library, 1969.

Harris, Marvin. *Cows, Pigs, Wars & Witches: The Riddles of Culture.* New York: Vintage Books, 1974.

Hill, Frances. *A Delusion of Satan: The Full Story of the Salem Witch Trials.* New York: Doubleday, 1995.

Hirsh, Marilyn. *The Rabbi and the Twenty-Nine Witches: A Talmudic Legend.* New York: Holiday House, 1977.

Hopman, Ellen Evert. *A Druid's Herbal for the Sacred Earth Year.* Rochester, VT: Inner Traditions, 1995.

Hutton, Ronald. *The Pagan Religions of the Ancient British Isles: Their Nature and Legacy.* Oxford: Blackwell, 1992.

———. *The Triumph of the Moon: A History of Modern Pagan Witchcraft.* New York: Oxford University Press, 2000.

Jong, Erica. *Witches.* New York: Harry N. Abrams, 1981.

Judith, Anodea. *Wheels of Life.* St. Paul, MN: Llewellyn Publications, 1987.

Karlsen, Carol F. *The Devil in the Shape of a Woman: Witchcraft in Colonial New England.* New York: W. W. Norton & Co., 1987.

Kittredge, George Lyman. *Witchcraft in Old and New England.* Cambridge: Harvard University Press, 1929.

Kluckhohn, Clyde. *Navaho Witchcraft.* Boston: Beacon Press, 1967 (first published in 1944).

Kors, Alan C., and Edward Peters. *Witchcraft in Europe 1100–1700: A Documentary History.* Philadelphia: University of Pennsylvania Press, 1972.

Lax, Roger, and Frederick Smith. *The Great Song Thesaurus.* New York: Oxford University Press, 1984.

Leek, Sybil. *The Complete Art of Witchcraft.* New York: World Publishing Co., 1971.

———. *Diary of a Witch.* New York: NAL Signet Library, 1968.

Lethbridge, T. C. *Witches.* Secaucus, NJ: Lyle Stuart, 1969.

Levack, Brian P. *The Witch-Hunt in Early Modern Europe.* London: Longman Group UK Limited, 1987.

Levi, Eliphas. *The History of Magic.* Translated by A. E. Waite. London: Rider and Company, 1957.

McCoy, Edain. *A Witch's Guide to Faery Folk.* St. Paul, MN: Llewellyn Publications, 1994.

Malinowski, Bronislaw. *Magic, Science and Religion.* Garden City, NY: Doubleday Anchor Books, 1948.

Markale, Jean. *King of the Celts.* Rochester, VT: Inner Traditions, 1994.

Martello, Dr. Leo Louis. *Witchcraft: The Old Religion*. Secaucus, NJ: University Books, 1973.

Mather, Cotton. *On Witchcraft: Being the Wonders of the Invisible World*. Mt. Vernon, NY: Peter Pauper Press, 1950 (first published in 1693).

Monaghan, Patricia. *The Goddess Path: Myths, Invocations and Rituals*. St. Paul, MN: Llewellyn Publications, 1999.

Monter, E. William. *Witchcraft in France and Switzerland*. Ithaca, NY: Cornell University Press, 1976.

Monter, E. William, ed. *European Witchcraft*. New York: John Wiley & Sons, Inc., 1969.

Morrey, Teresa. *Witchcraft: A Beginner's Guide*. United Kingdom: Hodder & Stoughton, 1996.

Murray, Margaret A. *The God of the Witches*. London: Sampson Low, Marston and Co., Ltd., 1933.

————. *The Witch-Cult in Western Europe*. London: Oxford University Press, 1921.

Newcomb, Horace, ed. *Museum of Broadcast Communications Encyclopedia of Television*. Chicago: Fitzroy Dearborn Publishers, 1997.

Parker, Derek, and Julia Parker. *The Power of Magic: Secrets and Mysteries Ancient and Modern*. New York: Simon & Schuster, 1992.

Paulsen, Kathryn. *The Complete Book of Magic and Witchcraft*, rev. ed. New York: Signet/New American Library, 1980.

Pickering, David. *Cassell Dictionary of Witchcraft*. UK: Cassell, 1996.

Price, Charles Edwin. *The Infamous Bell Witch of Tennessee*. Johnson City, TN: Overmountain Press, 1994.

Ravenwolf, Silver. *Teen Witch: Wicca for a New Generation*. St. Paul, MN: Llewellyn Publications, 1998.

————. *To Ride A Silver Broomstick: New Generation Witchcraft*. St. Paul, MN: Llewellyn Publications, 1993.

Regardie, Israel. *Ceremonial Magic: A Guide to the Mechanisms of Ritual*. Wellingborough, Northhamptonshire, England: The Aquarian Press, 1980.

Robbins, Rossell Hope. *The Encyclopedia of Witchcraft & Demonology*. New York: Crown, 1959.

Robinson, Enders A. *The Devil Discovered: Salem Witchcraft 1692*. New York: Hippocrene Books, 1991.

Rosean, Lexa. *Easy Enchantments: All the Spells You'll Ever Need for Any Occasion*. New York: St. Martin's Griffin, 1997.

Russell, Jeffrey Burton. *A History of Medieval Christianity: Prophecy and Order.* New York: Thomas Crowell Company, 1968.

———. *A History of Witchcraft, Sorcerers, Heretics, and Pagans.* London: Thames and Hudson, Ltd., 1980.

———. *Witchcraft in the Middle Ages.* Ithaca, NY: Cornell University Press, 1972.

Scot, Reginald. *The Discoverie of Witchcraft.* Yorkshire, England: E. P. Publishing, Ltd., 1973 (from the 1886 ed.; first published in 1584).

Segan, Lore, and Maurice Sendak. *The Juniper Tree and Other Tales From Grimm,* vol. 2. New York: Farrar, Straus and Giroux, 1973.

Seligmann, Kurt. *The History of Magic and the Occult.* New York: Random House, 1997.

———. *Magic, Supernaturalism and Religion.* New York: Pantheon Books, a Division of Random House, 1976.

Sharpe, C. K. *A History of Witchcraft in Scotland.* Glasgow: Thomas D. Morison, 1884.

Smith, Susy. *Prominent American Ghosts.* Cleveland: World Publishing Company, 1968.

Spanos, Nicholas P., and Jack Gottlieb. "Ergotism and the Salem Village Witch Trials." *Science,* Vol. 194 (December 24, 1976): 1390–1394.

Spencer, Baldwin, and F. J. Gillen. *The Native Tribes of Central Australia.* London: Macmillan and Co., 1938.

Starhawk. *The Spiral Dance: A Rebirth of the Ancient Religion of the Great Goddess.* San Francisco: Harper & Row, 1979.

Starkey, Marion L. *The Devil in Massachusetts.* New York: Alfred Knopf, 1949.

Stephens, Walter. *Demon Lovers: Witchcraft, Sex, and Belief.* Chicago: University of Chicago Press, 2001.

———. "Witches Who Steal Penises: Impotence and Illusion in *Malleus Maleficarum.*" *The Journal of Medieval and Early Modern Studies,* Volume 28, Number 3 (Fall 1998): 495–529.

Stone, Merlin. *When God Was A Woman.* New York: Dial Press, 1976.

Stutley, Margaret. *Ancient Indian Magic and Lore.* Boulder, CO: Great Eastern Book Co., 1980.

Summers, Montague. *The History of Witchcraft and Demonology.* London: Kegan Paul, Trench, Trubner & Co., Ltd., 1926.

Telesco, Patricia. *A Victorian Grimoire.* St. Paul, MN: Llewellyn Publications, 1992.

———. *Spinning Spells, Weaving Wonders: Modern Magic for Everyday Life.* Watsonville, CA: Crossing Press, 1996.

————. *Urban Pagan: Magical Living in a 9-to-5 World.* St. Paul, MN: Llewellyn, 1993.

Tuchman, Barbara W. *A Distant Mirror: The Calamitous 14th Century.* New York: Alfred A. Knopf, Inc., 1978.

Upham, Charles. *History of Witchcraft and Salem Village.* Boston: Wiggin and Lunt, 1867.

————. *Salem Witchcraft.* Williamstown, MA: Corner House Publishers, 1971.

Valiente, Doreen. *An ABC of Witchcraft Past and Present.* Custer, WA: Phoenix Publishing, 1986 (first published in 1973)

————. *Witchcraft for Tomorrow.* Custer, WA: Phoenix Publishing, 1985 (first published in 1978).

Walker, Barbara. *The Women's Encyclopedia of Myths and Secrets.* New York: Harper & Row, 1983.

Wedeck, Harry E. *A Treasury of Witchcraft.* Secaucus, NJ: Citadel Press, 1961.

Weinstein, Marion. *Earth Magic: A Dianic Book of Shadows,* rev. ed. Custer, WA: Phoenix Publishing, 1986.

————. *Positive Magic,* rev. ed. Custer, WA: Phoenix Publishing, 1981.

Weisman, Richard. *Witchcraft, Magic and Religion in Seventeenth-Century Massachusetts.* Amherst: University of Massachusetts Press, 1984.

Williams, Selma R., and Pamela J. Williams. *Riding the Nightmare: Women and Witchcraft.* New York: Atheneum, 1978.

INTERNET RESOURCES

Internet Medieval Source Book
http://www.fordham.edu/halsall/source/witches1.html

Malleus Maleficarum
http://www.paganteahouse.com/malleus_maleficarum/

The Witchcraft Bibliography Project
http://www.hist.unt.edu/witch.htm

Index

&